COAST DEFENCES OF ENGLAND AND WALES

COAST DEFENCES OF ENGLAND AND WALES
1856-1956

Ian V. Hogg

David & Charles
Newton Abbot   London   North Pomfret (VT)   Vancouver

0 7153 6353 0

© Ian V. Hogg 1974

All rights reserved. No part of this publication
may be reproduced, stored in a retrieval system,
or transmitted, in any form or by any means, electronic,
mechanical, photocopying, recording or otherwise,
without the prior permission of David & Charles
(Holdings) Limited

Set in 11/13pt Plantin 110
and printed in Great Britain
by John Sherratt and Son Ltd
Park Road Altrincham Cheshire WA14 5QQ
for David & Charles (Holdings) Limited
South Devon House Newton Abbot Devon

Published in the United States of America
by David & Charles Inc North Pomfret
Vermont 05053 USA

Published in Canada by Douglas David &
Charles Limited 3645 McKechnie Drive
West Vancouver BC

CONTENTS

	Preface	9
Chapter One	The Plans	13
Chapter Two	The Iron Age	27
Chapter Three	Construction and Progress	45
Chapter Four	Completion and Dissolution	76
Chapter Five	The Thames and Medway Defences	93
Chapter Six	The Portsmouth and Isle of Wight Defences	121
Chapter Seven	The Plymouth Defences	168
Chapter Eight	The Milford Haven Defences	205
Chapter Nine	The Lesser Fortresses	221
	Epilogue	234
Appendices	List of Coast Defence Works	236
	Details of Armament	247
	Bibliography	255
	Acknowledgements	256
	Index	259

LIST OF ILLUSTRATIONS

Photographs

	Page
A 68-pounder Converted gun on wooden traversing slide, open embrasure	33
The 9.2in BL gun on barbette mounting	33
Rear of the half-demolished casemates of Shornmead Fort	34
Casemates of Cliffe Fort	34
Rowner Fort, Portsmouth (Photo: G. Z. Trebinski)	51
Bembridge Down Fort caponier (Photo: G. Z. Trebinski)	51
Armstrong's Protected Barbette position, Puckpool (Photo: G. Z. Trebinski)	52
Fort Albert, Isle of Wight (Photo: G. Z. Trebinski)	52
Hurst Castle (Photo: Aerofilms)	101
Bovisand Fort casemate tier	102
Experimental casemates of the same pattern, after attack on trial	102
Agaton Fort and Ernesettle Battery, Plymouth (Photo: Aerofilms)	119
Plymouth Citadel (Photo: Aerofilms)	120
Haxo Casemates and expense magazine, Fort Efford, Plymouth	120
Entrance to Crown Hill Fort, Plymouth	169
A High Angle emplacement, Tregantle Down Battery	169
Practice at Renney Battery, 1953	170
Hubberstone Fort, Milford Haven (Photo: Aerofilms)	187
The 6in BL gun on disappearing carriage	188
A 6in disappearing carriage emplacement, Slough Fort.	188

List of Illustrations

Drawings

		Page
1	Experimental casemates at Shoeburyness	31
2	Built-up construction of a 9in RML gun	38
3	Simple plan of Grain Fort	48
4	Section of the iron shielded face of Picklecombe Fort	53
5	The installation of guns at Picklecombe Fort	54
6	The 7in RML gun and its mounting	56
7	Lt-Col Shaw's Muzzle-pivoting carriage	59
8	Moncrieff's disappearing carriage	61
9	Section of the armoured face of Horse Sand Fort	65
10	10in BL gun on barbette mounting	71
11	The 4.7in QF gun on central pivot mounting	73
12	The 9.2in BL gun on barbette carriage	80
13	The 9in High Angle RML gun	85
14	Plan section of Horse Sand Fort armour	130
15	Plan section of St Helen's Fort armour	134
16	Ground plan of Southsea Castle battery	138
17	The 13in mortar	164
18	Ground plan of South Hook Fort	213
19	Sectioned view of the Dover Turret	224

Maps

1	The Thames and Medway Defences	95
2	The Spithead and Sandown area Defences	128
3	The Portsmouth Harbour Defences	142
4	The Needles Passage Defences	148
5	Plymouth—the original defensive plan	175
6	Plymouth—the final construction	179
7	The Pembroke and Milford Haven Defences	209

The Garrison Gunner is, in my opinion, most necessary as a deterrent; his usefulness is like that of a notice that 'A Fierce Dog is on the Premises'

> Lt-Col Sir George Clarke, KCMG, RE, in an inaugural lecture to the Malta Naval and Military Society, 28 December 1893

PREFACE

Twenty years ago I was a student on a field artillery Long Gunnery Staff Course, the prerequisite course of instruction before becoming an Assistant Instructor-in-Gunnery; referred to by one wit as 'twelve months hard labour followed by solitary confinement for life'. As part of our larger education we visited Plymouth Citadel, then the home of the Coast Artillery School, for a week of indoctrination, and on the first day we were addressed by an instructor who began his exposition of 'the coast gunnery problem' by observing that the going rate for anti-aircraft artillery shooting was about a thousand rounds per aircraft downed; that field artillery invariably fired a few ranging rounds before getting fairly on to the target; but that coast artillery hit the target with the first shot fired. I would have been more inclined to believe him had I not recognised him as having been my battery commander in horse artillery some four years previously, and such fanatic embracement of a new faith made me a trifle wary.

The next day we were taken to Renney Battery and watched a 6in gun blow a fast moving target out of the water with the first shot.

I would not go so far as to say that I was converted on the spot, but I certainly regarded the 'concrete gunners' with a little more respect, and the remainder of the visit unfolded a new world, one with incredible machinery, enormous guns, and labyrinthine military architecture. Unfortunately, being a dedicated field gunner at the time, most of the impressions were eroded by time-honoured repartee involving such pivotal themes as concrete, the marking of waves on the map, and the difficulty of removing seagull droppings from the ordnance.

About seven years later I was undergoing another course of instruction in Pembrokeshire, and in the course of an idle Sunday afternoon drive, discovered Hubberstone Fort. This was the catalyst which revived memories of Plymouth and introduced me to the deserted fortifications surrounding the country, for in the intervening years coast artillery had ceased to exist. The size of the fort; the immense effort which must have gone into building it, arming it and manning it; the architectural intricacy of it; the fact that from the top of its casemates I could see more works which appeared to be equally derelict; all these things made me wonder just how many of these forts existed, who built them, when, why, how they had been armed, and a thousand other questions.

From then on my spare time was devoted to delving into old records, questioning old coast gunners, and travelling about to find and examine more forts. The magnitude of the task of actually locating and inspecting every one defeated me in the end, and I have had to rely on assistance in some areas. It was during this search for information that I discovered many more people with greater or lesser interest in the Victorian coast forts, and also discovered that nowhere was there any sort of connected narrative describing the works which ring the country; every minute detail had to be dredged out of reams of reports, sometimes ostensibly dealing with other subjects but containing, in throw-away fashion, some nugget of information. However, the nearer one gets to the present day, the more difficult this becomes; up to 1900 the records are fairly verbose, but after that the first inklings of 'security' creep in, and the references get more and more oblique. Unfortunately the Fort Record Books, the 'official diary' of each work, which record every change in structure or armament, are still classified documents, and thus I have not been able to confirm one or two items which remain conjecture.

As a result of all this activity, I came to the conclusion that, since there were others as interested as I, and since they might not have the facilities to delve into records which I was lucky enough to have, it might be as well to get it all down on paper, and so this book began to take shape. It would be presumptuous to say that it contains all there is to be said on the coast fortresses; that would take volumes. But if it manages to answer some of the questions which originally confronted me, then the aim is achieved. It is, due to my own predilections, about the things of coast defence—the works and armament—rather than about the men and the higher strategy. For those who wish to read of this aspect and to see coast artillery as a whole, throughout the ages and the Empire, and set against the strategy and politics of the times, I can only recommend they obtain a copy of *The History of Coast Artillery in the British Army* by Colonel F. W. Maurice-Jones, published by the Royal Artillery Institution. This excellent work deals with the wider aspects, while I have confined my attention to a much narrower field. The coast defences manned by the Royal Regiment of Artillery stretched from the Thames to Hong Kong in one direction and to Vancouver in the other, with countless forts and batteries guarding dockyards, ports and coaling stations in between.

1
THE PLANS

The British Isles have always been a standing invitation to an invader. The long coastline, indented with inlets and creeks, offers a host of possible landing places, and it is remarkable that so few attempts to exploit the possibilities are recorded. The Romans, having achieved a landing, were alert to the possibility of a repetition by someone else, though it is difficult to say who might have attempted such a feat. Even in those days, carrying a force across the Channel and landing it, even unopposed, would have required a certain amount of organising ability, and there is little evidence that the contemporary continental tribes were capable of the necessary co-operative effort.

Nonetheless a number of Roman fortresses were built so as to protect their more valuable ports; a chain of forts began at Brancaster (Branodunum) in Norfolk and stretched round the vulnerable south-east coast as far as Portchester (Portus Magnus) in Portsmouth Harbour. Traces of other works which appear to have had a defensive role have been found at other points all round England and Wales, as at Cardiff, Saltburn and Robin Hood's Bay, though there is a strong possibility that most of these were, in modern parlance, observation posts rather than defensive works.

For the question arises of how the Romans proposed to use their forts. As will later become apparent, the basic object of a coast work is to prevent the enemy gaining a foothold on the land by stopping him at sea, and no weapon capable of doing this was to be available for another 1,400 years. Ballistae and catapults, efficient as they may have been against land defences, were quite useless against moving ships, so there appears to have been no means of actually preventing a landing. It follows from this and from consideration of the design of the works, that these forts were less 'defences' than 'redoubts'; in other words, on the approach of an enemy the population of the port, with their valuables, cattle, stock-in-trade and other moveable possessions, would have withdrawn into the fort and closed the door behind them. The Legionaries and local auxiliaries would then have manned the walls, and the empty port would have been left to the depredations of the raiders.

Raiders from the North became the principal bugbear, to such an extent that shortly after AD 293, Diocletian, in his re-organisation of the system of government and control, appointed a 'Count of the Saxon Shore' to control the defence against Saxon raiders. This appointment controlled both land and sea defences, a sort of combined operations commander.

Eventually, as Roman power declined and the Saxons landed and occupied, the Roman defences fell into disuse. The Saxons seem to have been the first people to appreciate that a vigorous sea policy is the best form of coast defence; and left little in the way of land works.

The Normans took over many of the Roman remains and erected their own defensive works within the original trace, often assimilating some of the Roman work. Thus at Portchester, where the Norman keep was erected in the north-western corner, together with its inner bailey, and the rest of the enclosure was used as the outer bailey. Cardiff castle is another example of this technique.

During the Middle Ages defences were few, but periodic scares led to the hurried erection of works here and there. A small redoubt was built at Scarborough in the time of King Stephen and later improved on by Henry II. Cooling Castle, in Kent, was begun in 1380; overlooking Cooling Marshes and the sea reach of the Thames, this was specifically intended as a defence against French invasion. As with the Roman works, no offensive weapon could be mounted, the castle simply acting as a base or redoubt for a body of defensive soldiers. However, it probably qualifies as the first defensive work on the Thames Estuary.

Dover, from its position, was obviously a likely landing place for any invader or raider, and Henry I began by replacing the Roman works with a masonry structure. This was continued by Henry II who erected a keep and other structures and formed the nucleus of Dover Castle.

Portsmouth had declined in importance since Roman days, and only began to revive in the twelfth century, being granted a charter in 1194. Edward IV began the construction of towers at the harbour mouth, which were continued by Richard III and completed under Henry VII. Subsequently Edward VI built a further two stone towers and suspended a boom between them, one of the earliest applications of this form of defence.

It was Henry VIII who revitalised coast defence. One of the best descriptions of the situation comes from Lambard's *Perambulation of Kent* of 1576:

> King Henry, having shaken off the intolerable yoke of Papism, and seeing that the Emperor was offended by the divorce of Catherine, his wife; and that the French king had coupled the Dauphin his son to the Pope's niece and married his daughter to the King of Scotland, so that he might more justly suspect them all than safely trust any one: determined by the aid of God to stand upon his own guards and defence, and therefore with all speed and without sparing any cost he built castles, platforms and blockhouses at all needful places in the realm.

In addition to this incentive, Henry had an advantage denied his predecessors—gunpowder. The gun, primitive as it was, had already demonstrated its power and caused builders of land castles to modify their techniques, and Henry adapted his coast works entirely to the use of cannon; for now, for the first time, it was possible to install a weapon which could reach across the water and strike the attackers before they were within bowshot. The design he adopted was usually a variation of a central, circular or rectangular keep with large part-circular bastions arranged regularly around it. These formed platforms for guns on their roofs and the interiors were provided with casemates—vaulted chambers with an opening through which the gun could fire—on the lower levels. These casemates were even provided with chimneys to extract the gun smoke, a refinement which was ignored by later casemate-builders, as we shall see. This form of construction ensured the maximum field of fire from the parapet guns and also enfiladed the walls by the fire of the casemated pieces. The forts were then further secured from land attack by a wet ditch or moat surrounding the walls, with admission to the work over a drawbridge. Probably the finest remaining example of this type of work is Deal Castle, but others were built at Sandown, Walmer, Folkestone, Rye, Calshot, Cowes and Camber sands, to name but a few.

During the following years the defences largely remained as Henry left them, except for a few small modifications and additions. Probably the most significant was the building of Upnor Castle by Elizabeth I in order to protect Chatham Dockyard. This proved its worth in 1667 when the Dutch, with four men-of-war, three armed 'yachts' and two fire-ships, stormed the Medway. A chain-link boom across Gillingham Reach was broken by the men-of-war, which then turned and silenced the small batteries at each end. The fleet then began to play havoc with the shipping in the Medway burning everything they could reach and virtually destroying Chatham Dockyard. Eventually the guns at Upnor were manned, and under their fire the Dutch were driven off. The subsequent uproar was spectacular. Samuel Pepys records how he was assailed by the wives of sailors, who asserted 'This comes of not paying our husbands!', since the irruption of the Dutch had been entirely due to the absence of any sort of viable fleet. This in turn came back to the spendthrift habits of Charles II and the reluctance of Parliament to grant money for the country's defence, leading to the laying-up of ships and the non-payment of sailors. But in the aftermath of the Medway raid, the money was found from somewhere, and in a very short space of time sixty guns were installed at Woolwich to defend the approach to London, while existing but derelict works at Gravesend and Dover were hurriedly put in order and strengthened. The stable door having been securely bolted, the country slept once more.

The strengthening of the navy and the long peace after the Treaty of Utrecht had its inevitable effect and by the end of the eighteenth century the defences were once again in a run down condition. It must be borne in mind that there was no standing army to maintain or man them, and they were largely in the charge of local councils, sometimes with an invalid master gunner in nominal charge. While the local authorities might well have some thought for their charges, the actual business of producing men to keep them in order and the provision of sufficient money to pay for the maintenance was another matter.

Events in France, with the early rumblings of disquiet which led to the Revolution, caused some concern, and in 1779 Thomas Blomefield, the Inspector of Royal Artillery, was despatched to report on the state of the country's defences. We shall note some of his remarks in more detail later, when dealing with specific defences, but a few extracts here will give some idea of the state in which he found things:

> Dover. The bores of the guns are much damaged from the want of Tampions [ie the muzzles had not been plugged and rainwater had accumulated in the cannon barrels]. The Lieutenant-Governor represented the danger of the Weather Cock on the Tower immediately over the apartment where 1,300 barrels of powder were deposited, as it might attract Lightning.
> Hythe. A thin brick parapet as scarce affords any cover to the guns, and the platform which is paved with brick is incapable of supporting the weight. The carriages are much decayed and the guns damaged by rust.
> Portland Castle. No repairs having been done to the Castle for thirty years past, the roof admits the water in several places and the timber is much decayed. The firing of guns on the usual Festivals breaks the windows and shakes the building very much, for which reason it would be advisable to discontinue the practice.
> Upnor Castle is at present only used as a magazine. There are however eleven very old nine-pounders let into a frame of wood to fire on Rejoicing Days. They are very dangerous

guns, a man having actually been killed in attempting to re-load one of them when His Majesty was at Chatham. It is proposed to remove them entirely, as the neighbourhood of so large a magazine is certainly a very improper place for a battery.

This was a depressing picture, admittedly lightened here and there by reports of defences in better order, and the Board of Ordnance took steps to implement many of Blomefield's recommendations to close down useless works, move guns, renew guns and provide personnel, so that in 1784, on another tour, he was able to report:

'Hythe. Six 18-pounders. The guns and carriages are in exceeding good order.' Which was an improvement on his comments of four years earlier.

Whether or not Blomefield's report started things moving, there followed considerable public discussion of the state of the defences in consequence of the French Revolution, and particularly a strong demand for improving the defences of Plymouth and Portsmouth. Considerable expenditure was mooted, strongly backed by Pitt himself, but in this affair he met his match. The navy had not shone particularly well in the recent American wars, but Lord St Vincent was still a powerful figure, and his representation that the navy was capable of keeping the invader away from England's shores was accepted. To placate the objectors, some minor works were put in hand at Plymouth until the clamour died away, and these were probably never even armed. However in a very short time the activity of Napoleon and the considerable threat of invasion led to many more batteries being built in the period 1795–1803.

The long peace of 1815–1854 saw another lapse into somnolence, and very little was done to maintain the coast defences, but the Crimean War was the match which lit a slow-burning fuze. The fruitless operations of the combined fleets against the defences of Sebastopol made it obvious that a well-constructed and well-armed fort could stand off a fleet and take its toll against what seemed to be overwhelming odds. The French used armoured 'floating batteries' at Kinburn and this also pointed a

THE PLANS

lesson for the future. With the small amounts of money voted annually, together with one or two special estimates, the army managed to find enough to begin some additions to the defences of the south coast, and these were given fresh urgency and the whole question of defence brought into sharp focus by the action of the French in 1858 when they laid down their first iron-clad warship *La Gloire*. By following this with others of similar type they rendered the Royal Navy's wooden walls obsolete overnight and also posed a gunnery problem in how to defeat such protection. England's seagoing reply was to lay down the ironclads *Warrior* and *Black Prince, Defence* and *Resistance,* and to begin a series of trials of guns against armour plate in an endeavour to try to find the best combination of ordnance and projectile with which to arm the new vessels. The army also took an interest, since they too were going to be faced with the task of arming the defences with something suited to the new threat.

The sight, or even the thought, of these French ironclads lying at anchor in Cherbourg Harbour, fifty miles from Portsmouth, with the prospect of their foraying across the Channel or making offensive sweeps against merchant shipping led to an invasion scare of panic proportions. Under the direction of Lord Palmerston, a Royal Commission was appointed on 20 August 1859 'to Consider the Defences of the United Kingdom' and with the publication of their report the era of intensive coast fortification began.

It might be said at this juncture that the popular appellation of 'Palmerston's Follies' to the coast forts, notably those of Portsmouth, is not quite fair to that gentleman. In order to placate public opinion he was virtually forced to create the Royal Commission; having done so, when Parliament approved its recommendations he was in no position to countermand their wishes. Indeed, he had pruned the original estimates by over a quarter before presenting them to Parliament, as will shortly be seen. He then died in 1865 before most of the forts were built, and he cannot be blamed for the subsequent expenditure and building.

The document produced by the Royal Commission was a voluminous report (Cmnd 2682) and was to have far-reaching effects, so it is worth considering it in some detail. The commission consisted of the following Members:

Sir Henry David Jones, Major-General, Kt, CB
Duncan Alexander Cameron, Major-General
George Eliot, Rear Admiral of the Blue
Sir Frederick Hallett, Kt, Major-General, Indian Army
Astley Cooper Key, Captain RN
Lt-Col John Henry Lefroy, RA, Colonel of the Army
James Ferguson, Esq

Of this party, without doubt the most significant members were Cooper Key and Lefroy. Cooper Key was an ardent technical reformer, and the records of the Ordnance Select Committee of the period are rarely devoid of some mention of his name when questions of naval armament were being discussed. Lefroy was one of the foremost artillerymen of his, or any other, time. He made his mark early in life by being one of the young officers who founded the Royal Artillery Institution, one of the first regimental bodies to devote itself to professional studies. In 1843 he had sledged across Canada to Hudson's Bay to take observations of the magnetic pole which remained the standards for many years. He had been responsible for introducing new artillery techniques and, after his duties on the commission were over, went on to greater things. He became Director-General of Ordnance in 1868, Governor of Bermuda in 1871, was knighted in 1877, became Governor of Tasmania in 1880; he died in 1890.

It might be added that 'James Ferguson, Esq' was not without some influence on the Commission; he represented the Treasury.

This group were charged to enquire 'into the state, sufficiency and condition of the Fortifications existing for the Defence of Our United Kingdom and an examination had into all works at present in progress for the improvement thereof, and consideration given to the most efficient means of rendering the same complete, especially all such Works of Defence as are provided for the protection of Our Royal Arsenals and Dockyards', and to offer 'such suggestions as may seem to you meet as, regard

THE PLANS

being had to the works completed and in progress, and to the ordinary number of Our Royal Artillery voted by Parliament, will render Our United Kingdom in a complete state of defence'.

At first glance this seems to be an all-enveloping charter, but on closer examination, two things stand out; firstly the accent on 'Our Royal Arsenals and Dockyards', and secondly the apparently casual note that suggested improvements had to bear in mind 'the ordinary number of Our Royal Artillery voted by Parliament'. In other words, there was to be no increase of the strength of the regular army to man any proposed defences. This was to be a fundamental feature of the subsequent plans.

The Report, published on 7 February 1860, began in the best military fashion by defining the object to be attained by fortifying any place:

(a) to enable a small body of troops to resist a superior force, or
(b) to enable partly trained bodies of men to contend successfully with those more perfectly disciplined than themselves.

It then proceeded to insert the thin end of a very substantial wedge, rendered necessary by the wording of the commission's charge:

> There seems to be no reason to doubt that such troops as may be got together from the disembodied or less perfectly trained portion of the militia with local or other volunteers would, with an admixture of Regular soldiers, be able to defend our Dockyards against very superior numbers when fortified with due regard to these principles.

After discussing various forms of defence proposed in the past, the commission pointed out, by way of an example of their problems, that the coastline from the Humber to Penzance is 750 miles long, on 300 miles of which they considered a landing might be feasible. They considered that such an extended line would be impossible to fortify entirely so as to prevent a determined enemy from landing, and thus 'were of the opinion that the fortifications of this country should be confined to those points at which an enemy would strike, and of harbours whose possession would give him sure bases for operations in positions favourable to his designs'.

They then gave reasons for believing that neither the navy, the regular army, the volunteer force, or any combination of these, could be relied upon as being sufficient in themselves to prevent invasion; considered the provision of 'floating batteries' modelled upon the French pattern used in the Crimea, and discarded them until some authoritative statement could be made upon their utility; and finally recommended a chain of forts to cost £10,390,000, of which sum £1,885,000 was for the purchase of land, £7,005,000 for the erection of forts, £500,000 for their armament, and £1,000,000 to be reserved for the provision of a 200-gun force of floating batteries, if considered a suitable form of defence after examination by a special committee.

The specific recommendations for each of the fortress areas will be dealt with in greater detail when discussing these areas later, but a summary of the expenditure proposed will not be out of place here.

Area	Purchase of Land £	Construction of Works £	Money already Authorised but not voted £	Total £
Plymouth	755,000	1,915,000	350,000	3,020,000
Portsmouth	330,000	2,070,000	400,000	2,800,000
Pembroke	150,000	450,000	165,000	765,000
Portland	100,000	150,000	380,000	630,000
Thames		180,000		180,000
Medway	50,000	400,000		450,000
Chatham	180,000	1,170,000		1,350,000
Woolwich	300,000	400,000		700,000
Dover	20,000	150,000	165,000	335,000
Cork		120,000		120,000
Armament of Works:				500,000
Floating defences:				1,000,000
Grand Total:				11,850,000

THE PLANS

(The difference between this figure and the £10,390,000 quoted earlier lies in the inclusion here of money already authorised for defence in Parliamentary estimates but which had not actually been voted—ie money promised but not yet in the army's hands.)

By way of softening the blow, the commissioners went on to explain that the taxpayer would not be expected to foot the bill all at once:

> Judging by the progress of works already undertaken, those which Your Commissioners recommend may very well be executed within three years, but it would be desirable to allow three years and a quarter in order that contractors may have the benefits of the months from April to June in the fourth year. Payment will therefore be extended over four years. The entire expenditure may thus be apportioned as follows:
>
> | First year: | £3,675,000 |
> | Second year: | £4,381,000 |
> | Third year: | £2,686,000 |
> | Fourth year: | £1,108,000 |

Then came a further insertion of the manpower wedge:

> *Manning* Your Commissioners, having carefully considered this question, are of the opinion that the description of the duty and amount of training required for the service of Garrison Guns are comparatively of so simple a nature that to employ solely for that purpose a highly trained and specially educated body of men such as now compose the Royal Artillery is not absolutely necessary . . . We feel justified therefore in expressing a belief, which is supported by evidence before us, that previously untrained men of average capacity can be taught the ordinary duties required for such service in about a month and that in about three months such men might be made capable of performing the duties necessary for the efficient working of Garrison Artillery in the contemplated works, when supported by a due admixture of fully trained men and commanded by properly qualified officers.

It is said that in later years, when Todleben visited Portsmouth and saw the chain of forts there, he exclaimed 'Where in God's name do they expect to find the soldiers to man them?' If he had read the above paragraph he would have known: from the ploughboys, dockyard mateys and other indigenous population of the area, volunteered in time of peace, likely pressed in time of war, and all cemented together by a thin paste of regular gunners. It is difficult to reconcile the statement that serving garrison guns was 'simple' with the one pointing out that the Royal Artillery was composed of 'highly trained and specially educated men'. And while the service of the contemporary muzzle-loading smooth-bore gun might be said to be simple, this state of affairs was not to last for long, and Cooper Key and Lefroy must have been aware of the likelihood of more complex weapons coming into use very soon. It looks very much as if the experts were outvoted on this score, and the tempting but deceptive policy of manning complex weapons with half-trained men was accepted as a viable proposition.

It would not be out of place to point out here that this policy was not confined to the United Kingdom. An American board of enquiry in 1885 recommended the provision of 3,319 guns to defend 27 ports in the United States and proposed manning them in much the same way. But the United States Artillery were not slow to point out the drawbacks:

> It is unnecessary to say that these guns, numerous as they are and formidable as they ought to be, are only buried capital unless they be properly manned—not merely *manned* but *properly* manned. To take a man from the plow and set him to run a locomotive would be deemed criminal by any intelligent man, but the criminality is trivial compared to setting him to operate any of the great engines of war now included in the term cannon.

Finally the question of armament was approached:

> The new works recommended to be undertaken involving the provision of extensive armament and large artillery equipments, we have directed our enquiries into the question of providing them and the extent of the existing store. In respect of expense, that proportion which is not pro-

vided for in Engineer Estimates appears to amount to about £167 per 68-pounder smooth-bore gun; it is less for the smaller natures.

The reference to Engineer Estimates refers to the fact that this costing included various aspects of installation which were chargeable as engineer services rather than as Artillery equipment.

> We are not prepared to say precisely how many guns should be placed in some of the proposed works of defence; this will depend upon the nature of the work in each case and is a detail to be hereafter arranged between the proper departments. Upon a general estimate however we are led to believe that the works herein proposed will require for their armament not less than 2,500 pieces of artillery . . . Taking these at an average of £200 each, as a proportion of them will be rifled ordnance, the estimated expense under this head will be £500,000.

Although we shall be looking more closely at weapons in a short time, it is worth noting here that as the commission were sitting, the Armstrong breech-loading rifled gun was entering service with the army and navy, and the whole gunmaking industry was on the threshold of technical advances which were to render most of the world's artillery obsolete thrice over within the next generation. In the costing of the forts and other works the commission were reasonably close to the right figures —a good deal closer than any present-day committee would ever hope to come, for prices were much more stable in those far-off days—but in the matter of ordnance and mountings there was to be an escalation beyond their wildest surmise. By 1874 the Director of Artillery was recommending the provision of guns costing over £8,000 each.

The report was not accepted without some argument. At this time it was customary for public-spirited citizens who felt they had something of vital importance to say to publish pamphlets urging their point of view, and a small number appeared on this vexed question. Some of them predated the publication of the report and after the publication of the Report of the Royal Commission, more pamphlets were published, either decrying the whole thing, or urging complete and immediate acceptance of the recommendations in toto. One interesting counterblast was a pamphlet entitled 'Comments on the Report of the Defence Commissioners, with an Analysis of the Evidence' by Sir Samuel Morton Peto, MP for Finsbury. Sir Samuel was an engineering contractor turned politician who deserves to be remembered, if for nothing else, as the builder of Nelson's Column in Trafalgar Square. He had been an extremely outspoken critic of defence matters in Parliament, and in the public press, but when invited to appear before the commissioners and state his objections, he 'declined to appear' as the Report quaintly puts it. His excuse, elaborated in his pamphlet, was that he really didn't believe in the whole thing, since in his opinion the navy were perfectly capable of looking after the defence of the country, and any further expenditure on land defences would be sheer waste. This was no doubt true in many respects, but his opinion was somewhat biased by his belief—testified to by a number of witnesses before the commission—that it was impossible for a fixed gun to hit a moving target.

After considering the report, the government decided to raise the necessary money by a loan, but before placing it before Parliament they made a reduction in the estimates by cutting out a number of the proposed works. Six forts at Portsmouth were removed from the plans, 15 works of various sorts at Plymouth, 10 at Pembroke, 1 at Portland, 4 at Chatham, and the whole of a projected defensive ring around Woolwich. This immediately shaved the cost by £3,930,000. With this settled, Parliamentary approval was obtained, and work began.

2
THE IRON AGE

We have seen in the previous chapter that the catalyst which provoked the reaction and led to the 1859 Report was the construction of ironclad vessels by the French Navy, and we must now digress from the activities of the castle-builders to see just what caused the commotion and the problems it posed, and see what measures were proposed to deal with it.

In 1812 one John Stevens of New Jersey designed a ship with a gun battery protected by inclined plates, and by 1841 he and his sons had made some fundamental discoveries about penetration of iron plate by the spherical shot of the day. It must be borne in mind here that 'armour' during the nineteenth century, until the development of Krupp's and Harvey's face-hardened steel plates in about 1890, meant nothing more than ordinary iron plates of massive thickness.

After hearing reports of Stevens' work, the British Admiralty, in about 1840, made various experiments to test the reaction of round shot against iron plates, and these led to the conclusion that iron was not a suitable material for warships; unfortunately the precise results which gave rise to this opinion are not to be found, but I suspect it was based less on the performance of shot than on the difficulties of using the material itself.

But in 1855, as already mentioned, the French employed 'floating batteries' encased in iron at Kinburn in the Crimean War. These were simply special vessels shielded with iron and acting solely as floating gun platforms for heavy armament. They were towed by men-of-war, or could manoeuvre in smooth waters by use of their small steam engines, but their purpose was simply to bring heavy firepower to bear on a point and not to act as ships of war. It was this class of vessel that the Royal Commission had referred to a special committee and for which it had earmarked £1,000,000, should the idea prove worthwhile. (In the event, the committee reported against them and nothing more was ever heard about floating batteries as far as British defences were concerned; what happened to the reserved million pounds is not quite clear, but it seems likely that it was made available for the other works of defence.)

From 1856 to 1859, when the ironclad first raised its head, experiments were made in England using the 68-pounder smoothbore gun to attack four inches of iron, for this was considered to be the greatest thickness of iron which could be applied to a ship and still allow it to float and manoeuvre. The naval constructors of the day had soon determined that a layer of iron alone was useless, and it was necessary to 'back' it, or support the rear face, by a layer of about two feet of oak or teak wood. As a result of these shooting trials, conducted by the inevitable committee convened for the purpose, it was considered that $4\frac{1}{2}$in of wrought iron, backed by 18in of teak was, for all practical purposes, proof against any weapon at a range of 400yd or more. It was this conclusion which led to the specification for the first British ironclads—the 'Warrior' class—calling for construction from $4\frac{1}{2}$in iron plates, fastened together by $1\frac{1}{4}$in diameter bolts and backed by 18in of teak and $\frac{1}{2}$in iron inner skin, all supported by iron ribs 18in apart. The inner skin plate was to prevent splinters of teak being propelled into the vessel by the impact of shot which did not penetrate. This form of construction was most important in future development, since a number of butt targets were built identically and used for comparative trials of guns and shot for several years, always being referred to as 'Warrior targets'; the expression is frequently found in records of the 1860s.

Although this construction at first appeared satisfactory, time and further trials showed a number of defects. The through bolts, by piercing the face of the plate, rendered it liable to crack if struck near the bolt hole, and the bolts themselves, if struck, were converted into missiles which punched their way through the backing and inner skin to do great damage within the ship. The wood backing itself tended to rot away behind the plates, necessitating expensive replacement from time to time; and the tongued and grooved edges of the plates meant that it was impossible to remove a damaged plate without docking the ship and doing extensive dismantling, and, moreover, tended to spread the effect of a shot's impact to the adjoining plates.

So far the benefits of iron plate construction had gone to the navy, but it was now argued that if a foreign power had ironclads, it followed that they would mount guns sufficiently powerful to defeat similar vessels, and thus it might be a good idea if the land defences were sufficiently well armoured to counter such a threat. The design advocated was to build the major structure of the forts from masonry but to face the casemate with ironplate armour, with an aperture through which the gun could fire. A 'Special Committee on Iron Plates' was assembled, and under their direction various designs of casemate, built to plans prepared by the Board of Fortification and the Royal Engineers, were erected at the Gunnery Establishment at Shoeburyness and provided with various types of iron shield. They were then subjected to fire from various representative weapons at close range to determine their resistive power. The results were sometimes remarkable.

One of the first difficulties the committee had to overcome was the question of obtaining sufficiently large forgings. These enormous sheets of iron, of such thickness, had never been required commercially and their production was difficult and expensive.

They therefore went to the ironmasters of the country and enlisted their aid, seeking their opinion as to the best type of iron plate to resist shot. To quote their report: 'The great diversity of opinion among so many practical men could only be accounted for by the fact that none of these gentlemen had ever had an opportunity of witnessing the effect of a shot upon an iron plate, and this, in some measure, explains the very small progress that had been made.'

As a result, when experiments were scheduled, the ironmasters were invited to attend and watch their products being tested, a practice which did much to assist them in overcoming various defects and which also inspired a friendly spirit of rivalry and competition between them. This practice of inviting manufacturers to see their equipment being tested has been followed ever since in British service, and without doubt has been of considerable value to both sides. It has also given rise to some amusement, as when one manufacturer was being led to the site of a trial for his first time and a 9.2in gun was fired close by. 'Good God!' he cried; 'I didn't know it had to stand up to THAT!'

After a series of simple trials against plates, which were mainly to help the ironmakers attain a consistent standard of manufacture, two casemates were assembled with iron shields. The masonry was 14ft thick, consisting generally of six to eight feet of granite backed by brickwork, the side walls and vaulting being of brick. The shield of one was a compound structure 12ft long by 8ft high and 21in thick (including 7in of teak), while the second shield was of solid rolled iron plate, 7ft high, 6ft wide and 13.5in thick. Two guns were mounted in the casemates and operated back and forth and fired, to prove that the designs were practical, and then the trial began.

The face of the work was attacked by a battery of 7in, 8in, 9in and 10in guns at ranges from 600yd to 1,000yd, firing a variety of shot. The general result of the trial was that after 33 hits the work began to become untenable; after 54 hits the guns would have been silenced; and after 86 hits, of which 22 were on the iron, the masonry front was virtually destroyed but the shields still offered a fair amount of protection.

'The issue of this experiment was of the utmost importance to the Service,' said the official report, 'because on it were based the decision that (1) our most advanced and important sea forts should be protected by walls entirely of iron armour, and (2) that for other coast batteries masonry might be used but that every casemate of these should have a shield affording protection against fire *at least* equal to that of its own gun.'

Thus in 1865 the form of the defences was finally agreed upon, though by this time half the forts had been built and had to be

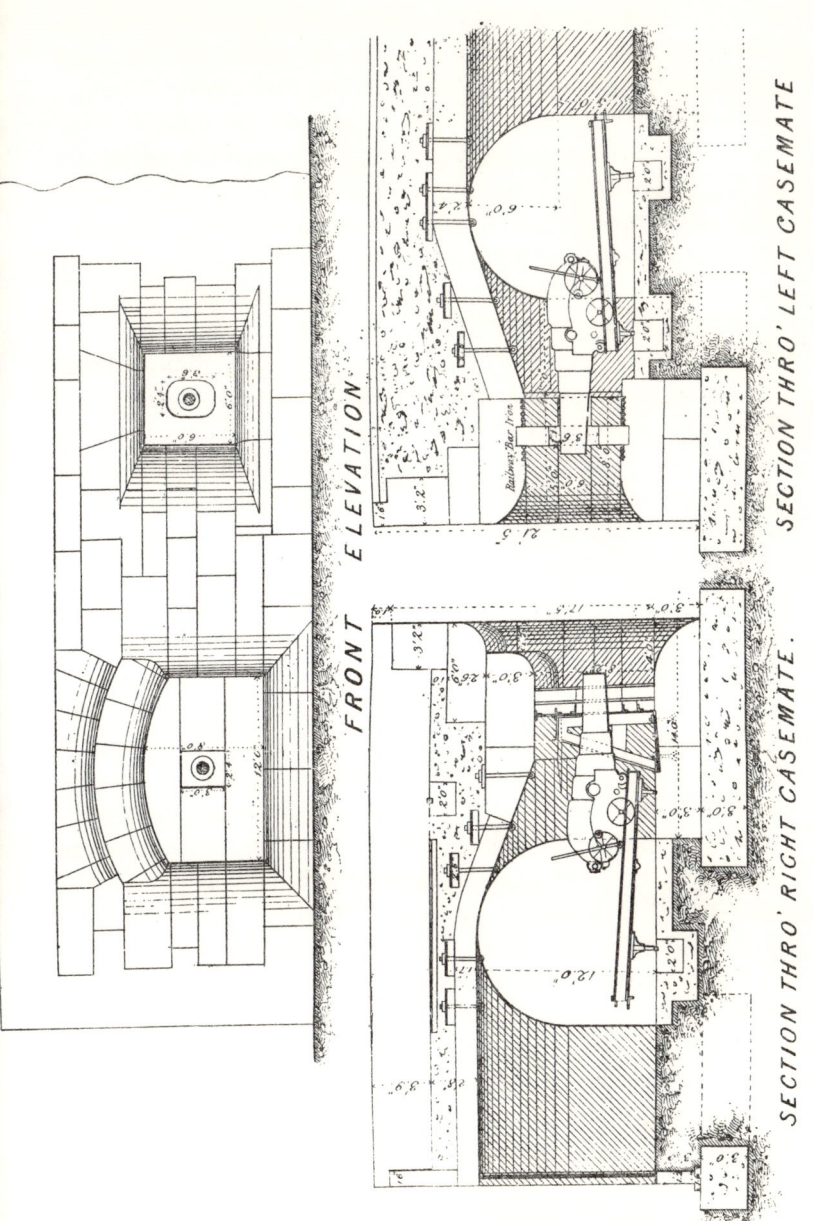

Experimental casemates erected at Shoeburyness in order to test the iron shield construction

modified to take the new shields. But at least it meant that construction could move ahead, for the whole programme had been delayed while this matter of protection had been thrashed out.

Unfortunately it wasn't as easy as that. The long saga of the leapfrog ascendancy of attack and defence, which has continued into the era of missiles and anti-missile-missiles, was beginning, and almost before the fort architects had completed their drawings the guns were getting bigger, the shot heavier and the propelling charges more powerful. The protection which looked so good in 1865 looked less attractive in 1866, and by 1867 trials were once more under way to discover a better form of protection. The difficulty was that drawing a thicker plate into the plans was relatively easy, but getting a thicker plate made was extremely difficult. The homogeneity of the metal was in doubt and the thickness of the plate led to deeper joints and thus greater points of weakness in the finished structure. An argument arose as to whether multiple plates would afford the same amount of protection; would three 5in plates provide the same degree of defence as one 15in plate? A small trial showed that a 7in thickness of iron disposed as a single plate, as two plates of equal thickness and as three plates of equal thickness, instead of giving resistance in the proportion 100 : 50 : 33 as might be expected, gave effects of nearly 100 : 95 : 88. Then another test showed that a 10in plate failed to stop a shot which had been stopped by two 5in plates. Finally a test of a 15in plate in comparison with three 5in showed that while the single plate had a slightly better resistance to single strikes, the multiple plate resisted a series of strikes much better. Further tests showed that separating the individual plates by a space of about five inches, by inserting some elastic material, prevented the plate breaking under attack by absorbing some of the energy of the blow. Iron concrete, made by mixing together iron swarf, asphalt, bitumen and pitch, gave the best results, though bricks in asphalt, concrete and hardwood were also satisfactory.

These results were communicated to the architects and in due course this 'sandwich' method of construction was adopted in many forts, although several of those already built had to be

Page 33 (above) *Taken about 1875, this shows a 68-pounder converted gun on traversing slide and carriage, in an open embrasure;* (below) *in contrast, this photograph from the 1930s shows a 9.2in* BL *gun on barbette mounting at Penlee Point Battery, Plymouth*

Page 34 (above) *Rear view of the half-demolished casemates at Shornmead Fort, Thames defences. This well illustrates the enormous thickness and massive construction of a casemated work;* (below) *the rear of the casemates at Cliffe Fort, Thames defences, with the remains of a 6in central pivot mounting above*

content with the simpler shields of the earlier solid pattern, for the task of replacing them would have necessitated completely dismantling the works.

Turning now from protection to attack, we should consider the ordnance of the time and the means available to the artillery for attacking armour. Since the invention of the gun, except for a few aberrant attempts, the weapon had been a muzzle-loading smooth-bore firing a spherical shot or 'cannon ball', and when the Defence Commissioners sat this was still the standard weapon. And, as we have already seen, the commissioners visualised arming the works with the 68-pounder smooth-bore and possibly a few of the new rifled guns. Sir William Armstrong had put forward his rifled breech-loader (RBL) gun in 1854, and a series of trials began which lasted four years. In 1858 the usual committee was formed to examine a number of rifled gun designs which had been put forward as alternatives to Armstrong's system, and in November of that year they reported, recommending the Armstrong design for adoption. In November 1859 Armstrong was appointed Superintendent of the Royal Gun Factory, Woolwich, and manufacture began.

The principal features of the Armstrong guns were that they were rifled; that they were breech-loaders; that instead of being cast in one piece, as almost all guns had been up to that time, they were built up by shrinking a number of tubes one upon another; that they were made of wrought iron instead of bronze or cast iron; and that they fired an elongated projectile. Let us examine these features point by point.

They were rifled; the interior of the gun bore was grooved in spiral form with a large number of shallow grooves, and the projectile was coated with a lead alloy sheath. The rifling grooves bit into the sheath as it was propelled up the bore, and thus the projectile was gyroscopically stabilised in flight, improving range, accuracy and regularity of performance.

They were breech-loaders; the rear end was open, terminating in a mortice-like slot. A loose 'vent-piece' or 'wedge' was dropped into this slot after loading, and clamped in place by a heavy screw. The escape of gas from the gun chamber to the rear was prevented by a copper sealing ring in the face of the vent-piece.

They were built up; Armstrong calculated the amount of strength necessary in the various parts of the weapon. He made the gun barrel and then made additions in the form of tubular jackets or 'hoops' which were machined to close tolerances, heated, dropped over the barrel or previous hoop, and then allowed to shrink tightly into place as they cooled. In this way he built up the requisite thickness of metal and at the same time, by virtue of the shrinkage placing the inner layers under compression, added to the ability of the whole structure to withstand the force of the explosion inside the chamber, all without adding excessive weight.

They were made of wrought iron; previously guns were made from cast iron or cast bronze. Armstrong felt that these materials were old-fashioned and weak. Steel was in its infancy and seemed to be impossible to produce homogeneously in large enough pieces; wrought iron was the material of the age, so wrought iron it would be. It also had the virtue in those pre-high-explosive days that if the gun was too weak to withstand the force of the explosion within it, it split gradually, whereas guns of cast iron, bronze or steel invariably split apart violently and dangerously without warning.

They fired an elongated projectile; the spherical projectile restricted the weight of shot by simple physical laws. Given a sphere of a certain size, you automatically arrived at the weight of shot for the gun, which is why all smoothbore guns are referred to as 'something-pounders'. But an elongated spun projectile could be varied in size, short or long, to produce whatever combination of weight and calibre was desired. (The fact that there were limitations on the length of the projectile which had some important effects on stability did not become apparent for some years.) Note, however, that the tendency to refer to guns as 'pounders' did not vanish with the smoothbores; the last of this line, the famous 25-pounder, is still in use today.

Altogether, the Armstrong gun had captured the market, but nevertheless the forts of the day were generally armed with the 68-pounder, a gun which was everything the Armstrong was not.

It had entered service in 1846; it was a cast iron smoothbore of 95cwt firing a shot about eight inches in diameter. It was cheap, it was simple, it was robust, and above all else it was there, in store, in quantity. The new Armstrongs were going to arm the horse and field artillery and the navy, and garrison artillery was a long way down the priority list. Eventually numbers of Armstrongs were allocated to forts, particularly once the navy had realised their limitations, but it was principally installed as a shell gun and not as an armour attacker.

For the principal defect of the Armstrong, technically speaking, was the relative inefficiency of the vent-piece in sealing the breech properly. Erosive wear occurred in the copper facing ring, vent-pieces were sometimes jammed, and on other occasions were blown out violently due to inability to secure them properly due to wear. This led to the tactical failing, which damned them in the eyes of the navy and the garrison artillery: the breeches were insufficiently strong to withstand the firing of the heavy charges of gunpowder necessary to propel a shot with sufficient velocity to smash through armour plate. The 68-pounder could defeat plate; the Armstrong could not, except in very large calibres which had only been made experimentally and which were doubtful manufacturing propositions at the time. Fortunately for the garrison gunners, by the time the forts were ready to be armed the science of gunnery had taken another turn and they were about to receive the weapons which represented a great improvement, from their point of view, over both the Armstrong system and the smoothbores—the rifled muzzle-loading (RML) guns.

The defects of the breech-loaders, both in England and in other countries, had led to considering a reversion to muzzle-loading, but the advantages of using elongated projectiles and rifling were too great to be given up, and the RML system was developed more or less simultaneously in both England and France. Instead of a large number of relatively fine grooves in the barrel, three deep grooves were cut, and the projectile furnished with two rows of soft metal studs, offset so as to match the rifling twist. The power charge was loaded into the gun via the muzzle and rammed down into the chamber; the projectile was

ROYAL GUN FACTORIES.
ORDNANCE WROT IRON MUZZLE LOADING GUN 9 INCH 12 TONS R.

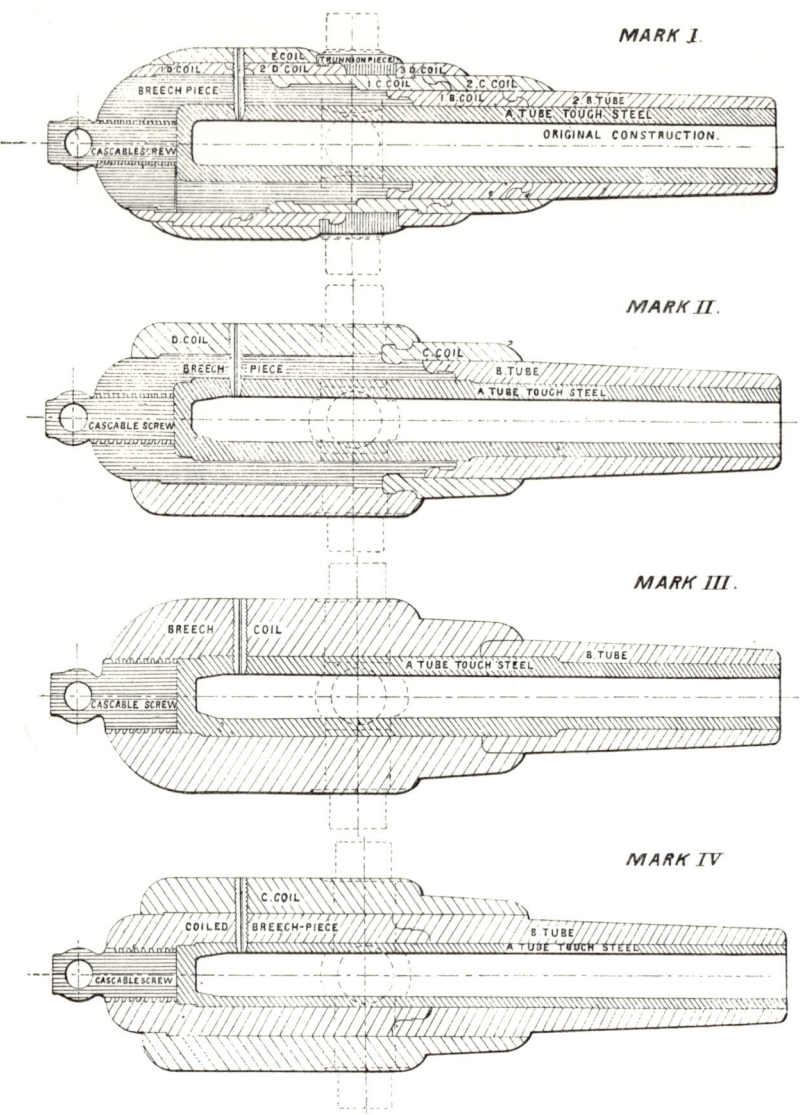

then inserted, base first, so that the studs engaged in the grooves, and rammed home so that the studs rode down the grooves until the projectile was in the proper place. On firing, the projectile was propelled up the bore with the studs riding in the grooves and thus imparting spin.

It is customary nowadays to point to this reversion to muzzle-loading as the classical example of the dead hand of reaction stifling progress and holding back the technical advancement of the army. But the same sort of thing happened elsewhere; the French went through three complete changes of equipment in ten years; the Austrians changed their system of artillery four times in eight years, as did the Germans. Experience had to be bought dearly in the matter of selecting ordnance. On the evidence and experience available in 1866 (for the Armstrong gun had been used on active service in China and New Zealand by the army and in Japanese waters by the navy), the decision to adopt the RML system was perfectly justified, and it was the only way by which guns of the requisite power could be produced.

In addition to the advantage of rifling, another feature was taken from the Armstrong gun; the system of built-up construction from wrought iron. This had proved its worth through several destructive trials and henceforth no gun would be made from a single piece of metal until the time of World War I, by which time metallurgy had made considerable advances.

An interesting problem now arose; with the introduction of RML guns, large numbers of smooth-bores were going to be made obsolete. Would it not be possible to convert them into RML by grooving the barrel? Being cast guns they would not have the strength of the newer built-up weapons, but they could still be usefully employed as shell guns and for land defences. After a number of experiments had been made, a Captain Palliser of the 18th Hussars invented a method which involved boring out the old gun barrel to remove erosion marks and then inserting a wrought-iron rifled liner. This was a sliding fit in the gun body and was then expanded into place by the simple expedient of firing a heavy proof charge. Trials showed that this liner so strengthened the guns that the conversions were more powerful than the original smooth-bores, and over 2,000 of these 'rifled converted' guns were made, both for naval use and for coast defences.

With the gun question settled—for the time being—next came the matter of the projectile. Hitherto the spherical ball had precluded any sort of scientific approach, but with the adoption of the elongated projectile there were several options open. Should the head be sharply pointed? Hemispherical? Flat? Recessed? Oval? Should the projectile be long in relation to its calibre, or short, or was there an optimum length? Should the gun be rifled to spin it rapidly or slowly? The only thing certain was that the propelling charge was to be the maximum the gun and projectile could stand, in order to extract the utmost velocity from the combination.

As in every other field of experiment, ammunition design relies on the maxim that if you ask the question properly in the first place, you're half-way to getting the answer, and the fundamental question in the ammunition world is 'What do you want to do to the enemy?' Loose answers such as 'destroy him' or 'sink him' won't do, as these early experimenters were soon to discover, and very quickly the question of attacking plate with the RML guns resolved into two schools, 'racking' and 'punching'.

The racking advocates contended that the system of attack best calculated to defeat armour plate was to smash a heavy shot against the structure so as to 'rack' or strain the whole of it and thus initiate its collapse. Penetration, of course, was advantageous, but the racking action would quickly bring about the demolition of the structure without the shot necessarily striking any particular part of the target or even piercing its skin.

The punching school on the other hand insisted that the object was to penetrate the plate cleanly and rely on the shattered fragments of plate and backing, plus fragments of the projectile (which usually broke up in passing through the armour) to damage material and personnel behind the protection. In other words they were out to attack the men, while the 'racking' party were out to attack the structure.

This, of course, led to the championing of two distinct approaches, the racking school favouring heavy guns firing massive bolts of iron at medium velocities, and the punching school arguing for less calibre and more velocity. Eventually a series of trials were performed at Shoeburyness which rather confounded the racking advocates. A 'Warrior' target was used, and a 7in RBL gun firing a 110lb shot against it at 1,175 ft per sec. The effect was relatively insignificant, the official report saying 'Made a slight indent. A bolt was started.' A 68-pounder smoothbore was then fired, with a velocity of 1,425 ft per sec, which smashed the plate and threw pieces off the back with damaging effect. More argument ensued until Lieut W. H. Noble of the Ordnance Select Committee proved to the doubters that it was the time taken to attack the plate which was significant, rather than the weight of shot. The amount of work done is a multiple of shot weight and velocity, and taking this as a guide—which the rackers had done—one would expect the 7in (110lb × 1,175 = 129,250) to be better than the 68-pounder (68lb × 1,425 = 96,900). But as Noble showed, the amount of time involved, i.e. the striking velocity, was a factor which materially altered this concept, since at low velocities the plate virtually had time to adapt itself to the blow and spread the load, whereas the high velocity shot took it, as it were, by surprise.

The application of this theory of delivering the shot at the highest possible velocity and not necessarily one of the highest calibre, and the gradual decline of the racking theory took one or two years to gain acceptance, but it was soon demonstrated that high velocity shot perforated and did damage behind the plate, and forward-looking thinkers were already contemplating the development of projectiles containing explosive which would penetrate and then detonate, giving even greater effect behind the target plate.

The next two questions to be answered were much more amenable to settlement; the first was what material was to be used for the projectiles, and the second was what was the best shape for penetration. In order to settle the first, shot from chilled cast iron, cast steel and forged steel were obtained from the most prominent manufacturers of the day—Krupp and Gruson of Germany, Finspong of Sweden, Terre-Noire of France, and such English makers as Vickers, Cammel, Hadfield, Firth and Landore-Siemens. All were made to the same size and shape and all were fired under identical conditions at identical plates specially made for the trial.

After intensive tests it was shown that against wrought iron armour the chilled iron shell gave the most consistent results, and this was adopted as the future standard. This material was developed by Major Palliser, the same officer (now promoted) who had suggested the lining of smooth-bore guns. Ordinary iron projectiles deformed on striking armour, but Palliser was sure that hardening the head, or even the whole body, to a glass-like degree would be no drawback, since the stress on impact would be compressive and would tend to hold the projectile together and act as a hammer to drive the hard point into the plate. He therefore had a number of shell cast with the bodies in a sand mould—so as to cool slowly—and the noses in a water-cooled iron mould, so that this portion cooled very rapidly and thus took on the metallurgical quality he sought. Palliser's shot were so superior in penetration that they were immediately authorised for manufacture, and remained in service as the standard piercing projectile for many years.

The shape question was resolved in similar fashion by firing otherwise identical projectiles with different head shapes. Eventually an ogival pointed head struck on a radius of two calibres was taken as the standard and this too remained the service optimum for many years. It is interesting to see that when a change of shape was eventually made, it was to a head of 1.5 calibres radius, a figure which the committee had indicated as a possible alternative to their chosen figure.

Having decided on the form and shape of projectiles for the primary coast defence role of defeating iron ships, and the guns to fire them, the only question remaining was the close range defence of the works against storming parties. For this the smooth-bore gun was deemed sufficient, when loaded with case shot—a thin metal canister filled with musket balls which ruptured on firing and ejected the balls from the gun rather in the manner of an enormous shotgun. It was also decided to provide the heavier weapons with shrapnel shell in order to allow them to deal with small boat landing parties while still afloat, and for this it was necessary to redesign the spherical Shrapnel Shell to a pattern suited for use with RML guns. Colonel Boxer, Superintendent of the Royal Laboratory at Woolwich Arsenal, had spent several years improving Shrapnel's original projectile, and he now produced an elongated pattern which was to remain the standard design for as long as the shrapnel shell remained in service.

Certain other projectiles ought to be mentioned here as they spanned the period from smooth-bore to rifled guns and were to remain in service for several years. Prominent among them was 'Martin's Liquid Iron Shell'. This was an improved version of the old-time 'red-hot shot'; in earlier days it had been the practice to heat up iron shot in a furnace close to the gun. When a wooden ship appeared in range, the powder charge was rammed, followed by a wet wad, and then the red hot shot. The gun was fired immediately, and if the shot struck it was invariably successful in starting a fire on the vessel. Mr Martin, an employee of the Royal Laboratory, proposed in 1855 a hollow spherical shell lined with a mixture of loam and cow-hair (for insulation). A special furnace known from its designer as 'Anderson's Cupola', which was a ponderous and complicated portable blast-furnace, was located in the gun battery and operated by a squad of men to melt a supply of pig-iron. When a target appeared, the empty shell was filled with molten iron; the portion at the filling hole solidified almost instantly to give a self-sealing effect, and the shell was loaded and fired. From the gunner's point of view it was a good deal less hazardous to fire than the red-hot shot, and its effect at the target was to break up and scatter molten iron all over the ship, starting several fires.

During the 1860s this shell was issued to a number of coast batteries together with the necessary cupola for melting the iron, but it seems to have been unpopular with commanders, who were somewhat apprehensive of the dangers of a machine full of red-hot coke and molten iron in the middle of their batteries in action.

In 1864 reports were called for from station commanders, and their replies were far from enthusiastic.

Eventually, since Martin's shell could not be easily adapted to RML guns, and because of the decline in importance of wooden ships, and the fire of common shell being equally effective, Martin's shell became obsolete in 1869.

Common shell were simply shell filled with gunpowder and fuzed to burst on impact. Their name came from their 'common' use in various applications, as distinct from the specific use of piercing shot or shell. In smooth-bore days they had been spherical, with a wooden fuze, but in RML days they were gradually improved to the point where two types emerged, Common and Common Pointed. Common were nose fuzed for use against troops and light targets on land. Common Pointed resembled piercing shells, having sharply pointed tips, but they were of ordinary iron and had no piercing value. They were filled with gunpowder and fitted with a fuze in the base so that they could penetrate light targets, such as the upperworks of vessels, and then burst within the structure.

Having now examined what the defences had to contend with, and how they intended to set about it, we can now revert to the actual works and see what had happened to the recommendations of the Royal Commission.

3
CONSTRUCTION AND PROGRESS

Once the report of the Royal Commission had been accepted, survey parties descended on the selected sites, conferences were held, and contractors were appointed and given their instructions, all of which opened the door to an orgy of castle-building such as had never been seen before. Gangs of navvies, at a loose end now that the great railway projects were largely completed, found employment for their picks and shovels in excavating the enormous ditches and piling up the ramparts of the new works. Stonemasons were engaged by the score and quarries thrived. Some of the more remote works, where labour was scarce, were partly prepared by military labour or by convict gangs—notably the Irish forts, which do not come into our consideration here—but one or two of the English and Welsh works, notably Portland where the convict prison was conveniently located, were superintended in their early stages by armed warders rather than bowler-hatted gangers.

The *trace* of the work—the outline of its perimeter—depended upon its geographical situation and tactical function. In some cases it was possible to adapt the design to a fortuitous piece of terrain so as to achieve the desired defensive posture and save a good deal of engineering into the bargain. In other cases it was possible to excavate a large pit and build much of the work within it, leaving only the barrack above the surface, and protecting the seaward side of the pit with masonry. But in the majority of cases there was nothing to do but simply erect the fort in the middle of nowhere and trust to its intrinsic strength to defy attack. With the encroachments of the last hundred years—the last thirty in many cases—washing round them today, it is difficult to visualise these works as they must have been when they were first built, gaunt, grey, forbidding piles, remote from any dwelling and commanding the land and sea for miles around.

The trace, then, took a variety of shapes, but wherever possible two basic shapes were preferred; for forts basically commanding the sea, a curved seaward face joined by two *gorge walls* to give a segment or wedge effect. For forts whose primary function was landward defence, an irregular polygon was preferred. Where possible a standard pattern drawn up by the Board of Fortification was adhered to, with local modification as necessary. It must be borne in mind that in 1860 fortification was still an exact science; the teachings of Vauban, Coehorn, Carnot, Montalembert and other seventeenth and eighteenth century masters were still valid, and the military engineer of the day was still conversant with all the esoteric terms of a bygone age. In consequence, the description of a work often sounded like a heraldic charge in its use of unusual terms, and a noted authority, Major G. S. Clarke, writing in 1889, was irked enough to criticise 'Vauban and his school, in whose hands permanent fortification grew to be treated somewhat as a geometrical puzzle—a species of maze designed much on the principles which may have guided Henry's chief engineer in laying out the approaches to Fair Rosamunde's bower, and, on the whole, very little more successful in keeping out the invader.'

But Clarke wrote this thirty years after the Royal Commission Report, and as the builders assembled in 1860 the air was thick with talk of lunettes, hornworks, demi-bastions, tenaillieres, cavaliers, caponiers and every other sort of architectural oddity. Fortunately the Corps of Royal Engineers, who were to be responsible for the designs, produced a man with a mind of his own; Colonel, later Lieut-General, Sir W. F. Drummond Jervois, RE. Jervois was undoubtedly a fortress enthusiast; he has been described as being 'bound and determined to erect on any barren rock or parcel of land on which the Union Flag had been raised a lasting memento to his gifted skills wherein expense seemed a secondary consideration.' There is little doubt that his activities throughout the farther-flung outposts of the British Empire merit this rather uncharitable description, but in the planning of the English and Welsh works he was more circumspect. Parliament had voted the money, and with few exceptions the sites were within easy reach of Westminster should any of the purseholders take it into his head to step down and see how the plans were progressing. So Colonel Jervois could hardly let his engineering talent run wild regardless of expense. Furthermore, he was a professional to his fingertips in an age when professionally expert soldiers were a rarity, and he was fully aware of the imminent changes in ordnance. In 1860 the two technical corps of the British Army, the Royal Artillery and the Royal Engineers both had flourishing professional institutes devoted to discussion, lectures and the publication of professional papers on every aspect of contemporary warfare as it affected them, and there was considerable and useful cross-pollination between the two. Engineers read papers at Woolwich and Gunners wrote for the Engineers, and nothing but good came of it. Because of this awareness of the possible power of the artillery of the future, and because too of the Royal Commission's comments on the manpower situation, Jervois abandoned the convolutions of the classic fortresses as being too difficult to man, too vulnerable to powerful guns, and, of course, far too expensive in time and money to execute. He decided on the simple polygonal trace and then went to work within that boundary to produce the most effective defensive work possible.

The general plan adopted was to surround the work with a high granite *scarp* or exterior wall some ten or fifteen feet thick, backed by earthwork and surmounted by a rampart. Within this rampart *casemates*—arched chambers with gun ports—would command the faces of the work, supplemented where necessary by firing slits for musketry. On the rampart, platforms were prepared for additional guns firing through *embrasures* or in *Haxo Casemates*, strong granite shelters mounded with earth, open at the rear and with a gun port at the front, giving overhead protection to the gunners and gun inside. The seaward faces of the forts were generally of granite or Portland stone, casemated, with roofs of masonry, brick and concrete up to twenty feet thick to give *bomb-proof cover*. The land face would be surrounded by a *ditch*, usually thirty to forty feet wide and about the same in depth; at the angles of the trace, *caponiers*, granite outworks of one or two storeys, ran across the ditch. These were provided with musketry slits and embrasures for light guns so as to allow the occupants of the caponier to cover the bottom of the ditch with a hail of fire in the event of an attacker managing to descend the vertical *counterscarp* or outer wall of the ditch. In some instances *counterscarp galleries* ran from the outer end of the caponiers, behind the counterscarp wall, in order to allow the defenders even greater firing ability against attackers in the ditch. The ditch itself, according to terrain and locality, might be a *wet ditch*, ie flooded with water to become what is generally termed a 'moat', and thus form a greater obstacle; although this intention was sometimes frustrated by nature and dry ditches became wet while wet ditches refused to hold water.

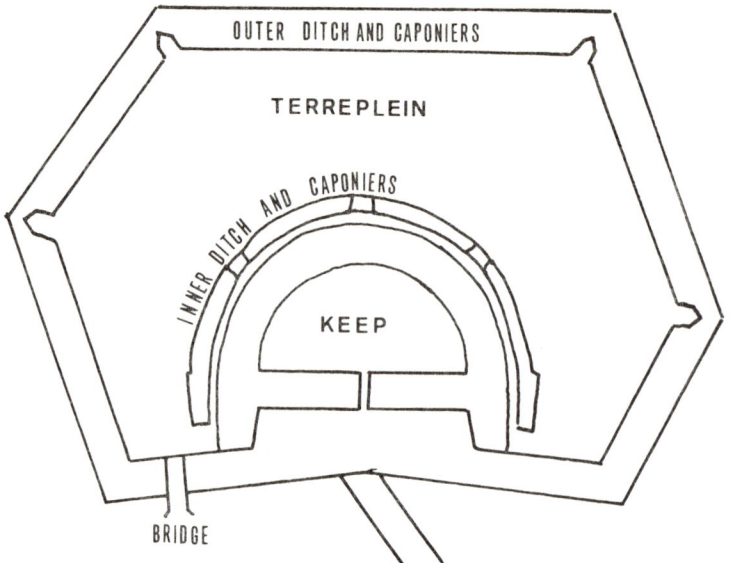

A simplified plan of Grain Fort, Thames defences, showing the principal features

CONSTRUCTION AND PROGRESS 49

Within the work, on the *terreplein,* there would be perhaps barrack accommodation for the garrison, generally mounded to be bomb-proof, or the accommodation might be incorporated in the mounded section behind the walls. Magazines, store-rooms, even wells were provided and positioned so that as far as possible they would be immune to enemy fire. In one or two cases some of the medieval castle spirit lingered with the provision within the fort of an independent self-defensible work, the *keep,* into which the remnants of the garrison could retire if the outer defences were forced, and there fight to the bitter end; this was usually positioned so that it could command the rest of the work and sweep the terreplein with fire. These however, were rare, since by that time it was realised that sealing yourself up in a keep while the enemy were prowling round with howitzers was simply presenting him with a well-defined and unmistakable target—a vertitable shell-trap as one critic put it.

This, then, was the basic plan. But implementing these plans took time. The commissioners had opined that the entire programme should take four years, but this was soon seen to be a forlorn hope. The magnitude of the works alone saw to that. Enormous ditches had to be dug, huge walls built, subterranean tunnels, chambers and magazines to be excavated, ramparts thrown up, and most of them in places difficult of access which restricted the engineers and contractors to the use of nothing more sophisticated than a horse and cart, a pair of sheerlegs and innumerable pairs of hands.

While the standard plan called for masonry works in the majority of places, where it was possible to raise the guns well above sea level so that there was no danger of ships bringing fire to bear on them from a superior level, the open battery was the preferred form. One advantage of this construction was that it provided effective armament in a good deal less time than would be needed to provide even the most simple masonry work; all that needed to be done was to level the necessary gun platforms, lay concrete, provide a masonry or concrete embrasure, and then mound the front with earth.

But while most of the works were scarcely past the foundation stage, second thoughts began to occur to the planners. As discussed in the previous section, the ironclad threat had led to numerous tests and trials, and the opinion arose that forts themselves had better carry as much or more armour than their potential enemies. The Spithead Forts, originally planned as masonry works, were completely transformed into armoured structures, and every casemated work was now reconsidered and the addition of armour to the casemates discussed.

1864, the year when construction should have been completed, came and went with the merest handful of works ready for occupation and with even less progress in the matter of arming them. By now the American Civil War was entering its closing stages and during that war a number of American coast forts had been engaged in conflict, and the reports of these engagements caused even more delay as their implied lessons were considered, deductions drawn and plans modified yet again. Most of the land fronts were strengthened, and the question was reopened on whether it might not be a better idea to build earth forts rather than masonry works, since American experience tended to show that earthworks were better at absorbing shot. The question inevitably arose as to whether it would be cheaper to demolish the granite structures and replace them with earthworks or to continue to improve the existing designs. The last course was finally adopted since it was considered that the seaward threat was the principal one, and providing the enemy's ships could be kept at arm's length by the provision of suitable guns, then the chance of their doing damage to a soundly constructed fort was minimal.

Work now concentrated on the installation of the armour shields in the forts, of the multiple plate pattern discussed in the previous chapter. Meanwhile, the question of armament was in debate. By 1866 as we have seen, the Armstrong gun was in decline, and the rifled muzzle-loader was accepted as the only possible armament which would defeat the ironclad. Therefore the forts had to be armed with a suitable RML gun and the weapons universally selected were the 7in of 7 tons and the 9in of 12 tons. The 7in could penetrate 7in of plate at 1,400yd range, while the 9in could penetrate 9in at 2,400yd, and this was con-

Page 51 (above) *The entrance and wet ditch of Rowner Fort, Portsmouth, showing the brick construction used in many of the land side defences there;* (below) *a good example of a dry defended ditch is this one at Bembridge Down Fort, Isle of Wight. The caponier is typical of the period*

Page 52 (above) *The remains of the only Armstrong protected barbette position in England, that at Puckpool Battery, Isle of Wight;* (below) *Fort Albert, Isle of Wight. The original brick-built work has casemates, while reinforced concrete parapets on the roof were for the protection of more modern armament*

sidered to be adequate performance against the iron ships of the day and those of the foreseeable future.

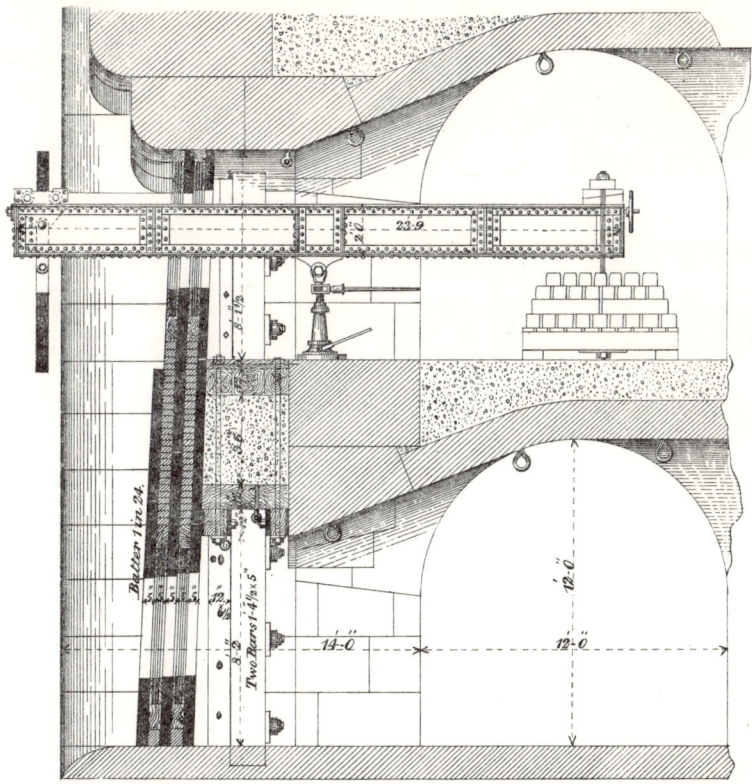

A sectioned view of the two-tier armour face of Picklecombe Fort, Plymouth, which also shows the method of applying the armour plates by girder beam and travelling carriage

The only drawback, of course, was that the weapons were heavier, more powerful and larger than the smooth-bores and Armstrong guns, and so the original gun strength could no longer be fitted into the works as planned. More changes had to be made, often losing one planned casemate of a work in order to make the remaining casemates larger, but at least sufficient prescience was employed to make the new casemates of ample size against the day when the wretched Gunners might desire to install a bigger gun; had this not been done at this juncture, it is interesting to speculate on the outcome. Would the forts have been expensively rebuilt to take larger guns in later years, or would the move to open batteries of barbette guns have come ten or fifteen years earlier than it did?

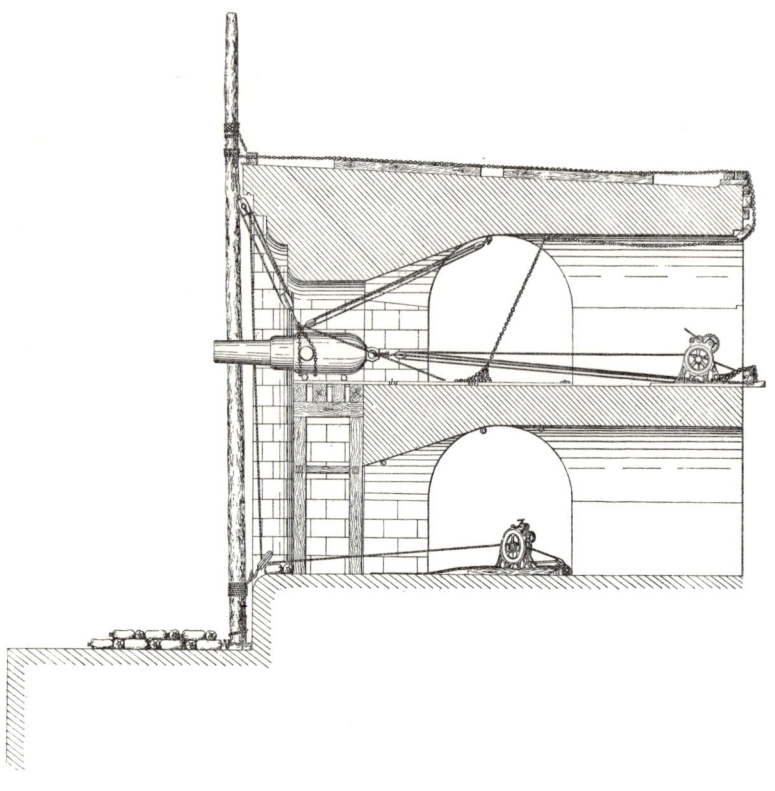

A sketch showing the arrangement of sheerlegs, spars, ropes and tackle to hoist the 9in RML *guns into position. Since the guns could only be brought by sea, to the face of the work, they had to be installed before the armour plate shields were fitted*

Eventually, by about 1872–3, most of the works were completed and the majority of the seaward defences were armed. These were the first priority and they were rapidly provided with

CONSTRUCTION AND PROGRESS 55

the latest weapons available. The Land-facing defences were less vital and at no time in their history did they ever receive their full allocation of guns. No more than a token number were installed, some of which were fired once in order to prove that the installations were serviceable, but the expense of completely arming the entire defence was as formidable as the problem of manning them in action. A little simple arithmetic shows the problem: casting up the guns demanded by the final plans gives the following numbers—and this is considering only the major fortresses—

7in 7 ton	642
8in 9 ton	12
9in 12 ton	403
10in 18 ton	165
12in 25 ton	25

Now consider the number of guns actually built, as given in various editions of the *'Treatise on Service Ordnance'*:

7in 7 ton	'numerous' (possibly 500)
8in 9 ton	'a few' (less than 12)
9in 12 ton	352
10in 18 ton	Possibly 50
12in 25 & 35 ton	33

Comparison of the two sets of figures shows a shortfall of 19 12in, about 115 10in, 51 9in, and probably about 120 7in. And it must be remembered that this comparison does not even begin to consider the number of guns demanded for works in Scotland and Ireland, the Channel Islands and the scores of forts throughout the Empire. Much of the deficit, of course, was offset by changes in armament—thus, works originally scheduled to mount 10in and 12in eventually received 11in or 12.5in—but even so the provision of land-side armament could never have been made to the planned scales.

Another consideration must have been the increased cost of ordnance by this time. It will be recalled that the commissioners estimated that the cost of the armament would average out at

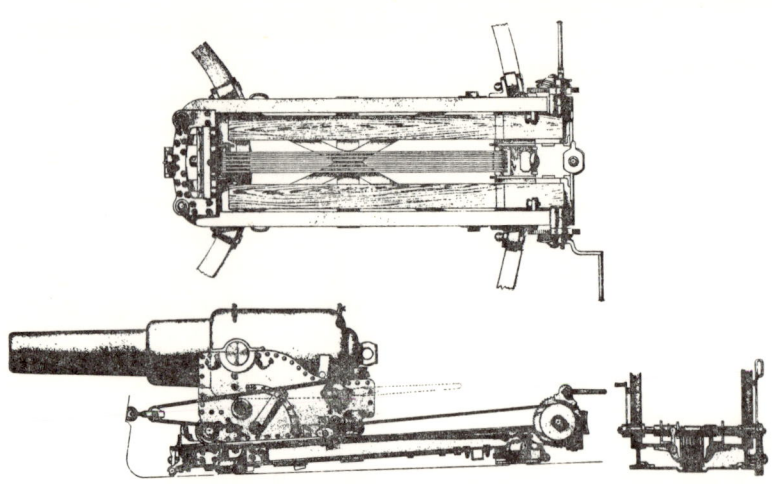

A 7in RML gun on wrought iron carriage and slide. The recoil was controlled—to some degree—by the interleaved plates between the carriage sides, known as a 'compressor'. This is actually a naval slide, land service types being rather higher-set on larger truck wheels

£200 per gun. Although figures are not available for all calibres, the rapid rise in cost due to the more complex construction of the new, more powerful guns is exemplified by the 10in 18 ton Mark I of 1868, which cost £1,250 for the gun and £577 for the carriage, with every round of ammunition costing £4.4.0d. A more interesting and enlightening set of figures was produced by the Director of Artillery in 1873 when comparing systems of construction, in which the cost of a work per gun mounted was calculated. This was arrived at by dividing up the work into the proportions chargeable to each gun of the basic structure, magazines, shields, parapets and so forth, and gave these values:

An open battery emplacement with magazines, but without shield	£590
An open battery emplacement with magazines and with iron shield	£2,425
An open battery emplacement with magazines, shield and splinterproof overhead cover	£2,642
A casemate and shield, magazine, lifts etc.	£3,849

CONSTRUCTION AND PROGRESS 57

To these should be added the cost of the gun and platforms:

9in 12 ton RML gun	Approximately	£800
9in casemate carriage and platform		£379
9in dwarf carriage and platform (for open batteries)		£448

It can be seen from this table that the cost of iron shielding considerably increased the price of a gun position, by £1,800 in the case of an open battery, and the relative costs of open batteries and casemates were sufficiently divergent to warrant more reliance being placed on the open battery form of construction if it could be shown to be as tactically effective. As it turned out the advantages were to become apparent in other directions too. In a number of works open batteries had been chosen largely because the terrain prevented the use of extensive casemated works and because the guns could be placed well above water level and thus would not be exposed to raking fire from ships. When the works were completed, the guns mounted, and firing practice took place, the casemates displayed the disadvantages which had been known prior to the decision to build in this form but which had been accepted as the price which had to be paid to obtain the necessary degree of protection. The casemates were restricted areas in which to contain a heavy gun and its detachment, and careful drill was necessary to obtain the desired rate of fire without the men getting in each other's way, or, more serious, getting in the way of twelve to eighteen tons of recoiling gun. On firing, unless the wind happened to be in a favourable quarter, the casemate rapidly filled with fumes and smoke which almost choked the gunners and made it impossible to lay the gun over the open sights. The stark outline of the casemate gave the enemy a well-defined target at which to take aim, and the effect of a projectile, be it a rifle ball or a cannon shot, which passed through the shield port and entered the casemate to ricochet around inside, was far more devastating than it would have been in an open position.

To try and mitigate some of the worst effects of fumes and smoke, most casemates were open at the rear. During normal times this aperture was closed by a wooden frame-work with windows and doors to give some shelter to the occupants, since the casemate was also the living quarters of the gun detachment. But as trials soon showed, the effect of firing a heavy gun inside the casemate was hardly compatible with a flimsy wood and glass structure, and during practice the windows and doors were generally removed, while standing orders provided for the removal of the entire wooden frame in time of war.

To try and prevent casualties from enemy fire the 'mantlet' was developed. This was a thick curtain of woven rope suspended inside the casemate shield and mounted on rings running on a 'mantlet bar', very much like a massive curtain rod. Two mantlets were hung in each casemate and pulled close about the gun's chase so that small arms fire or splinters of metal or masonry struck from the outer face of the casemate by enemy shot would be caught in the rope weave and prevented from entering. Moreover the mantlet tended to keep out some of the smoke and fumes, though due to its proximity to the gun muzzle it was easily ignited by the gun flash unless kept constantly saturated with a solution of calcium chloride. Final experiments with mantlets were made in 1871 and issues began in the following year, every iron shield being eventually fitted.

As a result of these various defects of the casemate, a number of inventors considered the problem of how to protect the gun and its detachment as much as possible without unduly hampering their activities. One of the first ideas to be put forward was the 'Muzzle Pivoting Carriage' of Lt Col G. Shaw, RA, who submitted his ideas to the Ordnance Select Committee in 1863. The principal feature of his idea was that the axis about which the gun elevated and depressed was no longer at the trunnions, or the point of balance of the gun, but on an imaginary line passing through the muzzle. Thus the casemate port had only to be big enough to admit the muzzle without having to provide room for it to elevate and depress, which of course reduced the chance of enemy fire entering. Used in conjunction with a carriage having an 'A' pivot, in which the traversing pivot was vertically beneath the muzzle through the centre-line of the shield, Shaw's design ensured the minimum space for enemy fire to enter.

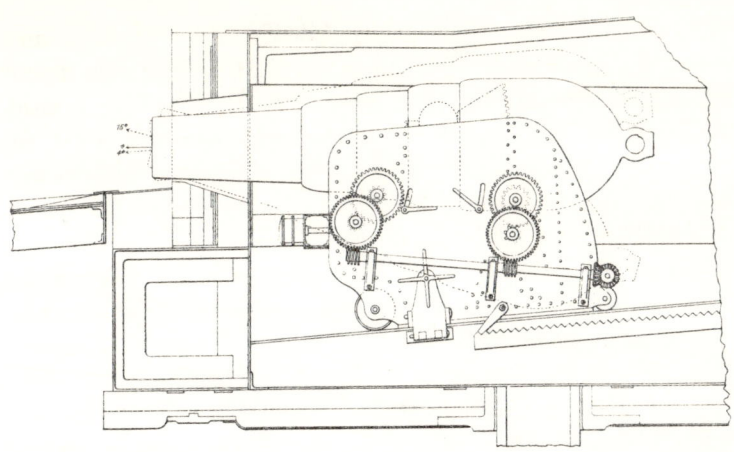

Lt-Col Shaw's design of muzzle-pivoting carriage. By operating a handwheel the shaft was rotated to turn the spur gears, which operated on two racks and lifted the rear of the gun about its pivot at the muzzle

After about six years of desultory trials the inevitable Special Committee was convened, and in March 1870 they submitted their report. They were 'unanimously of the opinion that no system of muzzle-pivoting for guns mounted in coast batteries is desirable' largely on the grounds that it 'interfered with the efficient working of the gun'. When examining the matter the Committee had been informed by Colonel Jervois, who was at the time Deputy Director of Works, that certain forts were already in course of construction with the shield ports made as small as possible in anticipation of the adoption of muzzle-pivoting carriages; this made no impression at all. 'The Committee desire to record their opinion that it would be far preferable to increase the size of the ports rather than to provide special carriages for these forts.' His Royal Highness the Field Marshal Commanding-in-Chief, the Defence Committee, and finally the Secretary of State for War concurring, the muzzle-pivoting carriage was officially dead.

It refused to lie down though. The Admiralty decided to use some, and then, two years later, Colonel Jervois returned to the arena with the news that he had completed two forts with small ports. 'It becomes a question of whether the guns should be so mounted or . . . looking to the desirability of arming without delay, service casemate carriages blocked up . . . should be employed as a temporary measure'. This caused a flutter in the Director of Artillery's dovecote, but a Lt Col Inglis was resourceful enough to produce an up-to-date design, which was followed soon after by a design from the Royal Carriage Department which used a single hydraulic jack beneath the gun breech to lift and lower it about the muzzle pivot. Both designs were put in hand immediately so that a comparative trial could be made. Within a short time the tests had been done and a design incorporating features of both models, using a hydraulic jack to lift the gun but with screw-jack 'followers' to take the strain when firing, had been put into manufacture, and by 1874 the carriages were en route to the forts. It was 1920 before these designs, officially known as 'Small Port Carriages', were to be declared obsolete, and the basic principle was revived in the 1960s to provide a suitable mounting to allow machine guns to be fired from helicopter windows.

But the muzzle-pivoting carriage was only a palliative for use in certain places, and by no means cured the basic defects of the casemate. While the restricted port lessened the chance of a missile's entry, it complicated the carriage design and slowed the service of the gun, and it did nothing to keep out the smoke and fumes. It was only adopted in small numbers of defences which were so sited as to be staringly obvious close-range targets. The real answer was to hide the weapon away completely until the time came to fire it, then expose it and fire, and then conceal it again while re-loading went on, all of these activities to be carried on in the open where smoke and fumes could disperse easily and there was ample room for the men to move about. Basically this came down to a question of lowering the gun behind a parapet, and it had been tried before; as long before as 1835 a Colonel De Russy of the US Artillery had designed a gun carriage on eccentric wheels so that as it recoiled to the rear it was also lowered behind the parapet. While theoretically workable it was impractical and never succeeded in catching anyone's fancy.

The problem was finally solved by a resourceful Scotsman, a member of a Militia Coast Artillery Battery. The Proceedings of the Ordnance Select Committee, Vol III p 182 record 'Report No 3705, 3 April 1865. A Protecting Barbette Traversing Carriage proposed by Captain*'. (The Committee were always reluctant to identify the author of any scheme they were about to condemn.) Their summing-up must have dismayed the inventor, who was in fact Captain Moncrieff of the Edinburgh Militia Artillery: 'The Committee are of the opinion that, although somewhat ingenious, the arrangement is too complicated to be serviceable ... The advantage which Captain * expects to realise by this method of mounting ordnance is much over-rated and, in the opinion of the Committee, is quite incommensurate with the expense which would attend its introduction. Entertaining these views, they recommend that no further encouragement be given to him.'

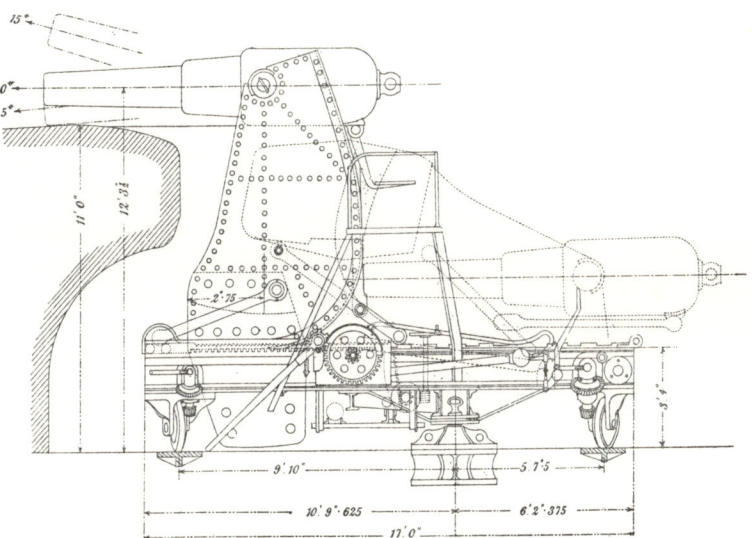

Moncrieff's disappearing carriage for the 7in RML *gun, Pattern II. The dotted lines show the position of the gun behind the parapet for loading*

'Although somewhat ingenious' was the under-statement of 1865. Moncrieff's design was outstanding. The gun was suspended by its trunnions on top of two iron-plate arms or 'elevators' which had curved rear surfaces.

From the gun a small sub-carriage or trail with rollers rested on an inclined plane. The bottom of the elevators was joined to form a box containing ballast, and the whole affair was mounted on a traversing carriage and concealed in a pit with a 9ft $10\frac{1}{2}$in parapet over which the gun barrel protruded. When fired, the recoil force caused the gun to move back, rolling the elevators back on their curved surfaces, lifting up the ballast counterweight. The gun sub-carriage ran down the inclined plane and as the gun reached the bottom, movement was halted by a pawl arrangement working on the elevator arms. The gun was now completely below the level of the parapet and could be loaded in perfect safety by the detachment. When ready to fire, the pawl was released and the ballast weight pulled the front end of the arms down, bringing the gun back above the parapet to be aimed and fired. Note that Moncrieff had solved not only one problem but two; not only had he found a method of concealing the gun, but he had also found a method of absorbing the recoil force, and putting it to some useful work, a trick rarely done since.

In spite of the committee's down-turned thumb, Moncrieff seems to have managed to get some interest going, largely by publishing papers on his system in the Journal of the Royal United Services Institution and in the 'Proceedings' of the Royal Artillery Institution. These must have caught the official eye, for by 1868 he had a prototype carriage built to mount a 7in gun and this was fired at Woolwich in May of that year. After that, things moved quickly. In 1869 proposals were put forward for mounting Moncrieff carriages in every possible (and some highly improbable) works, for in spite of the observations of the committee it was shown that a pit with a Moncrieff's mounting was a good deal cheaper than a casemate with armoured shield. By 1870 trials of a 9in RML gun on a disappearing carriage (as the species of mounting came to be known) were in hand. Moncrieff's original design, which entered service at 'Pattern I' was later improved by removal of the sub-carriage into 'Pattern II'. The mounting of 64-pounder, 7in and 9in guns was approved, but only two 9in were ever built, the extra power of that gun leading to an extraordinarily heavy mounting. Pattern I was officially introduced in December 1871, and 20 were made for 7in RML guns. Eleven of these went to Cork Harbour defences and the remaining nine to Flatholme Island in the Bristol Channel. About 45 Pattern II were made, some of which mounted 64-pounder guns, and of these 16 were installed in Britain, the remainder going overseas, most of the 64-pounder models to Malta. In the first flush of enthusiasm over 170 Moncrieff mountings were proposed in the United Kingdom alone, so the question might fairly be asked, 'Why, if they were so good, were only 65 ever made?' The answer is, of course, that while plans were afoot to employ the Moncrieff principle, the gun designers were at work preparing heavier and more powerful guns. The 9in RML was marginally stable on a much heavier mounting, and since it appeared that nothing less than 10in or 12in guns were going to prove acceptable as armour-piercers, and since these were far too heavy and violent for a Moncrieff carriage, the intentions had to be considerably modified.

By this time however, Moncrieff had turned to hydraulics and had produced a design of wheeled mounting for a 6.6in siege howitzer in which the gun recoiled on arms and was cushioned in its downward movement by an hydraulic ram, which then stored up energy to push the gun back up into the firing position. This was accepted for service with siege trains and a number found their way into forts for land-side defence as 'moveable armament', to be deployed within the fort in case of attack or taken outside in a flying column when needed. One might have expected Colonel (as he had then become) Moncrieff to have adapted the earlier coast design to hydraulics, but for reasons best known to himself he moved away from the idea to begin design of a mounting for a high-angle coast defence howitzer which was later widely adopted in the United States. The next step in disappearing carriages for British service was to come from another direction.

To return to the 1860s: while the choice of design was largely between casemated works or open batteries, there was a third pattern which, due to its enormous expense and complication, was restricted to use in very special applications. This was the armoured fort. Not a masonry work with iron shields, but a completely wrought iron structure, a skeleton frame clad in an armoured skin, with the guns in iron casemates firing through ports. These were built where it was necessary to place a work in a waterway because the limited range of the guns of the time made it impossible to close the water gap by batteries on each shore. It followed from their position that an attacking ship might be able to come quite close, and thus the works had to be as strong as possible. Four such works were built, together with three which were cross-breeds—masonry on the landward side and armour on the seaward side, since their proximity to the shore and the position of sandbanks and reefs ensured that no warship would be able to get behind them and attack the masonry face.

The four totally iron works were all in England; Plymouth Breakwater Fort, No Man's Land and Horse Sand Forts in Spithead Roads, and Portland Breakwater Fort. The cross-breeds were two in the Spithead area, St Helen's and Spitbank Forts, and one in Bermuda, Fort Cunningham. Except for the latter, a fuller description of their construction and features, since each differed slightly from the others, will be found in the chapters devoted to the various areas, but generally the system of construction was to build, with the aid of divers and caissons, a solid masonry foundation ring about twenty feet into the bed of the sea at the chosen location. This ring—usually about fifty feet thick—was then filled with clay and shingle, and the whole capped with a massive concrete bed. On this would be built the lower wall of the fort, of granite, and this carried the gun floor some ten feet above the high water mark.

With this foundation, the skeleton of the fort was built with wrought iron girders and three, four or even five layers of armour plate, with layers of iron concrete in between, applied to the outer surface. Inside, the 'usual offices' of shell hoists, fire control

CONSTRUCTION AND PROGRESS

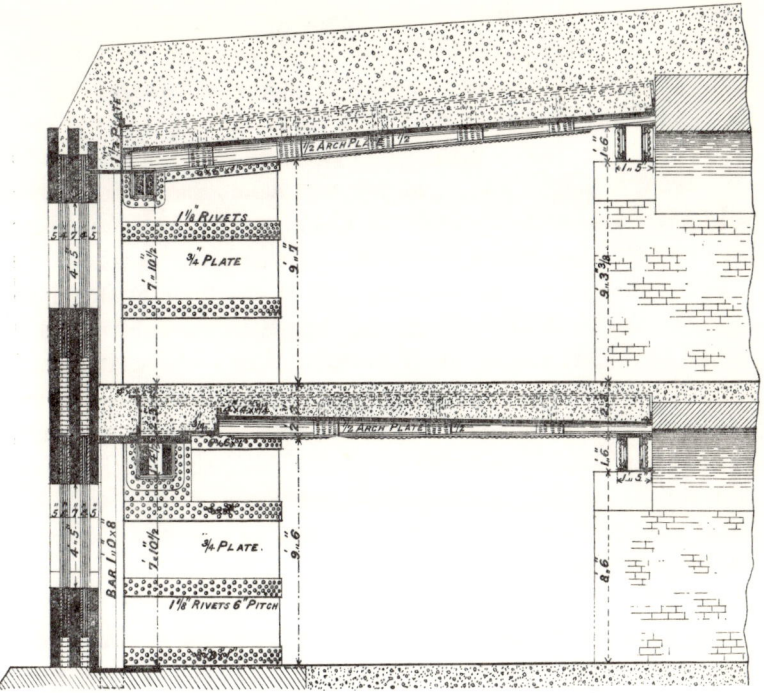

Sectioned view showing the system of construction of Horse Sand and No Mans Land Forts in Spithead Roads. (See also figure on page 130)

rooms, stores etc, would be carried in a central masonry core upon which much of the structural skeleton rested. The magazines were in the granite basement, partly below water level, and the guns were in iron casemates spaced around the perimeter of the fort, with the gun ports about twenty to twenty-five feet apart.

It has proved quite impossible to arrive at an exact cost for these iron structures, due largely to the complex accounting system in which different parts were charged to different accounts and became inextricably mixed with the costings of other works, but one thing is quite certain—they far exceeded the estimates of 1859. The entire Spithead defences, including five iron forts, two completely new land works, and the renovation of two older works, were estimated at £1,100,000. From various sources it is possible to make a reasonable estimate of what an iron fort must have cost; thus, an entry in the Encyclopedia Britannica (9th Edn, 1879) estimates the cost of one iron shield as £5,000 per gun. We have already seen that a 10in RML gun complete with carriage cost £1,827; a 12.5in RML cost £3,205 and the carriage £1,070, a total of £4,275 per piece. The cost of the foundations and masonry structure has been estimated at approximately £20,000. Taking Horse Sand as a specimen, these figures indicate that had it been built to the original plan for 120 guns it would have cost about £700,000; this, as much as tactics, may have been a considerable factor which led to amendment of the plans. As actually built it carried 25 10in and 24 12.5in guns, and on this basis the estimate becomes £437,775. Calculating on a similar basis for the four Spithead Forts gives a total of £1,052,279 which leaves very little change out of the original estimate for building the other works.

By today's standards, of course, a million and a bit is petty cash; even allowing for the relative purchasing power of the pound in those days, the bill translates into some £7 million, a sum which today would be voted away without second thought to produce seven miles of motorway or alleviate the difficulties of a nationalised industry. But in those days the pound was worth twenty shillings and it was a respectable gold coin. With this sort of arithmetic being done by a variety of interested persons, doubts began to be expressed about the value of such expensive exercises. And so, in 1869, a second Royal Commission was formed 'To Enquire into the Construction, Condition and Cost of the Fortifications erected, or in course of erection, under 30 and 31 Victoria and previous statutes.' Or in other words to go over what had been recommended by the 1859 Commission and see what was being done and whether the taxpayer was getting his money's worth.

The 1869 Commission went about their task with considerable thoroughness, visiting every work and examining it, making recommendations here and there for improvement, but generally approving of what they saw:—'The work has been well and skilfully constructed and there have been no failures' was a common remark—and made a painstaking examination of the expenditure which had been incurred. Unfortunately, of course, by this time the iron forts were still in the planning stage and their expenses were not available to be exposed to view: in most other projects the Commissioners expressed themselves satisfied that the work had been performed within the estimates, and in those cases where the estimate had been exceeded they were notably adept at so confusing the issue that a layman would scarcely have guessed that anything was amiss. In the intervening years there had been a number of supplementary votes and estimates for military purposes, against which some of the work could be fairly charged, so that in the end it would have needed an astute accountant to say exactly how the balance sheet should have been struck.

The 1869 Commission took reams of evidence from a variety of interested parties, including the major figures in the civil engineering profession and leading military experts, all tending to show that the expenditure was being kept in reasonable bounds and that the works were being constructed in such a fashion as to be effective defences. They also went very deeply into the Moncrieff mounting problem, and it is largely due to them that large numbers of Moncrieff mountings were proposed for the works, since it appeared that a saving of no less than £194,159 could be made by adopting this type of mounting in preference to shielded works.

But they were by no means complacent, and by no means 'going through the motions': nowhere was this more apparent than in their dissection of the magazine arrangements in the proposed works. In their investigation they had been profoundly disturbed by the apparent lack of concern shown over safety arrangements in the magazines of the new forts. Most were detached rooms in the rear of the work in which shell and cartridges were stored, sometimes segregated, sometimes not, or a cellar from which ammunition was issued through doors opening directly on the outside world. Illumination was by oil lamps, usually placed within a glass cylinder so as to prevent them being knocked over or inadvertently coming into contact with a gunpowder cartridge. Broadly speaking the arrangements had been left to the individual contractor, who, basing his work on a few simple guidelines, built what he felt to be sufficient to the task and within the estimate given.

Quite rightly, the Commissioners were perturbed by this, and they set about laying down a standard pattern of construction in which safety came before convenience. Lights were removed from the magazines and placed in a separate 'lamp passage' so that they shone through thick plate glass ports to illuminate the interior of the magazine, but without danger of gunpowder dust meeting the flame. Cartridges, shell and fuzes were rigorously segregated, and ammunition went from the magazine to issue rooms via hatches with flame-proof shutters. From the issue rooms it then went to the guns by lifts or hoists or man transport, the cartridges and shell still taking different routes, not to meet until they were actually at the gun.

This plan was so well conceived that, with little modification it remained the basic design for underground magazines for the rest of coast artillery's days. Additional funds were urged, and eventually voted, and the magazines in every work were either built to or altered to the desired standard.

With the publication of the 1869 Report, public opinion seems to have been placated; there appeared to be a potential threat to the Nation, and the measures taken and the expenses incurred seemed justified. One must also remember that at the same time as the builders were at work in Britain they were also at work in every port and coaling station in the Empire, piling granite upon granite, putting guns behind iron shields and running up enormous bills at the same time; the expenditure in the United Kingdom was only part of the story, and some of the overseas works were so involved and expensive that they were the constant target of Parliamentary watchdogs. Works at Quebec had cost £249,456; at Halifax £193,500; St Lucia and Barbados £470,000, while the defences of Bermuda were such that one exasperated MP stood up in Westminster to ask, of the kingpin of the Bermudan defences, 'Is Fort Cunningham made of gold?'.

CONSTRUCTION AND PROGRESS 69

But in spite of such sniping, the builders went ahead, satisfied that their efforts had been examined and approved.

By this time, too, the mechanical engineers were getting into their stride and beginning to solve a number of long-standing problems with varying degrees of ingenuity. Methods of controlling recoil were developed, beginning with crude friction brakes and then passing to hydraulic cylinders of simple design which were gradually refined and improved. With the muzzle loading guns all that was wanted was that the gun should be brought to a stop at full recoil so that it could be loaded before being run out once again, but with the advent of breech-loading it was possible to develop systems which both controlled the recoil and ran the gun out so that it was ready to fire as soon as it was loaded.

'With the advent of breech-loading . . .' It had to come sooner or later. The big rifled muzzle-loaders were getting bigger, as the ships of war they had to deal with got thicker. By this time some knowledge of ballistics had been acquired with a succession of experimental guns which showed that the easiest way to achieve velocity and smashing power was to make the gun longer and allow the explosion of the cartridge to exert its fullest effect on the shell. Moreover, instead of old-fashioned gunpowder charges, new-fashioned gunpowder in which the powder was moulded into prism shape and pierced with holes had been developed, which allowed a modicum of control of burning and allowed the pressure to be generated more evenly and over a long period, which also argued for longer guns. Increasing the charge in a short gun did little good, since the powder had no chance to burn before the shell left the muzzle, so that lumps of burning powder were ejected which was not only wasteful, but caused fires and other commotion.

With longer guns muzzle loading began to be a complicated business, demanding hoists to lift the enormous shells up to the muzzle, steam or hydraulic powered rammers to ram them home, and increasingly complex emplacements to contain all the necessary appliances. The zenith was reached with the 17.72in 100-ton guns, two of which were emplaced at Gibraltar and two at Malta (where they remain to this day). In order to load, a system of machinery known as the Armstrong Protected Barbette was installed in which steam driven lifts brought the ammunition up to a port in the side of the emplacement. The gun was traversed and depressed into alignment and the cartridge rammed home with a steam rammer. The rammer then retracted, the lift moved up to present the shell to the muzzle, and this in turn was rammed. The rammer retracted once again, the lift descended, and the gun traversed back to the firing position. All this took time; in an open barbette position it was capable of being supervised, but in other applications it was fraught with hazard.

A similar system was in use in the Royal Navy ships which carried heavy RML guns in turrets. After firing, the guns were run into the turret by hydraulic gear, the turret traversed and the guns depressed until their muzzles were aligned with an armoured structure on the deck outside which contained the ammunition hoists and rammers. There they were re-loaded, acting on instructions telegraphed from the turret. One ship so equipped was HMS *Thunderer* which had a turret carrying two 12in 38-ton guns.

On 2 January 1879, *Thunderer* was engaged in firing practice. The two 12in guns had been loaded, trained and fired. One, in fact, misfired, but the explosion of the other gun masked this, and since the guns were automatically run in hydraulically the lack of recoil went unmarked. The guns were then traversed, re-loaded, re-trained and fired once again. The double-shotted gun which was now loaded with a 110lb powder charge, a 688lb Palliser shell, an 85lb powder charge and a 575lb common shell, burst when fired, killing eight of the ten men in the turret and mortally wounding another. On the deck outside two more were killed and a further thirty-five were injured. Numerous theories were advanced as to the cause of this disaster, but it was conclusively proved that double shotting was the culprit by taking the other gun out of the turret, installing it in a blast-proof cell at Woolwich, double loading it and firing it, whereupon it burst in an almost identical fashion.

This was undoubtedly the final straw. Although the original

CONSTRUCTION AND PROGRESS

decision to revert to muzzle loading had been sound enough, given the state of the art and the requirements of the services at the time, by 1880 the gunmakers had had time to experiment and perfect their designs. They had been pressing for trials of their new products for some time; Sir William Armstrong had offered a 7in breech-loader in 1871, but it was refused.

By 1878 the drawbacks of the muzzle-loading system had become so obvious that Sir Frederick Campbell, the then Director of Artillery, submitted a memorandum to the Secretary of State for War to say that he had, after careful consideration of the whole matter, given instructions to the Royal Gun Factory to prepare a design of breech-loading gun to use the interrupted-thread screw-breech system. With the ice thus broken, things began to move rapidly. A 10in breech-loader was ordered for coast defence, and in June 1879 a Committee on Ordnance was appointed to give their opinion on whether breech-loading or muzzle loading was more suitable; the Admiralty spurred them on with a memorandum pointing out that 'The Navy could not wait for the best gun that laborious and prolonged investigation and experiment could produce, but dealing with the information they possess and the experience they have acquired, the Committee were asked to give the navy the best gun that could be made by the time the ships were ready to receive them.'

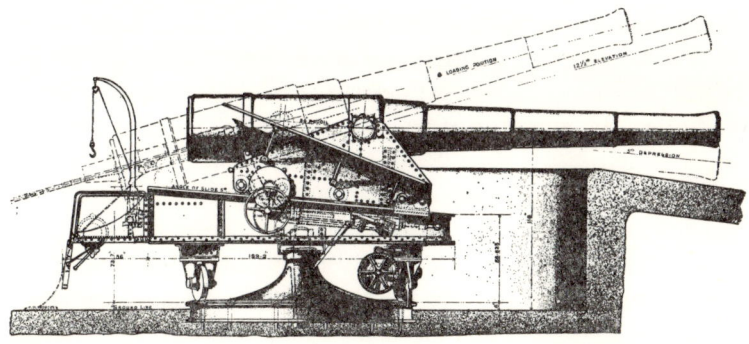

An early pattern of barbette mounting carrying a 10in BL *gun. Recoil is absorbed by a hydraulic buffer, but the gun was returned to the firing position by gravity*

The Committee recommended, in the following month, the manufacture of a 12in 43 ton breech-loading gun since this would not only be suitable for ships but would also suit the Spithead Forts. They also recommended a 10.4in gun for general coast defence use, and, in answer to an Admiralty request for a gun to compare with Krupp's contemporary 24cm (9.45in) model, they recommended a 9.2in of 18 tons, thus marking the conception of the gun which eventually became the coast artillery's standard weapon.

In the meantime, Armstrong took advantage of the favourable climate to present two breech-loaders, one 8in and one 6in, for trial. The 8in was a resounding failure, but the 6in stood its trials well and a number were purchased for use by the Royal Navy. The Royal Gun Factory was then given the task of producing a similar but more powerful model, and this was the birth of the other standard coast artillery gun. Of course, the complexity of construction of these breech-loaders put the price up; whereas the 10in RML had cost £1,250 and its carriage £577, the 10in BL cost £4,000 and its carriage another £1,000. The price of ammunition went up too; every time the new 10in went bang it now cost £11.7.0d instead of £4.4.0d.

So far, it might have been observed, all the coast defence guns had been heavy weapons, dedicated to the task of attacking iron-clad ships. But in the late 1870s and early 1880s another type of potential target made its appearance—the torpedo boat. With improvements in the self-propelled torpedo, numerous navies began developing light and fast boats which could either harry a fleet at sea or, more threateningly for England, dash across the Channel and into a defended harbour, loose off a few torpedoes at moored warships, and dash out again, their high speed and manoeuvrability preserving them from damage by the ponderous heavy guns of the forts. The navy were the first to appreciate the new threat to their ships at sea and provided themselves with a number of Hotchkiss and Nordenfeldt 3-pounder and 6-pounder guns, which became known as 'Quick Firing' (QF) guns. These were an important innovation. Their breach mechanisms were simple sliding blocks which could be worked remarkably quickly, and the ammunition was a 'fixed round' in which the shell was attached to a brass cartridge case containing the propelling charge and the ignition primer. In one movement one man could load the gun, and the rate of fire, for those days, was astronomical: the 3-pounder could fire 30 and the 6-pounder 25 shots a minute. The army then took notice of the threat to the dockyards, stimulated by reports of French naval exercises of the early 1880s, from which it appeared that cross-channel raiding was considered a feasible proposition.

The navy had their QF guns in 1884 but the Army had to wait; there were no funds available. It was not until 1888 that the 'Stanhope Programme' to improve the inner defences of harbours was approved, and £790,000, spread over three years, was allotted to cover provision of QF guns and controlled torpedoes. By 1892 all the provisions of this programme had been made; the 6-pounders and a newer and heavier 12-pounder had been installed at the most important harbours. In later years more were provided, and as the potential enemy got larger and heavier so did the guns; 4in, 4.7in and finally 6in QF guns were provided.

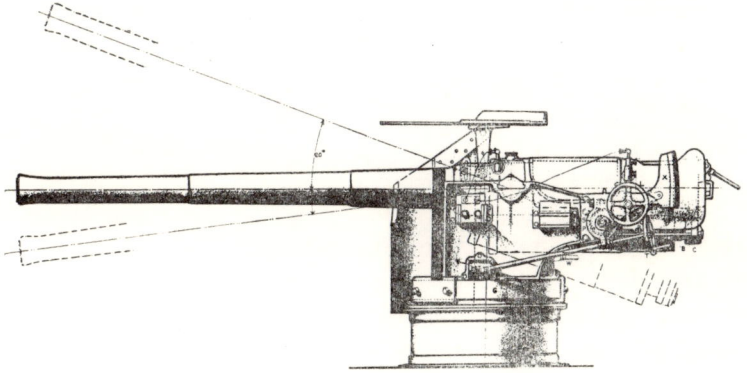

A 4.7in QF *gun on central pivot mounting. Recoil is axial and controlled by hydraulics and springs to give very fast reaction and thus speed up the rate of fire*

But before leaving the muzzle-loading era entirely, it will be of interest to pause and examine the 'Great Picklecombe Experiment' of 1872. At the time, the Ordnance Select Committee had a number of sub-committees working on a variety of aspects of defence, and one of these was the 'Committee on the Working of Heavy Guns'. This committee decided that with the armament of the major works completed, one such work should be manned on a war footing and put through its paces to see whether it could in fact produce the results expected of it. The fort selected was Picklecombe, in Plymouth Sound, and on 27 and 28 November 1872, under the watchful gaze of the committee, the alarm bells rang and the fort went into furious action.

After the noise died down and the smoke cleared away, the committee 'were of the opinion that the arrangement of the battery is satisfactory and convenient for the working of the guns . . .' but the body of their report abounds with so many 'ifs' and 'buts' that one is entitled to a certain amount of doubt.

> The issue hatches for cartridges are too high . . . The cartridge cage to be modified to prevent it catching on the side of the lift . . . The present arrangement of shell lifts will not admit of a supply . . . being kept up as fast as the guns can be worked . . . Some of the panes of glass forming the roof of the verandah were broken by concussion, producing dangerous splinters . . . When the side sights of guns were used they fouled the ports . . . which necessitated laying by the centre sights which only provide for 5 degrees of elevation . . . The laying was interrupted by the smoke of guns discharged from adjoining casemates . . .

Little things, taken individually, but several pages of little things add up to some major inconvenience. Probably the worst feature of the whole affair was the rate of fire attained by the 9in and 10in RML guns. The average time required to get off one round of 10in was 1 minute 45 seconds. A little elementary trigonometry and arithmetic shows that given an arc of fire of 45 degrees, the gun could just manage to get off four shots at a target moving at the leisurely rate of 12 knots and at a range of 4,000 yards, before the target sailed out of the arc. It was this one plain fact which governed the amount of ordnance intended for the forts of this era. Only by providing an overwhelming number of guns could there be any hope of putting sufficient projectiles into an area to damage an attacking fleet in the time likely to be available. It had been shown by the middle of the 1880s that there was no difficulty in designing and building guns big enough to punch holes in anything afloat; the difficulty now lay in getting the guns to have the desired effect on their targets. The degree of importance which attached to this simple proposition can be gauged by comparing the number of guns calculated to be necessary to defend a given area in the age of eye-shooting muzzle-loaders and in the age of breech-loaders with gradually improving rates of fire and methods of fire control. Portsmouth is as good an example as any:

Weapons demanded by the 1859 Commission:
Spithead 915 guns
Needles 81 guns
A total of 996 guns varying from 7 to 12in

Weapons actually mounted in 1881: Rifled Muzzle Loaders 85
Converted rifled 233
Smooth-bore 119
A total of 437, from 7 to 12.5in calibre

Weapons mounted 1 August 1914:
9.2in BL 14
6in BL 16
4.7in QF 2
12-pounder QF 23
A total of 55, from 3in to 9.2in

Weapons mounted 1 August 1941:
9.2in BL 6
6in BL 14
12-pounder QF 8
6-pounder QF 8
A total of 36, from 2.244in to 9.2in

Somewhere along the line 960 guns have become redundant; but surely no one will argue that the danger in 1941 was only four per cent of what it was in 1859?

4
COMPLETION AND DISSOLUTION

With the breech-loading gun firmly established as the New Messiah, the question of how best to install it came under review once more. The casemate form of work was thoroughly discredited by now, and the success of the Moncrieff pattern of disappearing carriage led to it being touted as the likely standard method of installation for the future. The original Moncrieff designs, using counterweights, were unsuited to any guns heavier than the 9in RML, but there was no shortage of inventors who were willing to try and improve upon it. The Elswick Ordnance Company of Sir William Armstrong, Mitchell & Co were well to the front, producing a design which relied on a hydraulic ram to keep the gun elevators up and resist the recoil force. When the gun fired the arms were driven back, pushing a piston into a cylinder and forcing hydraulic fluid into a chamber containing compressed air. The entry of the fluid compressed the air yet more, and the combination of fluid passing through a restricted valve and the compression of the air brought the gun down gently behind the parapet. As it stopped, so a valve in the hydraulic system closed, trapping the compressed air and fluid, and relieving the ram of pressure so that the gun stayed down in position for loading. After loading was completed the valve was opened and the pressure of the air forced the ram out and thus raised the gun above the parapet.

The first tentative patents on this were taken out in 1869, even before Moncrieff's original design was perfected, and it may very well have been the existence of this patent which kept

COMPLETION AND DISSOLUTION

Moncrieff from further development of his original idea when hydraulics became more common. But it was not until 1885 that the hydropneumatic disappearing carriage was a workable proposition, and in that year a spectacular trial took place to demonstrate the tactical advantages. A pit was constructed on the tip of Portland Bill and a dummy 6in gun was assembled to a disappearing carriage therein. Mechanism was provided to raise the gun every two minutes to the firing position, remain in the 'up' position for 20 seconds, discharge a smoke puff, and then retire into its pit once more. HMS *Hercules* was then given carte blanche to bombard it and do whatever damage it could. The trial began with Gardner and Nordenfeldt machine guns firing hundreds of rounds without a single bullet striking the gun or falling into the pit. Then the ship's 10in RML guns began firing broadsides; the gun remained undamaged in spite of some apparently close shots. Then the ship's guns were allowed to fire independently under their own gun captains; this was even less effective. During all the heavy gun firing the ship's 6-pounder QF guns were allowed to shoot whenever they saw the gun raised, but not one hit was made on the gun, its carriage or its emplacement.

This was enough to convince the most sceptical critics. A ship confronted with a casemated fort had a target; but a ship confronted with a gun on a disappearing carriage only had a target for fleeting moments, and if, with everything in its favour, HMS *Hercules* still couldn't hit the gun, it certainly had no hope of doing it in war when the target, far from being a dummy, would be shooting back at the ship. The disappearing carriage was here to stay, and it was adopted for the 6in BL gun in 1886 and for the 9.2in and 10in BL guns in 1888. They were installed all over the world, though not many were in Britain. By then there was sufficient armament in most places, but one or two works which needed re-arming at that time were given disappearing carriages where the lie of the land made it advisable, notably in the Thames Estuary.

The disappearing carriage guns were to remain in service for many years, the last model being declared obsolete (in Mauritius) in 1926. But disillusionment had set in well before that date.

The truth of the matter was that the engineering wizardry of the Royal Carriage Department and Sir William Armstrong, Mitchell & Co, had, between them, blinded the gunners with science so that they had lost sight of their primary function, which was to shoot at ships and not stare open-mouthed as tons of ordnance swung and swooped through the air. The *Hercules* trial compounded the mischief, for in their agreement that the ship had never hit the gun, the observers failed to attach sufficient importance to the fact that it had not been able to hit the emplacement either, and that wasn't whizzing up and down. The chance of a ship in motion managing to hit a target as small as a gun on shore was so slender that it was not worth the mechanical complexity nor, and this was the essential point, was it worth the slow rate of fire caused by the time absorbed in the upward and downward movements of the gun. The other point against the disappearing carriage was not appreciated until many years later but it might as well be mentioned here, and that was the inability to produce a carriage which would allow the gun to elevate any more than 20°. In the 1890s this was of little consequence, but as fire control improved and the range of guns increased, the day arrived when greater elevation was wanted, and the geometry of the disappearing carriage just could not manage it. (I believe Americans, using a different design, just managed 30° with two 16in guns in Panama, but even that wasn't good enough by the time of installation, and no more were built).

In 1894, however, a stroke of good fortune fell the way of the gunners. Sir George Clarke, KCMG, FRS, RE, was appointed Superintendent of the Royal Carriage Department. Sir George, later to become Lord Sydenham, was an outstanding engineer and, like all good engineers, had a sound grasp of the need to apply basic principles. The purpose of a gun carriage, as he saw it, was to allow the gunners to shoot as rapidly and accurately as possible, and the weakness of coast artillery at this time was their inability to perform this fundamental requirement. He therefore set about the development of totally new mountings for coast artillery in which axial recoil with hydropneumatic recoil control was employed.

COMPLETION AND DISSOLUTION

Hitherto the traversing slide pattern had been almost universal for heavy guns; the gun was rigidly attached to a carriage which recoiled up the inclined plane of the slide, controlled by a hydraulic buffer. This had been slightly improved with the advent of the early BL guns by the adoption of the 'Vavasseur' mounting, in which the inclined plane section was on top of a rotating structure anchored in concrete, but the gun still recoiled up and down it. The new designs placed the gun in a 'cradle', attached a hydropneumatic system beneath, and slung the whole cradle in a traversing mounting. Thus the gun recoiled axially within the cradle, recoil distances were kept short, and the gunners could be clustered around the gun, protected by a shield, ready to load and fire as fast as the weapon could be pointed by the gunlayer. First came a central pivot mounting for the 6in gun, which made the 6in almost as easy and fast to operate as the 6-pounder, and then a series of barbette mountings for the 9.2in and 10in guns, with hydraulic power provided to supply the ammunition. With these the BL gun became as potent as the quick-firing guns. New emplacements were designed as deep concrete pits in which the mounting was protected while the shielded gun projected over the parapet. The target presented by these new designs was small—something like 18sq ft for a 6in gun—and the chance of an enemy ship seeing one, let alone hitting it at long range, was insignificant. Sir George's designs were so fundamentally sound that they remained in service with but small modification until 1956.

The guns were provided, the mountings perfected, the emplacements constructed; the detachments were highly skilled; two more expressions had to be added to the equation—the ammunition had to be effective and the gun had to be found a target and pointed accurately at it.

So far as ammunition went, improvement was a matter of degree and not of any new basic principle. The Palliser shot gave way to steel shot and shell; the studded projectile for the RML gun was first replaced with shell having 'automatic gas checks' which allowed the gun to be loaded from the muzzle but which were expanded by the cartridge's explosion so as to be forced

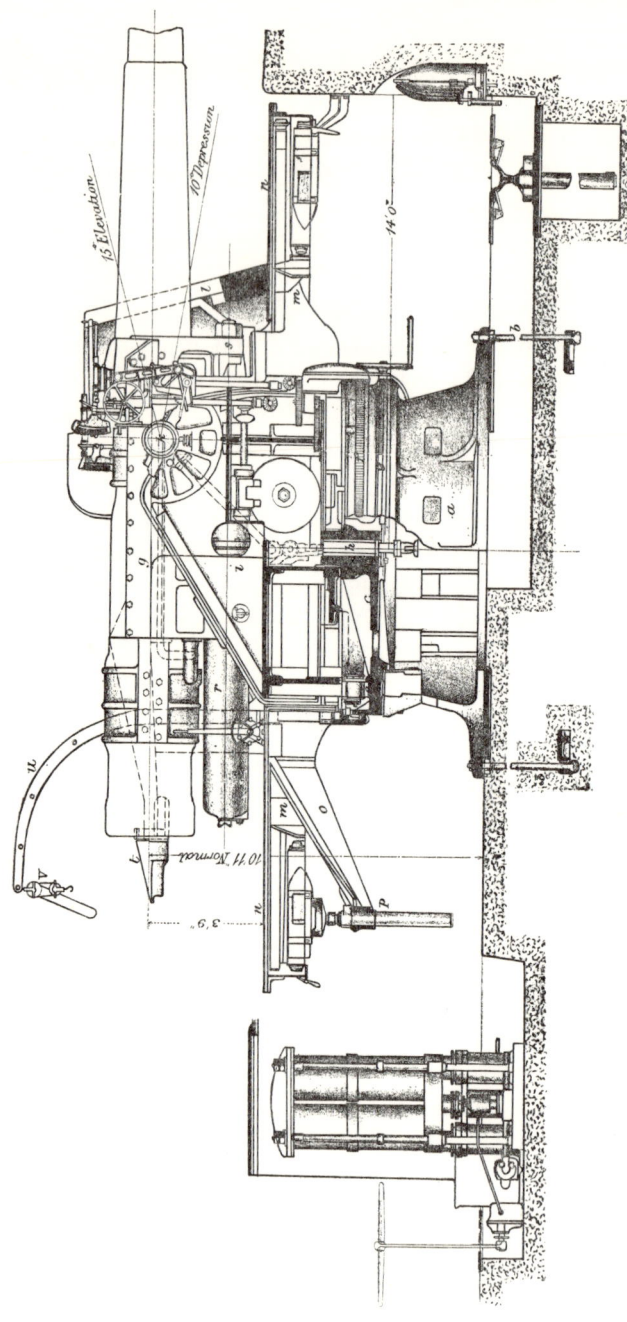

SIDE ELEVATION.

The 9.2in barbette mounting, a photograph of which is on page 33. Ammunition is lifted by the hydraulic press on the right, to be carried beneath the gun platform by trolleys, from which the press 'P' lifts it to the gun breech. The apparatus at the left is an hydraulic accumulator which stored power for the operation of the gun and hoists into the rifling and thus spin the shell. With this device it was possible to do away with the three deep grooves and rifle the gun with large numbers of shallow grooves—the 'polygroove' system. With the arrival of breech loading this gas check turned into the driving band, a band of malleable copper pressed into a groove in the shell body which would bite into the rifling and so spin the shell during its passage up the bore.

At the same time as the new guns and mountings were being designed, the Royal Laboratory, the section of Woolwich Arsenal responsible for ammunition design, had been experimenting with various high explosives and had eventually discovered that picric acid, melted and poured into a shell, was an efficient filling. Under the name of 'Lyddite', commemorating its development at the trials establishment at Lydd, it entered service in January 1896. At that time too, work had been going on into finding a propellant explosive more suitable than gunpowder and a combination of nitro-glycerin and nitro-cellulose extruded in the form of cords and hence called 'Cordite' was officially introduced in December 1893. This 'smokeless powder' was a vast improvement on gunpowder; relatively little smoke (smokeless, in this context, was an optimistic term) but much greater power made gunnery more efficient. Unfortunately it led to other difficulties in due course, notably excessive wear of the guns due to the high flame temperature of cordite which was something rather more than the melting point of steel, a problem which has never been entirely solved to this day.

In discussing the business of fire control, we must first step back briefly to the 1850s and consider the method in vogue at that time. A contemporary instruction merely said that on receiving orders to commence firing ... 'The Number One, after supervising the loading, will station himself to windward where he can best observe the strike of the shot, and give the necessary corrections'. That was really all there was to it; when an enemy ship approached, the Fort Commander gave the word, and from then on it was every gun for itself.

When the new works were built, such an individualistic approach was out of the question; the casemates were crowded enough without neighbouring sergeants wandering through looking for a windward viewpoint. Guns were now grouped under the control of an officer, who received orders from a commander in an observation post (or 'look-out' as they were then called) clear of the smoke, and the particular target for each group was defined and observations of the fall of shot passed down for corrections to be made. How the corrections and orders were passed down forms an interesting study in itself, and the reports of the Director of Artillery for 1870–80 are full of weird and wonderful systems of signalling, from trumpets and megaphones to speaking tubes and mechanical indicators.

But even had the communication been perfect, what was there to communicate? Little more than an educated guess; the observing officer had nothing more scientific or sophisticated than a telescope and his own experience, and while the training ammunition allocation was no more than three or four rounds per gun per year, the amount of experience he was likely to have in assessing the fall of shot was minimal. The principal demand was for some system of determining the range to the target, and a number of rangefinding devices were tried out in these years, almost all of which were based on having two observers, widely spaced, laying instruments on the target which were capable of measuring the two base angles of the triangle so formed. This involved a good deal of skill, and, of course, came back to the communication problem. Moreover, many coast works had terrain problems in finding the necessary piece of even ground, up to a quarter of a mile wide, to ensure that the two observers were given the best chance to make the system work. It was a Royal Artillery officer who finally solved the problem. Captain H. S. S. Watkin realised that if an observer was at a height above the waterline, this became the base of the measuring triangle, and a simple measurement of the angle of depression to the target would automatically give the range. The simplicity of this proposition was rather complicated by the curvature of the earth and the rise and fall of the tide, but corrections could be deduced and applied to allow for these factors. Watkin's Depression Rangefinder very soon became the standard equipment in every fort, relaying its information by electric telegraph to the fire controller.

Now another problem presented itself. The target was moving, and if the gun was fired at the target's present position, by the time the shell arrived the target had moved, and consequently the shell missed. Watkin now applied his inventive mind to this problem and eventually produced his 'Depression Position Finder'. This consisted of a telescopic sight allied to a plotting table and an electrical transmission system. It was installed in a well-concealed and protected 'cell' well clear of the work and manned by skilled observers. One kept the telescope trained on the target as it steamed along while the other read the plot which gave the target's position at a selected time corresponding to the shell's time of flight. The data on the future position was transmitted directly to the gun platforms and there displayed on dials, and on this data the guns were laid by scales on the mounting for elevation and bearing. The detachment were solely concerned with loading and firing as fast as possible and laying the gun to the data ordered. They neither knew nor particularly cared what the target was; indeed, with a gun on a disappearing carriage they were never likely to see it. When the gun captain signalled 'ready' to the position finder, the observer pressed a firing button and fired the guns at the precise instant calculated to produce target and shell in the same place at the same time. With minor variations the system remained in use for the rest of coast artillery's days, and it was marvellously effective.

At about the same time the basic principle of the depression range finder was applied to a gun sight for the shorter-range weapons, so that with the gun telescope pointed at the bow-wave of the target ship, the gun was automatically given the correct elevation to hit it; this was known as the 'auto-sight' and also remained in service until 1956.

It will be recalled that Colonel Lefroy hinted at the use of mortars as defensive weapons in the 1859 report, and mortars were specified as part of the armament of some of the works surrounding Spithead. In the ensuing years Lefroy wrote one or two papers on the subject of high angle fire and, along with other kindred thinkers, observed that warships were a good deal thinner on their topsides than they were on their armoured belts. Slowly the idea gained ground that, provided a reasonable system of fire control and aiming could be developed, there might be something in this idea.

In 1884 the Inspector-General of Fortifications suggested that it might be possible to use the existing, but by now obsolescent, RML guns in a high angle role, particularly as a means of attacking ships which might anchor out of effective range of the flat-trajectory guns in order to bombard shore installations. The Superintendent of the Royal Gun Factory gave as his opinion that the current 9in RML gun (which the IGF had suggested as a likely candidate) was insufficiently accurate for such an application and he suggested re-lining one and polygrooving it. A gun was duly re-lined and re-rifled and a carriage altered to allow the desired elevation, and on December 1884 a trial was fired at Shoeburyness, which, to everyone's surprise, gave remarkably accurate results at 10,000yd. Ever alert to the possibility of making a good thing better, the Ordnance Select Committee now suggested relining another gun to 10in calibre and trying that, in the hope that the bigger shell would produce better results at the target.

The initial enthusiasm slowed a little after this and it was the following year before the 10in was made and fired, whereupon trials for range and accuracy of both 9in and 10in guns were made. These were also satisfactory and in February 1886 plans were drawn up for installing one at a suitable fort where it could be controlled by the existing position-firing system and tried against floating targets in something approximating to service conditions.

Installation duly began at Warden Point on the Isle of Wight, and trials to develop a suitable fire control system continued off and on until 1890. Finally the results of all the different trial firings were studied and the decision was taken to install batteries of high angle guns at various locations where it seemed feasible for a bombardment fleet to anchor out of reach of the normal guns. The weapons were mounted behind cover so as

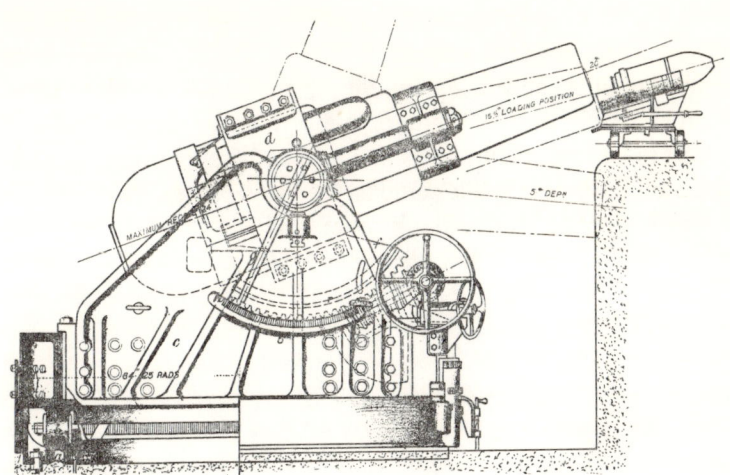

The 9in high angle RML *gun, as used at Tregantle Down Battery. Muzzle-loading was done from the top of the parapet, the gunners being concealed by an additional natural crest*

to be invisible from the sea, though this measure of concealment did not survive the first salvo, since gunpowder charges were still in use and a dense cloud of white smoke rose above the battery to advertise its position for miles around. Few of these batteries were installed in England and none in Wales, the majority of the installations being made overseas. The first batteries were built in 1893 and they remained in service until the early 1920s, since even a muzzle-loading projectile could still play havoc with the deck plates and upperworks of a Dreadnought.

They were later supplemented, and then supplanted, by a high angle design of 9.2in BL gun, a much more powerful and longer-ranging weapon, but relatively few of these were installed. Britain never took to the coast howitzer with much enthusiasm, certainly not as did other nations, notably the USA who installed hundreds of them and kept them in service until after World War II. The principal problem was fire control. It was a hard enough job to hit a moving ship when the shell's time of flight was 20 seconds, that is a 9.2in firing at 9,000 yd range. But with the 9in RML throwing its shell almost 15,000ft up into the air at its maximum range, the time of flight was never less than a minute, and a moving vessel could take avoiding action in that much time. Admittedly, the intended target was supposed to be stationary vessels intent upon bombardment, but they were unlikely to remain stationary for long after the first shots arrived. For all that, I think more could have been done with high angle guns in British service had there been sufficient finance to allow the system to have been more frequently used.

But the palmy days were drawing to a close in the 1890s. The Imperial Defence Act of 1888 allotted £3 million for the construction of additional fortifications at naval and mercantile ports throughout the Empire, and provided for the re-arming of most of the existing works. This was the starting point of the 'Stanhope Programme' previously mentioned, which provided numbers of quick-firing guns for anti-torpedo-boat defence, but the programme of re-arming the old works with modern BL heavy guns was so enormous that £3 million was spread very thin and the work progressed slowly. In many cases it was found impractical to try and install a modern gun and mounting in an old work; the amount of demolition and rebuilding necessary threatened to be a lot more expensive than building a completely new work somewhere else, and where space was available near the work, this was often done, a new barbette battery being installed. The gradual redundancy of the 1859 casemated works dates from this time, since it proved almost impossible to do anything with a modern gun inside an old casemate. In one or two cases, 'needs must when the devil drives' as the old saying has it, and some sort of installation was managed, but rarely with anything heavier than a 6in BL gun. Clarke's modern mountings were beginning to show what the modern coast gun was capable of doing, and there could be no backward step at this point simply for the sake of putting an existing work to use. The casemated works with their RML guns remained as auxiliary armament for many years, but the programme of re-armament begun in 1888 rendered them obsolescent.

In consequence, the funds allotted, which had been calculated on a simple one-for-one basis (even sometimes including an allowance for the scrap value of the replaced gun) were soon used up in the provision of concrete emplacements and fire control equipment, as well as for the new guns and their mountings and within a short time the army was back asking for more money with which to complete the programme. But they had, by the Barracks Act of 1890, just been given another £3 million to provide accommodation for their soldiers, and the demand for yet another handout was too much for some Members of Parliament who demanded some sort of an accounting. The outcome was a return showing 'Expenditure on Fortification and Armament since the Recommendations of the 1859 Commission' which revealed that the impressive sum of £12,154,416 had gone on works and another £5,484,810 on guns. Considering that Parliament had originally balked at £11 million, they had cause to sniff on finding over £17 million gone and the forts still not efficiently armed.

The brake on the big spending was also due to a fundamental change in defence strategy; by the end of the 1880s the Royal Navy was in a sorry state. The annual estimates had hardly changed in the previous forty years, and since the cost of warships had risen sharply, the number of new keels had declined in proportion. Other nations saw in this situation a chance to get ahead, and new building began both on the continent and in the USA. As a result of public concern over naval parity a commission was formed in 1889 to examine the Royal Navy and its role in national defence, and their report upset all previous theories by stating quite firmly 'the danger of invasion would better be met by increased naval expenditure than by costly shore defences'. Their opinion was endorsed by the rapid approval of the Naval Defence Act of 1889 which provided for ten battleships, nine heavy cruisers, 29 light cruisers and a host of supporting vessels, at a cost of £27,500,000. With this as a starter, the Royal Navy moved into the Big Battleship era with increasing speed—and expense. Ten more battleships were authorised in 1895, five more in 1896, four more in 1897, and three battleships and four heavy cruisers in 1897.

However, in order that the navy's rear should be protected, the Naval Works Act of 1895 authorised over £8 million for dockyard facilities and some defensive works to go with them; this Act was later extended by revised estimates every year, until by 1901 over £27 million had been authorised. The lion's share of this went to overseas bases, and for purely naval installations, but sufficient crumbs fell to allow the defensive works to be brought up to an efficient standard of armament; and by that time they needed to be.

As the new century dawned the defences were in a state of flux. The 1899 manual, writes Headlam, referred to a variety 'of BL, RML, QF and smooth-bore ordnance of 12.5in, 12in, 11in, 10in, 9.2in, 9in, 8in, 7in, 6in, 5in, 4.7in, 4in, 80-pounder, 64-pounder, 40-pounder, 32-pounder, 12-pounder, 6-pounder and 3-pounder calibres, with many marks of most—eg 7 marks of 9.2in BL gun—mounted on every variety of carriage and slide, common standing, casemate, dwarf, small port, central pivot, barbette, pedestal, Moncrieff and hydropneumatic disappearing.'

The 'Textbook of Service Ordnance 1893' which was the current guide, lists 54 RML guns, 7 RML howitzers, 11 RBL guns, 69 BL guns, 1 smooth-bore gun and 14 QF guns as being currently 'on the books', while the carriage and mounting inventory was so involved as to defy tabulation. The accession of funds under the various Acts of Parliament, although it did not entirely sweep away all the antiques, at least relegated them to the reserve and ensured that the first-line armament was the best available. The 12-pounder and 4.7in QF guns, and the 6in and 9.2in BL guns of the latest marks on the latest mountings were installed, together with position finders, communications and all the necessary accessories. By way of a final check, a 'Committee on the Armament of Home Ports' looked over the defences in 1905 and, generally speaking, found them satisfactory. It was the highwater mark of peacetime coast defence.

When the war broke out in 1914 the coast defences were at the peak of their form. Well armed, amply provided with ammunition, manned by highly trained men, they were ready and waiting. By and large, they went on waiting though on the few occa-

COMPLETION AND DISSOLUTION   89

sions when they were called on to fire they gave a good account of themselves. The relative proximity of the German High Seas Fleet led to the increase of defensive works on the East coast of England, particularly to cover the entrances to the Tyne and Humber. As well as barbette batteries, the Humber was given two iron forts on the sands behind Spurn Head, but these were of considerably simpler construction than the Spithead forts. An intention to improve the defences of the Tyne began with asking the United States Government for a supply of 14in guns on disappearing mountings, but these could not be provided and the plan was then adopted of building four batteries of 12in BL guns in ex-naval turrets. Due to various technical troubles, work on this project did not get under way until the war was almost over and they were scrapped in the 1920s before the installations were completed.

When the war ended there was the usual massive retrenchment in defences. It had been proved beyond all doubt that provided the Royal Navy was strong enough the chance of the coast artillery being called into play was slender, and the whole of the innumerable defence works were considered and their future prospects reviewed. As a first step the storekeepers had a field day going through their inventories and striking out weapons and equipment which had long been obsolete in practice but which had lingered on. In 1921-2 vast number of guns, all the smoothbores and RML guns and a number of the early patterns of BL guns were struck from the books, together with the variety of carriages and mountings which had supported them. All were declared obsolete, and either 'reported for disposal', which meant they were dismantled and returned to Woolwich for scrapping, or, in the charming Victorian phrase always used by the official publication, 'brought to produce', which meant that they were dealt with where they lay, the useful pieces being taken off and kept while the rest was disposed of locally. In many cases this disposal consisted of heaving the gun into the sea or into the fort ditch. When Stack Rock Fort went under the auctioneer's hammer in 1932 the Notice of Sale contained the following notes: 'In the Fort and included in this Lot are three old dismantled muzzle-loading guns each approximately 12 feet long and 20 tons weight.' In one overseas fort, I am reliably informed, the disposal of two 10in guns on disappearing carriages was done by opening the hydraulic valves and allowing the guns to sink into the pits, whereupon the pits were filled with sand and forgotten. My informant was the man who accidentally discovered them in the 1950s.

This clearance left a massive list of works without guns; most of the modern armament had gone into newer works, and the old casemated forts were now standing empty and of no defensive value at all. But the millions of pounds poured into them demanded some sort of recognition, and while many of the more remote and tactically useless were sold off—for sums which would not have paid for one of the original shields—as many as possible were put to use by other elements of the armed forces. The Royal Navy took over most of the works surrounding Portsmouth and put them to use as stores and barracks, instructional and experimental establishments. The serviceable works went into a state of 'care and preservation', for it had been decided that the reduced regular army could no longer man the fixed defences, and in the event of war they were to be the responsibility of the local territorial forces, as had usually been the case during World War I. To ensure regular maintenance an establishment of regular troops was located in each district whose job it was to continue to maintain the guns and works and to provide a trained nucleus of specialists to assist the territorials in training and on mobilisation.

In this fashion the defences rubbed along through the 1920s and 1930s until the threat of war became obvious. The time was not spent idly, however; in 1921 the turn of events in the Far East made the provision of a powerful fortress in Singapore a necessity; for political reasons nothing was done until 1932 when work finally began. This plan, demanding the latest armament and fire control methods, was a useful stimulus and the years of peace were fruitfully occupied in designing, testing and perfecting a variety of devices, weapons and tactical plans. So far as the United Kingdom went, little or nothing was done

COMPLETION AND DISSOLUTION

to provide new works, but the experimental work stimulated by the Singapore planning carried a useful fallout in allowing fire control to be improved and in developing the 15in long range guns and the twin 6-pounder anti-torpedo boat gun, both of which were installed in British defences in later years.

At the outbreak of war in 1939, England and Wales were defended by the following:

9.2in 29
6in 69
4.7in 8
12-pounder 31
6-pounder 2

which were grouped round the four great fortresses and the most important defended ports. The situation seemed a good deal less threatening than it had been in 1914, for the German Fleet had nothing like the power it had in those days, and the likelihood of raiding across the North Sea appeared to be much less.

But the collapse of France in 1940 changed the picture overnight. Very shortly, the German Army, an apparently invincible war machine, was poised on the shore across the Channel, making preparations to cross in force. As an anti-invasion measure, emergency batteries were installed on every likely invasion beach. The guns were collected from every possible source, large numbers being provided by the Royal Navy from stocks removed from scrapped warships in the 1920s. Installation was as simple as could be, slabs of quick-setting cement with anchor bolts to take the shipboard pedestal mountings in most cases; baulks of timber in others; a special prefabricated steel platform, the 'Arrol-Withers' was developed for the standard coast defence 6in gun; in one way and another several hundred guns of all calibres were hurriedly provided and installed, with fire control systems of greater or less complexity depending on what could be provided in the time available. By October 1940, 510 ex-naval weapons had been mounted and manned, and these were later added to by such diverse weapons as ex-American 75mm field guns on pedestal mountings. At one time there was even a suggestion to remove some 138mm guns from an interned French warship and mount those, but the question of ammunition supply threatened to be difficult, and when the guns were examined they were found to be almost worn out.

The major accretion of heavy guns was in the Dover area where they were emplaced less for coast defence as for the attack of German ships attempting to run the gauntlet through the Straits of Dover, and also to counter-attack the German long-range batteries which had been installed on Cap Gris Nez. The first guns in the area were two naval 14in manned by Royal Marines, but these were later joined by two 15in, and batteries of 6in, 8in and 9.2in, all on long-range mountings.

By 1945 most of the Emergency Batteries were either dismantled or in the process of being dismantled. With the war over the fortresses and defended ports went back into hibernation, the armament being put into 'care and preservation' with maintenance by district establishments as in pre-war days. But the writing was on the wall; the vast development of air power, the sudden appearance of the guided missile, the wartime development of combined operations and beach landing techniques which could put a sizeable force ashore almost anywhere, and the nuclear weapon, all showed that landings on enemy shores could be made virtually at will, and without a ship ever getting within sight of the defences.

On 17 February 1956 the Minister of Defence rose in the House of Commons, the scene of so many arguments and debates on the subject of coast defences, and announced that in the light of modern weapon development there was no longer any justification for retaining coast artillery. On 31 December of that year the axe fell, and the coast defences of Britain ceased to exist.

5
THE THAMES AND MEDWAY DEFENCES

The Thames had been fortified to some degree since the earliest days. Some primitive defences already existed at Sheerness; Tilbury Blockhouse was constructed on orders of Henry VIII, and, later, Elizabeth caused Upnor Castle to be built, thus saving the day when the Dutch fleet sailed into the Medway in 1667.

Whether the Dutch raid was, in modern jargon, cost-effective, is arguable, but if it did nothing else it focussed attention on the state of the defences and caused some improvemests to be made at Sheerness and the construction of a tower off the Isle of Grain. A form of early warning system was developed in which the navy stationed a picket boat out to sea, from which the approach of a hostile fleet could be signalled. Thus, the Order Book for Sheerness Garrison for 1796: '27 August. As the utmost alacrity and attention becomes more necessary than ever in the Garrison, the officer on duty is to take care that the Main, Artillery and Line guards are fully and clearly instructed in the signals of alarm from the Sandwich Flagship at the Nore ... the Relief and Patrol, in going round, are likewise to have an eye to the Nore.'

The rise of Napoleon caused a flurry of activity. Batteries were built at Coalhouse Point and Shornmead, and another at Gravesend. Together with Tilbury Fort, the new works crossed fire, Coalhouse and Shornmead on a bend where the attacking vessels might be moving slowly, and Tilbury and Gravesend on a narrow stretch which should have improved accuracy. With these groupings in action it would be unlikely that any vessels would have got through to sail further upriver and attack the powder magazines at Purfleet or the Arsenal at Woolwich.

When the 1859 Commissioners reviewed the defences they found them composed of Tilbury Fort mounting 32 heavy guns; Gravesend Battery with 15; Coalhouse Battery with 17; and Shornmead with 13 guns. All were open earthworks mounting smooth-bores behind embrasures. The commissioners were of the opinion that while these were well sited they were insufficiently powerful, and recommended that they should be strengthened. Tilbury was strong enough but should be re-armed; Gravesend, Coalhouse and Shornmead should all be replaced by stronger works, and a new fort should be built at the south side of Cliffe Creek to form an anchor for a floating barrier between it and Coalhouse.

In the Medway the proposals were more extensive. The existing defences were firstly the open batteries of Sheerness, which had been built in 1780 to replace earlier works, and then strengthened in 1796 and 1825. They consisted of a line of bastioned earthworks with wet ditches totally enclosing the town and dockyard, with the remains of Charles II's battery at Garrison Point. Although described as 'well armed' on the land side, the ability of the guns was somewhat marred by the fact that a suburb known as Mile Town had grown up outside the defences, and the buildings so obstructed the fields of fire and provided such cover for an attacker that it was doubtful whether effective defence would be possible.

While the Garrison Point Battery and the 3-gun Grain Tower were capable of covering the navigable portion of the Medway entrance, their firepower was insufficient and it was recommended that a 'powerful casemated work' should be built to replace the battery on Garrison Point. To co-operate with this another casemated work should be built so as to enclose the existing Grain Tower; an open battery should be built on the southern part of the Isle of Grain, and another battery on the Medway end of the Sheerness land defences.

In order to secure the Ise of Grain, a fort was recommended on the highest part of the island to prevent an enemy landing

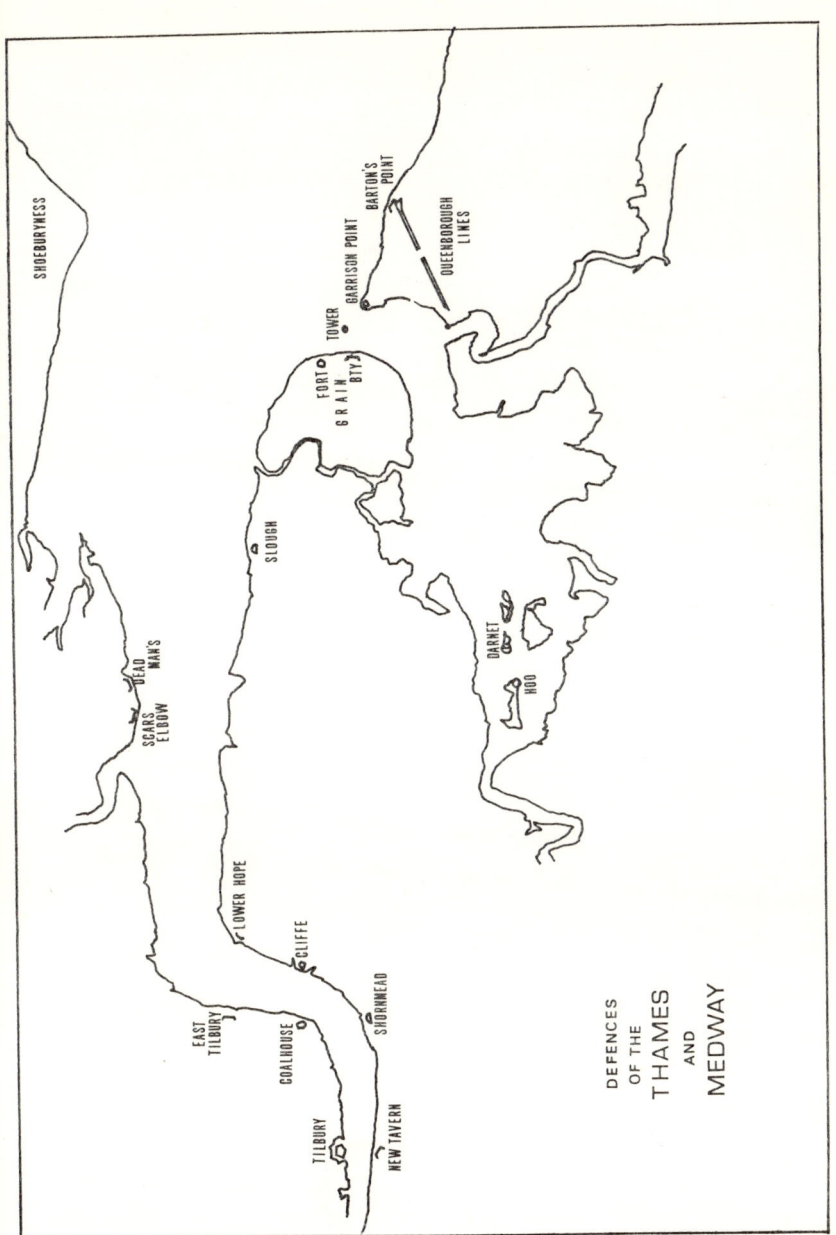

Map 1 The Thames and Medway Defences

on the island and also protect the rear of the open battery. Moreover it would also co-operate with another new work to be built at Slough Point, near All Hallows, facing the River Thames, in order to prevent landings from the Thames aimed at an overland attack on Chatham.

To overcome the difficulties caused by the Mile Town buildings a new defensive line across the neck of land behind Sheerness was proposed, but there was some question as to whether this would be better as a simple line of ramparts or whether three detached works well in advance should be built. After considering alternatives, the Commissioners recommended that redoubts be built on three hills about two miles from the existing lines.

Finally, by way of insurance, it was proposed that two works should be sited where they could block the Medway and form a last line of defence against the chance that an enemy fleet just might manage to get past all the formidable defences planned at Sheerness and Grain. One work was to be built on the tip of Okeham Ness and a partner on the opposite side of the channel on Burntwick Island.

All in all, the commissioners put forward quite a formidable programme, particularly in relation to the Medway, and indeed made it more formidable by recommending a chain of land defences around Woolwich and extending across country to Chatham in order to deny the road to London to any possible invader. Without taking these into account, the proposals outlined above were estimated at £630,000 for the purchase of land and construction of works. The proposed land defences would then add another £2,050,000 to that, and after that the question of armament would arise.

However, before the recommendations reached Parliament all the Woolwich and Chatham land defences were struck out, and the proposed strengthening of Grain Tower was also dropped. Work began on the rest of the plan in 1861, but during this construction work some changes were found necessary. Instead of the advanced redoubts planned for the land side of Sheerness, the plan reverted to a simple line of rampart and wet ditch, the 'Queenborough Lines', running across the Minster Marshes. The planned location of the two forts in the Medway was found unsuitable and fresh sites on Hoo and Darnet islands were selected.

In the subsequent years additions to these main defences came and went. In 1795 a battery of four smooth-bore guns had been located at Lower Hope Point; long abandoned, it was revived in the 1890s for a short time. Another new work was East Tilbury Battery, built downstream of Coalhouse Fort in order to replace the obsolete armament of that work in 1890.

It is surprising that the Commissioners did not apparently consider the utility of works on the north bank, particularly in the Thameshaven and Canvey Island area, where the channel was close to the shore. There is an interesting reference in the minutes of the Ordnance Select Committee (Vol III, 1865) to a balloon ascent from Woolwich in that year, in which the observer stated that his field of view was so great he could see Canvey Fort, but he appears to be the only person who ever did, since no record of a Fort on Canvey Island can be discovered. However, Canvey eventually got some guns; during World War I a 6in battery was installed at Dead Man's Point, and during World War II a 6-pounder battery at Scar's Elbow.

One of the most interesting features of the Thames defences was the existence of two Brennan Torpedo Stations. The original recommendation for Cliffe Fort called for a floating boom across the river to Coalhouse Fort. The practical difficulties of constructing and operating such a barrier were quite formidable; the old idea of heavy timbers reinforced with chain was hardly tenable in the age of iron ships. But the fortunate arrival of the controlled shore-based torpedo saved the day, and instead of the boom, a torpedo battery was built at Cliffe, oriented to Coalhouse.

The Brennan torpedo, invention of Louis Brennan, later better known for his various mono-rail trains and gyroscopically-stabilised vehicles, was patented in 1884 and purchased by the British Government in 1885. The weapon was a cigar-shaped device containing two reels of fine wire, driving, via a differential gear, a propeller and rudder at the rear, and carrying an explosive-filled warhead at the front. A short mast bearing a flag was mounted amidships. Launching was done from a railed ramp leading down into the water, and two steam engines in the fort pulled the wire from the torpedo reels. This drove the screw and imparted movement to the torpedo, and a gyroscope kept it upright in the water, with the tip of the mast and the flag visible above the surface. The controller watched the flag and steered the torpedo by altering the speed at which one or other of the steam engines pulled on the wire; thus speeding up one engine gave an increase in the speed of one reel in the torpedo, and this, via the differential gear, acted on the rudder. This weapon is, indeed, the true father of the many wire-guided missiles developed in the last thirty years, and undoubtedly qualifies as the first guided missile ever to enter military service.

The torpedo station at Cliffe was installed in 1886-7 and by 1890 was fully operational. Another was built at Garrison Point Fort to cover the entrance to the Medway. By 1900 the system had been abandoned, and today only the installation at Cliffe remains, that at Garrison Point having been dismantled.

Tilbury Fort (Six-figure National Grid Reference: 552 755)

Originally built on the orders of Henry VIII in about 1540, in 1588 it was the scene of Elizabeth I's review of the 117,000 man army raised against the possibility of invasion by the Armada. Under Charles I it became a regular Fort, bastioned and fully armed, in 1667. By 1716 the armament was listed at 161 guns, though this was reduced by the Board of Ordnance to 60. In 1805 it has fourteen 42-pounder, twenty 32-pounder and thirty-five 9-pounder smooth-bores, and by 1859 this had been reduced to thirty-two guns, trained down and across the river. Under the orders of the 1859 Commissioners it was extended in 1861; the old seventeenth-century powder tower was demolished and a new magazine built in its place, and an 18-pounder field gun battery was installed, but little else could be done until the new forts were completed, since stripping the armament out to rebuild the work would have left the Thames undefended.

In 1865 the armament on paper was an impressive sixty-six guns and eight howitzers, but the effective armament was reported as five 68-pounder RML, five 32-pounder smooth-bore, and four 10in smooth-bore, and how many of the remainder were serviceable was open to question. At this juncture it seems that the view was taken that since the armament was so defective it might as well be withdrawn and the fort rebuilt. In 1866 Parliament was asked for £50,000 in order to strengthen the river defences and add iron shields, but the Bill was withdrawn. By 1867 the Director of Ordnance was able to report that work was now in progress for re-arming Tilbury with heavy rifled guns, but progress was slow and it was not until 1872 that the guns were installed in the river face, leaving the land side still armed with smooth-bores which remained in place until 1888.

General Gordon, after his adventures in the Taiping Rebellion which earned him the sobriquet 'Chinese Gordon' was, as a Royal Engineer, appointed Commander, Royal Engineers, Sheerness in 1866. He became greatly concerned over the defences and under his urging new earthworks were built, to take brick emplacements for guns firing through embrasures to command the river; it seems that all the embrasures were not occupied though, since an 1880 return lists seven 9in and one 11in RML gun distributed through thirteen embrasures.

By the time the Commission on the Armament of Home Ports reported in 1905 Tilbury had been provided with two 6in BL converted guns in the south-east bastion and four 12-pounder QF on the curtain, their concrete emplacements being built over earlier RML positions. These remained until after World War II.

Today Tilbury Fort is a scheduled Ancient Monument, under the care of the Department of the Environment, and is in excellent repair. Many of the SB, RML and later emplacements can be seen, some with racers and pivots still in place. It is open to the public and is one of the oldest coast defences to be maintained in substantially its original form.

Coalhouse Fort (691 768)

Originally an earthen open battery constructed in 1795 and mounting four 32-pounders, these works were demolished in

1855 and a second open battery for 17 guns was built on the site. The 1860 report called for a casemated work with 28 guns, plus another 28 *en barbette* on the roof, all to be smooth-bore 68-pounders. The planned form was a straight row of casemates with an angled earthwork closing the gorge, but after the foundations had been excavated, in 1867 the design was changed to a curved casemate face with a bastioned defensible barrack closing the gorge. At the same time the plan to place barbette guns on the roof was abandoned, since the new RML guns promised to make up in firepower what might be lacking in numbers.

The 1869 Report suggested a change in armament to use 12 guns in the casemates and 8 on Moncrieff mountings, all to be 7in 7ton RML, though it is difficult to see where Moncrieff mountings could have been installed; possibly the plan was to place them on top of the casemates, as was done in some of the Milford Haven forts. However the plan was soon changed, to mount 11in and 12.5in RML in the casemates and 9in RML in the open batteries at the upriver end.

Seen from within, the fort is a two-storied erection, the lower level being magazines and storehouses. These are protected by 14ft of granite at the front, which in turn is overlaid by the earth glacis in front of the work. The next floor is the casemate level and gun floor, and the casemates are fitted with iron shields set in granite facings and closed at the rear by wood-framed windows and doors. The roofs of the casemates are vaulted with 2ft 6in of brickwork which are surmounted by another 2ft 6in of concrete and asphalt to form the roof. From the terreplein level, iron ladders lead up to the casemates and from there to an iron catwalk running round the face at roof level.

The defensible barrack in the gorge is on Kentish ragstone, selected in many of the Thames works for its convenience in supply, cheapness and also for its fortunate property of being less liable than granite to splinter into lethal fragments if struck by shot. The windows facing the land side are provided with loopholed iron shutters and the walls are also loopholed. A moat surrounded the front face and flanks of the work, 60ft wide and 8ft deep but the efficiency of this was somewhat vitiated by

Page 101 *Hurst Castle, in the Needles Passage. The original fort of Henry VIII is in the centre, with the extensive casemates at each side*

Page 102 (above) *The casemates of Bovisand Fort, Plymouth, showing the armour shields;* (below) *a contemporary drawing showing the effect on the experimental casemates at Shoeburyness after extensive firing trials*

THE THAMES AND MEDWAY DEFENCES

the presence of what appears to be a causeway at each end but which is, in fact, the old river wall which was considered too vital in its role of flood controller to be removed for a mere defensive whim. At either end of the work is a double-storied caponier covering both these causeways and the approach road. These were armed with machine guns, three being issued in 1890.

To revert to the main armament; by 1872 machinery for traversing the 11in guns was being installed—though 'machinery' in this context means little more than some fancy arrangement of ropes and blocks—and by 1880 there were thirteen 11in and four 12.5in guns in the casemates and three 9in in the open battery.

No change seems to have taken place for some time after this, but in 1892 a 10in BL on disappearing carriage was installed here for a three-month trial, though its exact position is not known. There is every possibility that it was not intended as authorised armament but was being tested prior to removal and installation at East Tilbury Battery.

In 1888, when re-armament with BL guns was contemplated, the first proposal was to retain the fort as a barrack and store but to emplace the new guns in pits alongside the work. This was soon found to be out of the question due to the soft ground giving no support for the foundations except at considerable expense and trouble, so the plan was adopted of filling in the alternate casemates with massive concrete piers to support the weight of four 6in BL on central pivot mountings placed on the roof. A number of the down-river casemates were bricked up and the earth glacis was piled up to roof level over them, and, at the up-river end, to shield level. This was completed by the early 1890s, though an 1895 return still mentions a number of RML guns in the fort and also shows that two 6-pounder Hotchkiss QF guns had been installed in a small open battery on the river bank, upstream of the main work.

The main armament was withdrawn in the 1920s and the fort used as a store. During the course of World War II it was occupied for some time at least by the Royal Navy, and there are the remains of light anti-aircraft gun positions on the roof. But its main defensive role was perpetuated when, in late 1940, an

C.D.—G

emergency battery of two ex-naval 5.5in BL guns was installed on the river bank and the fort used as accommodation and fire control room.

Today, after a spell as a shoe warehouse, the fort is derelict. The area has been landscaped into a park by the local authority.

East Tilbury Battery (693 776)

This work lies in private ground between the village of East Tilbury and the river. It was proposed in 1887 in order to strengthen the defence of the river with a work which would not be so vulnerable as Coalhouse. Construction was slow starting, due to legal difficulties over the title to the ground, but it was complete by 1890.

As originally laid out there were six emplacements of concrete, concealed from the river by an earth glacis. The two centre pits mounted 10in BL guns while the flanks each carried two 6in BL, all of which were on disappearing carriages. A 3-pounder was also mounted at the extreme right of the work and was probably a practice gun, since by this time the 3-pounder was no longer considered a useful offensive weapon, having been replaced in that role by the 6 and 12-pounder QF guns.

Towards 1900 the two 6in sections were remounted on barbette carriages, the 10in guns being left alone, being removed when the guns were declared obsolete in the 1920s.

The work was completed by magazines underneath the gun floors, supplying ammunition by tray lifts. Living casemates were built beneath the 10in battery, and the usual cookhouse, stores, offices etc, were on the inland side of a sunken way running the length of the work.

The battery remained in service until after World War II. At present it is derelict and considerably overgrown.

Scar's Elbow Battery (786 820)

Sited on the point of this name on Canvey Island, Scar's Elbow was installed in 1940 as an insurance against sudden forays by torpedo-boats. No gun then mounted in the Thames was fast enough to cope with these vessels, so a twin 6-pounder was installed here, together with five searchlights for illuminating the water.

The twin-six consisted of two 6-pounder barrels with semi-automatic breech mechanisms mounted close together in a single turret. Supplied with ammunition by a string of men passing the rounds from trolleys, although hand loaded a mounting could deliver a stream of aimed fire at over 100 rounds a minute in the hands of a skilled detachment.

Scar's Elbow battery was never called upon to demonstrate this ability, however, and was dismantled shortly after the war. The emplacement is visible.

Dead Man's Battery (791 822)

Sited on Dead Man's Point on Canvey Island, this work was installed during World War I in order to protect the northern bank of the river and as part of the general improvement of the East Coast defences. Two 6in BL on barbette carriages were installed in the usual concrete pits, together with a central magazine and the 'usual offices'.

In 1918 it was placed in 'care and preservation' status and remained so until 1938 when it was re-opened and manned until 1945. It was dismantled shortly after the war and now only the emplacements remain, overgrown and derelict.

New Tavern Fort (650 747)

This was originally known as Gravesend Fort and was built at the end of the seventeenth century. The Board of Ordnance reduced it from 17 guns to 10 in 1716, and in 1779 a new work, to be known as New Tavern Battery was begun, which was later armed with sixteen 32-pounders. The 1860 report recommended its improvement, but, like Tilbury Fort, the work was delayed by the need to retain it as a viable defence until the new forts downstream were completed and armed.

Work finally began in about 1869 with the installation of iron shields in the earthworks and the mounting of 12in RML guns, and by 1880 the armament was six 9in and one 12in RML. By 1887 another three 9in were authorised, but there is some discrepancy in the reports of that time, which refer to 11in and 12in guns indiscriminately; this may be due to the fact that either 11in or 12in guns could be fitted to the same mountings, or it may be due to a subtle matter of terminology; the 'approved' armament of the work was 11in, but what actually found its way into a fort wasn't always what had been approved in the first place, and it is quite likely that 12in were substituted for the 'approved' 11in. The whole question is academic though, as neither 9in, 11in nor 12in were ever mounted in any greater numbers than they were in 1880.

In 1895 two 6-pounder QF and three machine guns were on the 'approved' list, and though the machine guns were certainly issued, there is no record of the 6-pounders ever being installed. Shortly after this the RML guns were withdrawn and the emplacements altered to take two 6in BL guns. These remained in place until some time in the 1920s when the work was abandoned and the site reverted to the local council. It is now a formal pleasure garden, but there are one or two traces of former glory; the two 6in emplacements, an oddly detached iron shield, an old magazine building, all looking a little out of place among the lawns and rose bushes.

Shornmead Fort (692 748)

Shornmead existed as an open battery from 1795, mounting four 24-pounders, but its position on the bend of the river was so soundly selected that the 1859 Commission did not hesitate to recommend that it be replaced by a much stronger work. As well as its river defensive role it was to form the anchor of a line of works running overland to Chatham and Rochester, but these were never built, and only the river face of Shornmead was ever armed.

The building of the fort—a semi-circle of casemates with the gorge closed by a defensible barrack, and with open batteries at the upstream end of the casemates—was attended with a good deal of misfortune. The foundations sank, floors cracked, the whole work tilted, walls collapsed, and it was all of ten years before the fort was completed. It appears that in 1869 there was still considerable doubt as to how it might behave if it were to be loaded with large numbers of heavy guns, and it was recommended that the armament be five 7in RML on Moncrieff carriages and nine 7in in the casemates.

All seems to have come out well, however, as there is neither trace nor record of the Moncrieff mountings and there are twelve casemates, nine closely spaced on the right and centre flanks, two widely spaced on the left, and one turned at a full 90° to the rest of the work on the extreme right flank, giving flank defence. In addition there are three open battery positions on the left of the casemates. According to a return of 1880 there were eleven 11in guns in the casemates, the twelfth casemate probably being the right flank and probably armed with a 32-pounder SB gun. The open battery mounted three 9in RML.

No heavy BL guns were ever installed here, due probably to the general doubt as to what the foundations would stand. It would have been a colossal task to sink additional foundations outside the work for new gunpits and magazines, and the only modern armament ever installed was a small open battery built on the river bank, originally mounting two 6-pounders. These were removed in about 1913 and two 12-pounders provided in their place. These remained in place until World War II when they were reinforced by an emergency battery of two ex-naval 5.5in BL guns, and the work, as with Coalhouse, used as the accommodation for the battery. The guns were all removed shortly after the war but the ground on which it stands forms part of a military practice range and the fort was used by the Army School of Demolitions as a practice area during the 1950s, with the result that very little of it remains, all the barrack buildings in the gorge and the rear faces of the casemates being demolished. Only the granite face and armour shields remain intact, so that from the river the fort looks untouched. But if nothing else, the remains give an unrivalled opportunity to see just how thick and resistant and massive was the system of construction. The magazine level beneath the casemates is flooded and no longer accessible—evidence still of the problems which bedevilled the builders.

Cliffe Fort (707 768)

Cliffe was the child of the 1859 Commission: they recommending the building of a work there so as to form a triangle with Coalhouse and Shornmead for mutual support, and also to act as an anchor for a boom between it and Coalhouse.

Like most of the Thames works the building of Cliffe was accompanied by foundation troubles, slippage, cracked floors and walls, although this was eventually overcome and there is no evidence today of any liability to subsidence; even the magazines are perfectly sound and dry. The trace is approximately a 90° arc, the curved face being the casemates and the two straight faces bastioned walls, one forming a defensible barrack and the other being a gorge wall with entrance gate. The right flank casemate has an unusual form of iron shield with a shallow but wide slot in it, as opposed to the more usual rectangular, almost square, slot. Due to the growth of trees and bushes, it is impossible to see exactly what arc this covers, but it seems likely that this was a flank defence position similar to the right-hand casemate of Shornmead.

In front of the left flank there is an access slot in the glacis which allowed Brennan Torpedos to be serviced, the actual firing station being below the left-hand casemates, with the launching rails running through a deep cutting in the glacis to the river some hundred yards distant.

As with Shornmead, the delays in construction gave the authorities a chance to have second thoughts about armament, and whereas the original intention was a simple casemated battery, by 1869 it was proposed to re-equip with 7in RML guns, six Moncrieff mountings and seven in shielded casemates. But like everywhere else on the Thames, the Moncrieffs were non-starters here, and by 1874 the armament was 12in 35 ton RML guns. This was soon changed for the 1880 returns show six 11in and two 12.5in, and by 1887 the 11in had increased to nine and a pair of 9in added in the upstream open batteries. It is likely that three 9in were originally installed, but one would have been withdrawn when the Brennan torpedo was installed since it was one of the 9in magazines which was converted for the torpedo engine room.

An 1895 report refers to the provision of three 3-pounder QF here in the open batteries. It is difficult to see how three such guns could have replaced the 9in, and the probable answer is that they were supplied with the parapet mounting which could be readily clamped to the open battery embrasure without disturbing the major armament, and then used for practice. When this was over they could be unclamped and removed, leaving the 9in again ready for use.

A more interesting feature of the 1895 report is that it refers briefly to four 9in high angle guns in the list of approved armament, entering 'none' on the list of weapons actually mounted, and, under 'proposed armament', entering 'four 10in'. These are the high angle RML guns discussed in chapter four. There is considerable divergence of opinion as to whether these were ever installed, but I am of the opinion that they were. Some four hundred yards downstream of Cliffe Fort is a large erection which, at first sight, resembles a Mulberry Harbour cast ashore. On closer examination it can be seen that the rear or landward face is of masonry, casemated, and with signs of a series of gabled roofs. This original erection—possibly a casemated defensible barrack, though it is not mentioned on any records—appears to have been dismantled except for its front face and then, using this as a basis, a large concrete box has been built, some two hundred feet long, forty feet deep and thirty high, with passages and magazines beneath. Into this box was then thrown all the remains of the original building, plus more rubble, to make a solid structure.

Behind this, though the area is considerably torn up and overgrown it is possible to distinguish marks indicative of gun mountings of some type. The concrete 'thing' obscures this area from the river, and I believe that here a battery of high angle guns was installed in the middle 1890s. The guns probably remained there until 1922 when all the RML high angle weapons were declared obsolete.

Cliffe Fort itself was armed with modern weapons in about 1900 when two 6in BL and three 12-pounder QF were installed. The 6in were withdrawn in the 1920s but the light guns remained there until after World War II.

At the present time, Cliffe stands derelict, the basic structure sound though the barrack accommodation is ruinous.

Lower Hope Point Battery (716 787)

An open earthwork battery was built here in 1795 to mount four 24-pounder guns, and in a return of 1805 it was shown as being an outwork of Gravesend Fort. It does not feature in any records of the latter half of the nineteenth century, and all the evidence (which is very little) points to it having been abandoned some time before 1850. However it was revived in about 1898 and provided with two 12-pounder QF guns and a number of searchlights. They were certainly in position in 1905 and probably during the course of World War I, but they were withdrawn very soon after the war and the position abandoned. There is now no trace of the emplacements to be found.

Slough Fort (835 788)

Slough was another 1869 conception. Its purpose was mixed; partly to engage ships entering the Thames, partly to help Grain Fort in covering the Isle of Grain, and largely to prevent a landing on the desolate shores near All Hallows, which would have allowed an enemy to outflank the Medway defences and strike at Chatham. The area of Slough Point was the only part of the southern bank of the Thames not entirely flooded in those days, and it was thought that with a little more judicious flooding in time of emergency the fort would be able to control the only viable landing area. It was then intended to back this up with a

THE THAMES AND MEDWAY DEFENCES   111

line of works reaching back to Chatham, but this plan was abandoned due to its cost.

As first planned, Slough was to have seven casemates protected by iron shields in granite, with three more guns on the roof. Three officers, 1 NCO and 75 men were to garrison the work, though where they were expected to live is hard to establish, for Slough is undoubtedly the smallest Fort ever built in Britain, and it would be hard enough to find standing room for 79 men on the terreplein behind the casemates.

The plan is a simple semi-circle of casemates, with the gorge closed by defensible accommodation. A ditch surrounded the front and flanks and was later extended across the gorge, with a drawbridge affording access. The original intention was to arm with ten RBL guns, since the primary task was to oppose landings and not attack iron ships, but although these were supplied to the fort they were never mounted, and according to the report of the 1869 Commission were to be replaced with 7in RML.

Although Slough was built to schedule, it certainly came unstuck over its armament, for even the 7in never appeared. In 1881 a complaint was voiced that the place might be of some use if only the iron shields could be fitted, and in 1885 another complaint observed that the fort had never been completed; since the masonry was all there, this could only refer to the shields and the guns.

In 1888 a recommendation was made that the casemates should be closed at their fronts and the fort used as a base for moveable armament—four 16-pounder RML guns on wheeled carriages, three 3-pounder QF similarly mounted and three machine guns. The intention was to deploy these as necessary to counter a landing; the draining of the surrounding area had been going ahead steadily in the intervening years and the landing area available to a potential enemy was now much greater in extent than when the fort was originally projected. Moreover, as a cynic observed, the plan for flooding the marshes would meet with strenuous objections from the local inhabitants if it was ever tried. But it is doubtful whether this mobile column was ever provided, for very soon after this the plans were changed once more.

Now the accent was to be on coast defence proper, and the attack on ships was to be the primary role; the beating-off of landings was considered unnecessary if the landing vessels could be sunk in the channel before they got close enough to disembark their troops. And so four new concrete emplacements were built in 1890, two at each side of the fort. The outer emplacements held a pair of 6in BL and the inner pair of emplacements held 9.2in BL guns, all of which were on disappearing carriages. By 1895 the actual armament consisted of these four guns plus four 9-pounder BL guns on field carriages held in the fort for deployment in the event of landings, three 3-pounder QF on wheeled carriages approved but not supplied, and six machine guns.

The 3-pounders later appeared as pedestal-mounted anti-torpedo-boat guns and were placed on the roof, over the casemates, which had now been converted into accommodation for the maintenance party. The ditch was filled up at the rear of the work and the drawbridge dismantled, and a glacis of earth was run up to roof level at the front, completely concealing the face of the work. Finally, in about 1902, the two 9.2in and right-hand 6in positions were stripped of their carriages and converted into 9.2in barbette positions. The left-hand 6in equipment was left in place and was not dismantled until the work was finally abandoned in the 1920s; its toothed traversing ring can still be seen in the emplacement.

The work was abandoned in the late 1920s, and between 1930 and 1936 the casemates housed a small zoo. It was not used during World War II and today is in sound condition, privately owned, and forms part of a livery stable.

Grain Fort

Regrettably this work no longer exists, and had vanished from the scene before I began to take an interest in the area. It will be recalled that the 1859 Commissioners recommended a work here to protect the island and to act in co-operation with Slough Fort and Garrison Point. Construction began in 1861 and the work was completed in 1867. The original plan was for open batteries with embrasures to mount 16 guns pointing seaward and 12 more on the land face. The 1869 Report noted that this plan had since been changed and that it was now proposed to place 15 guns on Moncrieff carriages, presumably on the sea face, but this was never done, doubtless because of the discovery that the Moncrieff system was ill-suited to the heavier guns which Grain's key position warranted. By 1878 the sea face was armed with 11in RML guns and in 1885 their emplacements were improved by the addition of iron shields.

The trace of this work was an irregular heptagon with a semi-circular self-defensible keep within, all surrounded by a dry ditch protected by caponiers at the principal angles, with demi-bastions on the keep structure protecting the rear face of the gorge wall. The guns were emplaced on an upper terreplein, protected by the ramparts, and behind this was the inner ditch enclosing the keep, a two-storied brick structure with casemates and loopholes commanding the whole interior of the work. In addition, the inner ditch had counterscarp galleries and caponiers to protect it, from which passages ran beneath the terreplein to the outer ditch caponiers and the magazines. This subterranean system was somewhat compromised by a flight of steps leading up to the terreplein.

The armament of Grain underwent considerable changes over the years. The landward armament, from about 1877 onwards, appears to have been four 9in RML, with eight 64-pounder SB on the roof of the keep and an undetermined number of 32-pounders protecting the flanks and ditches. In 1888 the 11in RML main armament was planned to be replaced by two 10in BL on hydropneumatic disappearing mountings, and the mountings were installed in the following year, though the guns were some time in arriving and were not emplaced until 1892. These mountings were then changed for improved patterns in subsequent years; the Ordnance Board Annual Report for 1898 refers to the installation of Mark 3 mountings, and the Report for 1901 refers to their trial firing.

By 1905 they appear to have been dismounted once again, and in 1906 two 9.2in on barbette mountings were installed on the terreplein, and these remained the principal armament throughout both world wars, though some evidence suggests that the two 10in might have been hurriedly remounted in 1914 for the duration of the war.

Grain Fort remained manned from its first occupation until closed down in 1956 with the removal of the defences. During World War II numerous anti-aircraft guns were installed to augment the air defences of the Thames Estuary. The work was sold in 1961 and completely demolished in the following year to make way for the Kent Oil Refinery which now occupies most of the Island.

Grain Battery

This was an open battery for 14 guns bearing on the entrance to the Medway and was constructed at the same time as the Fort. It was then proposed to provide 10 guns on Moncrieff carriages, but these never materialised and eventually 11in RML were installed. These were replaced in about 1895 by 6in BL guns, a battery of four being installed. Like Grain Fort it had active status until 1956, was sold in 1961 and demolished in 1962.

Grain Tower (897 758)

This work was built late in the seventeenth century as support for Garrison Point and to prevent a landing on the Island. When examined in 1859 it was armed with three guns, probably 32-pounder SB, and it was recommended that it be rebuilt as a stronger, casemated work. But the government, probably feeling that there was enough heavy metal in the area already proposed, struck the item from the estimates and no work was ever done. In spite of this the tower was retained and the guns left in place for many years. It then, in the early years of the century, became a signal station, which it remains today, though during World War II a single 6-pounder was mounted on the roof.

Hoo and Darnet Forts *(796 704 and 807 707)*

These two works can be treated under one heading since they are almost identical and sited so as to operate together.

The two works were originally planned on Okeham Ness and Burntwick Island, each to mount 25 guns and to carry a boom between them to block the channel.

While the proposed sites looked sound enough on the map, examination of the ground showed them to be unsuitable, the principal difficulty being the question of securing sound foundations. The sites were changed to place the two works on Hoo and Darnet Islands, and it was intended that they should be circular casemated works with a basement floor for stores and accommodation with magazines beneath, surmounted by 2 tiers of guns, 9 on the lower floor and 16 on the upper, all to be provided with iron shields.

Building began in 1864 but soon ran into difficulties. The foundation would not bear the load of the proposed structure and in 1867 modified plans were approved and building began once more. The magazine and basement floor were as before, but with a single casemate tier for 11 guns above it.

The works appear to have been completed in about 1871 and were armed shortly thereafter. Hoo received eleven 9in RML while Darnet had eight 9in and three 7in RML. Provision was also made for anchoring the boom defence but there is no record of this ever having actually been fitted in place.

The two forts remained in the care of maintenance detachments until some time early in the present century when they were disarmed and abandoned. They remain abandoned today, in rather better condition than most of their contemporaries, since they are difficult of access and thus less vandal-prone. Darnet Fort now sports a large navigational signal on the roof.

Garrison Point Fort *(908 758)*

The relationship between Garrison Point at the tip of the Isle of Sheppey and access to the Medway was always fairly obvious but nothing was done until the enemy were almost at the door.

In the course of the Second Dutch War, with England at war with both France and Holland, it was finally decided to fortify the point, and early in 1667 work began on preparing emplacements. On 7 June the Dutch fleet under de Ruyter suddenly appeared in the mouth of the Thames. Since Charles II considered that the Dutch had been beaten in various sea battles during the previous year he had paid off the Navy, so there was no hope from that quarter. Sixteen guns were hurriedly mounted in the half-finished work and a scratch garrison of gunners, shipless seamen and local Trained Bands was assembled. On 10 June the Dutch arrived at the entrance to the Medway and three warships began bombarding the fort while a force of 800 soldiers and marines was landed to attack it from the rear. After about an hour, when nine of the guns had been put out of action, the garrison was finally overcome and left the work in possession of the Dutch, who held it until 21 June and then, after thoroughly wrecking it, sailed away.

This manoeuvre was, of course, in connection with de Ruyter's attack through the Medway to Chatham Dockyard previously mentioned. It gives Garrison Point the melancholy distinction of being the only coast defence work in England ever to have been captured and occupied by an enemy.

After this initial setback the works were rebuilt and in the forthcoming century further batteries built in the area, covering both the estuary and the Medway, plus a line of earthworks and a wet ditch to protect the town and dockyard from another attack. As already related, the efficiency of these works had declined over the years.

In 1859 it was recommended that a 'powerful casemated work' be built on the site of Charles II's ill-fated battery, to mount 36 heavy guns in two tiers protected by iron shields, and the roof to be prepared for two turrets each mounting two 12in 25-ton guns. The work was duly built to this specification, though the roof turrets, as in all other cases, never appeared, and by 1872 it was in full commission with a mixture of 9in and 10in guns in the casemates. These were shortly changed for heavier weapons, and in 1880 the armament was twenty-eight 9in, ten 10in, three 11in and three 12.5in, all behind iron shields. In view of the general difficulties suffered by the Thames forts in connection with damp and doubtful foundations, it is interesting to read a complaint from here in 1879 that the cartridge bags in the magazine were going mouldy.

In the early 1890s the armament was brought up to date by the installation of three 6in and four 12-pounder guns, and shortly before World War II 2 twin 6-pounders were added. Although no longer a defensive work it remains in the hands of the Ministry of Defence.

Cheyney Rock Battery

This was proposed by the 1859 Report as the northern anchor of the Queenborough Lines, a fresh alignment of ditch and rampart running across the tip of the island and sealing off the Sheerness area. It was intended to mount three 7in RML on Moncrieff mountings here. There appears to be no further record of the work and it has not been possible to discover any remains on the ground. It is therefore doubtful whether, in fact, it was ever built.

Barton's Point Battery (942 748)

In default, presumably, of Cheyney Rock Battery, the northern end of the Queenborough Lines had no major work. But in the late 1890s, when re-armament with modern weapons was being undertaken, a work was finally built here to mount two 9.2in BL guns and two 6in BL guns, all on disappearing carriages. The 6in were in place by 1901 and the 9.2in shortly thereafter, both being noted in the Ordnance Board Annual Report for 1905. A Practice Battery of two 6-pounder Hotchkiss guns was also installed at about the same time. The disappearing carriage guns were withdrawn in the 1920s when all this class of mounting was made obsolete, but the practice battery remained and was in fact used during the training season by the various territorial units in the area.

Fletcher Battery (008 730)

This work originated at about the same time as Barton's Point Battery, and for the same reason, to provide the mouth of the Thames with modern heavy armament which would have been difficult to install in the existing 1859 vintage works. It was completed by about 1918 and carried three 9.2in guns on barbette mountings. These remained in active status until 1956 when they were withdrawn and the work abandoned.

Warden Battery (020 726)

A third modern work, contemporary with Barton's Point and Fletcher Batteries, Warden was equipped with two 6in BL guns on central pivot mountings and two 12-pounder QF. These remained in place until after World War 1 but the work was then disarmed and abandoned and the land sold in the 1920s.

Page 119 *An aerial view showing Agaton Fort in the foreground and Ernesettle Battery behind*

Page 120 (above) *An aerial view of Plymouth Citadel, illustrating the bastioned trace;* (below) *a Haxo Casemate and its expense magazine, above the casemate tier at Fort Efford, Plymouth*

6
THE PORTSMOUTH AND ISLE OF WIGHT DEFENCES

Portsmouth Defences

Portsmouth, as befitted the premier naval dockyard, had always had some form of defence, even, as we have seen, in Roman times. When the 1859 Commission came to examine the current works there was already a certain amount in existence, and in the early 1850s more money had been voted for improvements which were then in the course of construction. Fort Blockhouse and the Point Battery opposite, housed in a tower whose origins dated back to Henry II, Southsea Castle, and some old batteries on Gilkicker Point were more or less serviceable. Fort Cumberland at the eastern end of Portsea Island defended the entrance to Langstone Harbour and in conjunction with Southsea Castle covered the shore of Portsea from the danger of a beach landing. There was, though, a large gap between these two works and two more were planned to fill it; Lumps Fort was already being built and the other, Eastney Battery, had not been begun.

In order to protect the western flank work was in progress on a rampart and wet ditch—the Stokes Bay Lines—running from Fort Monckton, near Gilkicker Point, to a battery in front of Gosport, and authority had been given for the building of another small work to be placed behind the centre of this line to act as a keep.

In order to deny the Spithead Roads to an enemy fleet, sanction had also been given to a plan to construct some form of ordnance tower on the shoals of No Mans Land and Horse Sands, points where the deep water channel was most constricted, narrowing to about 2,000yd.

The commissioners began their report by examining exactly what the defence of Portsmouth involved, and they broke the task down into five well-defined areas:

1. The immediate defence of the entrance of the harbour
2. The prevention of an enemy gaining a foothold on the shore
3. The protection of the anchorage at Spithead and the prevention of it being bombarded from the sea
4. The defence of the Needles Passage
5. The prevention of an enemy gaining a foothold on the Isle of Wight.

With regard to the first task it was considered that the existing batteries were sufficient, taking into account the twisting and difficult nature of the channels which would slow any ship attempting to run through. But as additional insurance it was decided to extend the Southsea Castle work by placing additional batteries on each flank and also to provide a floating boom to be hauled across the channel from Fort Blockhouse in time of danger.

When it came to denying the enemy a foothold, the Southsea shore with the two new works contemplated and the additional batteries would be well protected, but the Gosport side was to have a military road with a parapet on the seawards side which, like a similar proposal on the Isle of Wight, would allow a mobile column to deploy under cover to meet any threat to the area.

Next came the problem of the Spithead anchorage. Previous works had been built on the assumption that the threat was from short range fire from smooth bore guns, but the commissioners felt that due to improvements in artillery it was now vital to develop a defence system which would keep an enemy at arm's length and prevent him from taking up a position from which he could bombard the dockyard or anchorage at long range. The two towers proposed on the shoals, while a step in the right direction, were not deemed sufficient, since even with these fully armed and crossing their fire with the shore batteries, 'we are of the opinion that no practical amount of fire . . . can be depended upon to stop the passage of steam ships if the channel be sufficiently clear to allow of their proceeding at high speed.' The question of a floating boom was debated at some length, but providing a boom to cover the entire expanse of water between Portsmouth and the Isle of Wight was obviously unrealistic, and simply placing a boom across the deep water channel would be technically difficult and would be an insufficient defence anyway.

After studying charts of the area and assessing the likely points from which fire could be brought to bear on the anchorage, the commissioners recommended that the proposed works should be augmented by similar towers, one between Horse Sand and Portsea Island and one on the Spitbank Shoal, plus a casemated work on Sturbridge Shoal. These would then form a line across the roads and would be completed on the southern flank by shore batteries on the Isle of Wight in the area of Nettlestone Point. The more important of these towers were to be three-tiered works with additional guns on their roofs, so as to be able to bring the maximum fire to bear on any point.

Having taken care of the defence of the dockyard and anchorage, attention was now focussed on the possibility of an attack being made from the land side by a force landed elsewhere on the coast. This contingency had been studied in the past; a line of land defences had been begun on the northern edge of the dockyard in the time of James II and had been continued in a desultory fashion until the end of the eighteenth century. On the Gosport side a wet ditch and some earthworks had been constructed in about 1678 and these were extended to cover the area of Priddy's Hard in 1790. While these works as originally planned might have sufficed to stop an attack by foot soldiers, they were, by 1859, utterly useless in any respect. The spread of building on either side of the works had reduced their effectiveness by providing ample cover for an attacker on the one side while hindering the deployment of defenders on the other, and the line was so close to the dockyard area that it gave no protection against the fire of artillery which could be brought up close to it. It was now necessary to move the defensive line well out of artillery range.

The only existing works which were further out than the Gosport Lines were the Hilsea Lines, 'of weak trace and low profile', running along the northern shore of Portsea Island, and the remains of a fort dating from Charles II, both erected with the intention of denying a crossing of the narrow channel separating the island from the mainland. In addition, the 1850 scares had led to the erection of two forts between Gosport and the Solent: one of these, Fort Gomer, was completed, and the other, Fort Elson nearly completed when the commissioners inspected the district. Plans had been drawn up in 1856 for a system of works to strengthen the Gosport flank by placing three more forts between Gomer and Elson and then to connect the five by a line of earthwork and ditch; for a new excavation in the rear of Hilsea Lines to replace the earlier work; for the construction of a large and powerful fort on Horsea Island; and for a new fort in the Portchester area.

It is difficult to understand what was in the minds of the people who had produced this plan. If the Gosport flank works were meant to prevent an attack from the Solent, it would appear that the planners had given up hope of preventing a fleet passing through either the Needles or Spithead and were now concerned with trying to save what they could. The building of a work on Horsea tends to strengthen this opinion, since if the seaward defences were at all efficient, no enemy would have been able to reach this point. The only project which made any sort of sense was the strengthening of Hilsea Lines in order to prevent an overland attack.

Curiously though, the commissioners accepted the Gosport flank line, though their reasons were slightly different; they were less concerned with the prospect of an enemy landing in the Solent—their other dispositions fairly ruled that out—than with the likelihood of a land attack from the north making a sweeping movement to a flank and driving down the peninsula from the direction of Winchester and Southampton. For when the commissioners finally decided on their scheme of defence they envisaged an impregnable ring of works running from the Gosport shore at Browndown right around the north of Portsmouth to come to rest near Havant, a perimeter some ten miles long.

The crest of Portsdown Hill was chosen as being naturally perfect for siting such a defensive line and two systems were suggested. Firstly, to cut an enormous ditch 'after the manner of a railway cutting' running the entire distance and flanked at intervals by guns in caponiers. Secondly, to build a number of strong detached forts at intervals such that the intervening ground could be swept with fire. The first plan was objected to on the grounds that a resourceful enemy would eventually be bound to cross the ditch either by blowing down the sides or by filling it in at some point, whereupon the whole line would collapse; moreover such a work would be immensely expensive in labour and time and would demand an enormous garrison to man all the caponiers. The second course was accepted as being the wisest, demanding less manpower to defend and being a more flexible mode of defence, and four principal works were planned. Additionally, detached flank works at each end of the line would cover the approaches to the ridge from east or west, the eastern one overlooking the village of Bedhampton and commanding all the ground from the ridge to Portsmouth Harbour.

Finally, to secure the dockyard from long range land bombardment from the western flank, three more works were planned in advance of the Gomer-Elson line. One was to be in the Lee-on-Solent area, one at Stubbington and one near Newgate to link this line with the western outwork of Portsdown Hill.

By the time the Commissioners had finished with Portsmouth it was sewn up tight and the bill was quite impressive:

Spithead:

No Mans Land	120 guns	700 men	
Horse Sand	120	700	
Sturbridge Shoal	120	700	
Spitsand	60	300	
Intermediate work	60	300	
Southsea Castle	10		
Gilkicker Point	9		
Total	499 guns	2,700 men	£850,000

Outer Defences:

Crookhorn	30 guns	300 men	
Windmill	30	300	
Fir Clumps	30	300	
Nelson's Column	30	300	
Seven outworks	106	1,060	
Total	226 guns	2,260 men	£650,000

Gomer-Elson connecting ditch			£20,000
Lee-on-Solent Fort	30 guns	300 men	
Stubbington Fort	30	300	
Newgate Fort	40	400	
Total	100 guns	1,000 men	£350,000
Grand Total	825 guns	5,960 men	£1,870,000

In addition to this formidable reckoning, it was estimated that in the event of an attack, an additional 15,000 men would be needed to man the defensive works.

This was a sizeable pill to swallow, and it was an obvious target for the economising bound to follow. One is, indeed, tempted to speculate on whether the worthy commissioners had not, in fact, appreciated the point and over-planned so as to be sure to retain the necessary strength after an inevitable axeing; it certainly seems to have worked out that way.

Firstly the intermediate tower between the Horse Sand and Portsea Island was struck out, followed by the Spitbank Tower and the forts at Lee-on-Solent and Stubbington. This trimmed £460,000 from the estimates and at this figure it went to Parliament and was passed. But before any money was voted, more cuts took place. The line of earthworks from Gomer to Elson was abandoned, saving another £20,000, and exploratory surveys showed that the Sturbridge Shoal would not provide a firm enough foundation for any sort of work, so that too was struck out. But this latter excision left too big a hole in the defences and the work at Spitsand was now re-considered and approved, together with another similar work on Ryde Sand. More exploratory sinkings showed that Ryde Sand was also untenable, and finally a sea fort off St Helen's Point on the Isle of Wight was approved in its place.

With these details secure, work began in 1862, the delicate task of constructing the sea forts being under the direction of Mr Hawkshaw, CE. Sir John Hawkshaw, as he became in 1873, was one of the foremost civil engineers of the day, responsible among other things for Charing Cross and Cannon Street Railway stations and bridges in London, and for the railway tunnel under the River Severn.

Generally speaking, most of the work was completed by 1868–9, though in one or two cases there were difficulties which gave rise to delays, and it was 1871 before everything was ready. But of course, by then it was time for re-armament and redesign, and it was the middle 1880s before the defences finally settled down. After that the only work was to bring the armament up to date periodically, and little was done in the way of altering the works themselves. No work was ever planned or built after the 1869 Commission report, and, indeed, it is hard to say where one might have been fitted in had it ever been mooted.

Today, due to the ever-expanding needs of the services and the scarcity of land, almost all the Portsmouth defence works are in the hands of the Ministry of Defence, mostly occupied by naval establishments of one sort or another. The land defensive position on Portsdown Hill was abandoned in that role before World War I, though the forts were used as barracks accommodation by a variety of garrison artillery siege batteries for many years. They were generally closed down in the 1920s, but were taken back into use during World War II, since which they have remained occupied, many of them being extensively rebuilt inside to provide modern accommodation.

The Spithead Forts

These works, located in the sea across the Spithead Anchorage are so different from all other works in the area as to warrant grouping together. The principal works are Horse Sand Fort

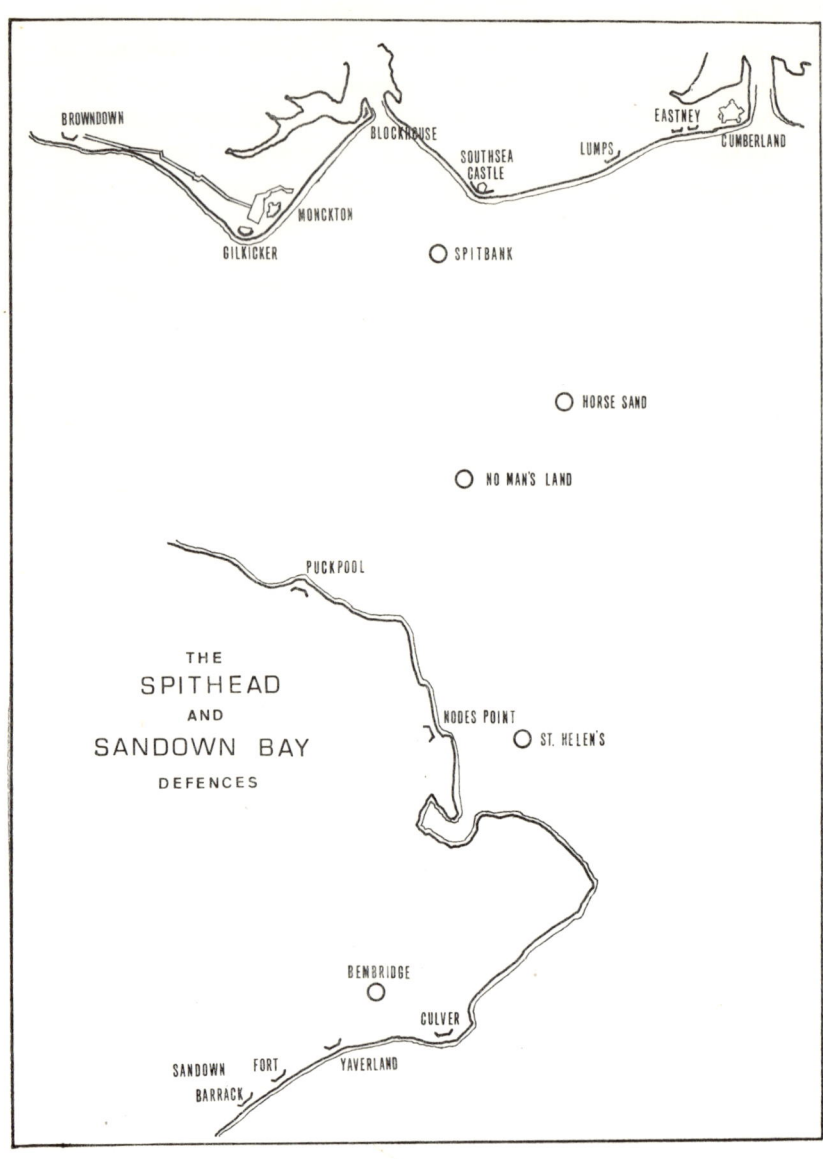

Map 2 The Spithead and Sandown area Defences

and No Mans Land Fort, two thousand yards apart. The foundations for these are granite and Portland stone masonry rings sunk almost twenty feet below low water mark and measuring 230ft in diameter. The ring of stone is 53ft 6in thick and the centre is filled with a mixture of shingle and clay upon which a thick bed of concrete was laid. Upon this bed a granite wall 14ft 6in thick, 100ft in diameter was built. The original intention was to construct the works entirely of granite, but before the foundations were completed, the decision to completely armour them was taken, and the iron armoured work was then built on top of the masonry foot-wall. From the concrete bed the masonry runs up to a point 16ft above the high water mark and at that level a circular baseplate of iron measuring 2in thick and 3ft wide was let into the masonry to form the basis of the iron structure. The outer edge of the plate was slotted to take the feet of upright armour bars which acted as backing and anchors for the outer armoured skin. To portion off the casemate sections, hollow steel casings 12ft deep, 7ft 6in high and triangular in form were now bolted to the base ring. On top of these casings rested a solid ring of 3in-thick iron plate, welded into a continuous ring running round the entire fort. Its outer edge was also slotted for the armour bars, which backed the plating throughout the height of both tiers of the work. Onto this plate were laid the outer ends of the support girders for the upper gunfloor, the inner ends being supported on the masonry 'hub' of the work. These girders were joined by arch plates to make a continuous surface, and onto this went 2ft 3in of concrete forming the gunfloor of the upper tier. The construction of the upper tier was the same; pier casings, 3in thick iron ring, girders and arch plates, this time surmounted by 4ft 6in of concrete to form the roof.

An interesting point about this construction is that no part of the floor structure or roof structure—ie the outer ends of the roof girders—was attached to the 3in-thick iron rings on which they rested, the surfaces being free to slide. The object of this was that should the outer walls be struck by a heavy shot, the movement would not be transmitted to the gunfloors and thus deform the racers or dislevel the gun mountings.

The armoured wall itself was of layered construction. The inner layer was five inches thick with a one-inch layer of wood and cement between it and the upright armour bars. This layer of plate was in two tiers and bolted to the pier casings. The middle layer was of plates stood on end, each 22ft 6in high and reaching from the granite base to the roof. The thickness varied, those plates in which ports were cut being 7in thick, those without ports 5in; the 7in plates weighed 18 tons each. The outer layer was of 5in thickness, again in two tiers. Each layer was spaced with about 6in of iron concrete and was bolted to the preceding layer. The total weight of ironwork in each fort was 6,214 tons, of which 3,764 tons—75 tons per gun mounted—was armour plate, the remaining 2,450 tons being the structural skeleton.

As a final touch the roof was reinforced and prepared to accept guns in turrets, to be added at some future time when the design of turret was finally decided.

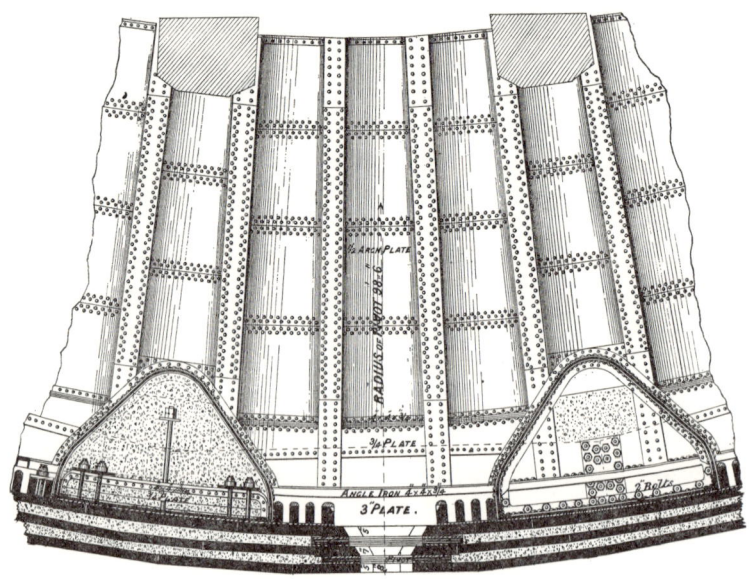

Overhead view of the armoured face of Horse Sand and No Mans Land Forts, showing the triangular casings between each casemate

Spitbank Fort was a work of somewhat different construction; only the seaward side was iron, the inner side being of masonry. The work was 150ft in diameter and the armour section consisted of two box girder arcs, one at the level of the floor and one at roof level, against which the armoured wall rested. The inner structure was built up of iron pillars in pairs between the gun ports supporting the box girders and roof, which was also of iron plate. The gun floor was 16ft above high water level and the armoured skin was made up of three layers of 5in plate, though fastenings were provided to take a fourth layer should it ever be deemed necessary.

St Helen's Fort is totally different from the others. The foundations were a ring of iron caissons sunk to a depth of 25ft 6in, and upon these a granite casemated work was built, having massive iron shields 20ft wide between masonry piers. These shields are formed of three layers of 6in plate separated by iron concrete and each shield contains two ports. Between the ports are pier casings of $\frac{3}{4}$in iron filled with concrete to back the armour and support the roof. The most unusual feature is that two of the shields were constructed so as to conceal only one gun each; the weapon was mounted to fire from either shield port.

Horse Sand Fort (655 949)

The original plan for this work was for a three-tier fort with guns and mortars on the roof but this was modified to a two-tier work with reinforced areas in the roof to take five turrets. The two tiers would mount forty-nine guns, and in addition to this armament it was to be a control station for a network of controlled submarine mines in the Spithead entrances. But although the fort was built according to this plan, it was some time before it was properly armed. It had been decided that the 12in 36-ton gun would be used in this fort but the normal casemate platform was unsuitable for the restricted space available, and in July 1872 the Director of Artillery convened a 'Special Committee on the Arming of Spithead Forts'. These gentlemen studied the drawings of the work and opined that the Sea Service 12in 35-ton gun on a 15ft platform looked as if it would suit the case. (Sea Service—ie naval—RML guns were generally slightly shorter than the equivalent calibre in Land Service—ie army—guns, due to there being less space available on ships). The Superintendent of the Royal Carriage Department was asked to produce a design, and on 30 September 1872 produced a drawing showing the 35-ton gun on a casemate platform of the pattern used with the 12in 25-ton gun. This was approved and these were provided and mounted in the fort by the summer of 1874, but before long the decision was taken to remove them and replace them with the new and more powerful 12.5in 38-ton gun. The 12in were taken out in 1877 and work began on remaking the gun floors and preparing them for the new racers and traversing arcs, but there was a considerable delay while a suitable design of carriage was being developed. In September 1878 the Inspector-General of Fortifications enquired plaintively if it had yet been decided how the guns were to be mounted, as the gun floors could not be completed until this question was settled; his problem was that once the design had been approved and the racers and arcs produced, they had to be set into the floors and anchored in concrete and lead, and it would then take some time for the concrete to harden to the point where it could take the weight of the guns and their mountings without shifting and thus upsetting the level of the weapons. His enquiry seems to have moved things along, for by the end of 1879 the fort had been provided with its new armament of twenty-five 10in on the upper tier and twenty-four 12.5in on the lower.

They were not left in place for long. That same year saw the Committee of Ordnance recommending the provision of the new 12in 45-ton BL gun which was then in the design stage. This was an extremely powerful weapon in comparison with the muzzle-loaders, and the usual pattern of carriage and slide would be incapable of withstanding its recoil within the dimensions laid down by the construction of the casemates, and so the Superintendent RCD was given the job of designing some completely new system of mounting these guns to allow them to be used here. He eventually produced the 'Yoke Mounting' in which a heavy iron yoke was attached to the foot of the traversing platform and ran in grooved racers in the floor and roof. The barrel of the gun passed through the hole in the yoke, and the piston rods of the hydraulic recoil buffers were attached to the body of the yoke. In this way the recoil stress was evenly divided between floor and roof, and the front end was secured from the likelihood of jumping up into the air when fired. Yet another Committee, this time the Committee on Heavy Guns, visited Shoeburyness in March 1881 to watch a test of this design of mounting in a mock-up casemate. After more work it was finally approved in 1884, and the platforms were built in two patterns, upper tier and lower tier, differing in the spacing of the traversing trucks so that they could be fitted to the existing racers laid for the RML guns to avoid rebuilding the gun floors for a third time.

With these weapons finally in place, the fort was more or less complete, since the turret installations were never made. In 1895 the mountings were fitted with hydraulic machinery to elevate and depress the gun, traverse the mounting, hoist the shells, open and close the breech, wash out the chamber and ram the shells, but this complication turned out to be more trouble than it was worth and in 1907 it was all removed and the mountings reverted to hand operation. Finally in 1920 the 12in guns were all withdrawn and the mounting declared obsolete, the upper tier being re-armed with 6in BL guns on central pivot mountings, which remained in place until the 1950s. Today Horse Sand Fort is a naval signal station.

No Mans Land Fort (639 937)

This is of the same pattern as Horse Sand, the only slight difference being that the foundations had to go deeper. But the rest of the story is the same as far as construction and armament is concerned. There appears to have been an experimental roof mounting in the early 1900s since the Annual Report of the Ordnance Board for 1900 records the supply of electric training motors for the mounting, and a very indistinct photograph taken before the time of World War I shows some sort of gun, probably a 6in BL on the roof. Beyond that no record has yet been found. As with Horse Sand, No Mans Land is in the hands of the navy.

St Helen's Fort (649 898)

This was intended to mount six heavy guns to seawards, behind the armoured face, and four lighter guns facing landwards from the masonry face to cover the beach area against a landing. Due to its large arc of fire seawards, two 10in guns were mounted on turntables so as to be able to fire out of either of the two ports of the shield, 60° apart.

The turntable was a massive steel plate structure 23ft in diameter, revolving about a central spindle and supported on conical rollers. Control was by hand gear engaging in teeth on the side of the platform, and it was locked in place by tumblers engaging in slots in the floor. The interesting feature is that the

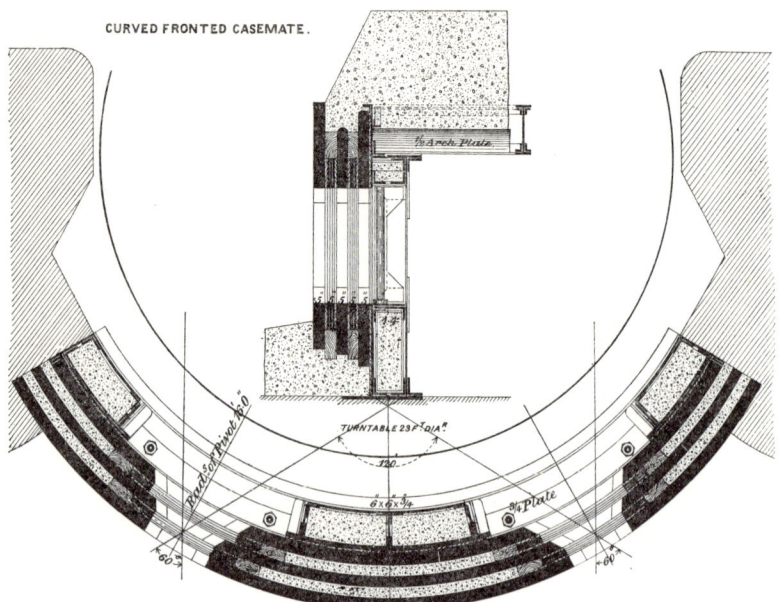

The armoured face of St Helen's Fort. One curved shield with two firing ports served one gun mounted on a turntable. The centre drawing is a section of the wall and port

gun was not simply clamped to this revolving table but mounted on its usual traversing platform, the racers and traversing arc being built into the platform. Thus at each port the gun still had its full 60° of traverse available, giving it a total of 120° coverage, and only two positions of the turntable were necessary.

The work was completed in 1871 and by 1880 had its full complement of two 10in 18-ton guns and four 12.5in 38-ton on the sea side. There is no record of the planned lighter ordnance for the land side ever being installed.

In later years the importance of this work declined with the activating of Nodes Point Battery, which mounted modern ordnance, and after the RML guns were withdrawn the fort was given up by the army in the 1920s. It was later taken into use by the Admiralty, in whose care it now is.

Spitbank Fort (636 971)

This was also half-armoured, with armour-defeating guns on the sea face and shell guns in the masonry face where they could command the Southsea beaches. The armament history, so far as the heavy guns go, is the same as that of No Mans Land and Horse Sand, nine 12.5in 38-ton guns being succeeded by nine 12in 43-ton BL in yoke mountings in the 1880s. The land side was provided with seven 7in 7-ton RML guns but these were withdrawn when the 12in were installed and from then on the land side remained unarmed. In the 1920s the 12in were removed and 6in BL guns installed; these remained until after World War II. Spitbank is now in the hands of the Ministry of Defence.

The Remaining Spithead Anchorage Defences

Fort Cumberland (683 993)

Fort Cumberland is a scheduled Ancient Monument and in addition is actively preserved both by being used by the Royal

Marines and by the existence of a Fort Cumberland Preservation Society. Built in 1746 and enlarged in 1794, the first official record of its defensive capability is its inclusion in a return of 1805 showing its armament as eight 24-pounder, forty-one 18-pounder, twenty-five 12-pounder and seven 6-pounder guns. As might be imagined from this list, it is a very large work laid out on the bastioned trace. The 1859 report noted it as being in existence and considered that no further work was necessary to make it any more effective, and except for rearming with newer weapons it was untouched. By the 1880s it was exclusively the domain of the Royal Marine Artillery, which it has remained ever since. There is no record of it ever being equipped with heavy ordnance for the attack of ships, and all the evidence points to continued prime use as a RM training establishment, with the secondary role of closing the entrance to Langstone Harbour in time of war. But when the breech-loading era arrived it was decided to put some modern ordnance into the work, and a battery of 6in BL on disappearing carriages was put in in the late 1890s. These remained in place throughout World War I and were removed in about 1924 when all these weapons were declared obsolete. Since that time it has been exclusively a Marine training centre and has not formed part of the defences.

Lumps Fort (658 984)

This work is something of a mystery; the 1859 Report refers to its construction being in progress at that time; the 1869 report reiterates this statement, referring to 'two intervening forts about to be constructed at Lumps and Eastney'. Yet a report in the records of the Board of Ordnance, giving returns of armament in 1805, includes under the heading 'Portsmouth Fortress' the item 'Lumps Fort—three 32-pounder guns'. It seems likely that an open battery had been built on this site during the Napoleonic Wars but had been allowed to fall into disuse during the intervening years. A return dated 1824 which lists the master gunners of various works shows Lumps Fort as being without one at the time; one can assume, therefore, that it had deteriorated over the years until by the 1850s it was not worth remodelling and was used as the site for a completely new work.

The new construction provided for 14 guns in embrasures and three en barbette, the scheduled armament being a mixture of 68-pounder smooth-bore and 7in and 8in Armstrong RBL guns. The work was surrounded by a rampart and ditch, but the 1869 Report noted that 'as the ditch will not retain water, it must be regarded as an imperfect obstacle.'

The armament actually installed was a mixture of 32-pounder SB and 7in RBL, and this establishment seems to have been singularly unfortunate in its gunnery. In 1867 a 32-pounder being used to fire a salute during the Naval Review of 17 July was so ineptly manned that the gun captain was blown over the parapet by a blank charge. Three years later a 7in Armstrong was rendered unserviceable by a common shell bursting in the barrel due to the fuze being improperly fixed.

Thereafter Lumps Fort seems to have played little part in the defensive role until World War I when it was armed with two 6in howitzers, which must rank as the most unlikely weapons ever found in a coast defence work. However, bearing in mind that Lump's principal role was beach defence, these two weapons firing shrapnel shell doubtless would have been as effective as more expensive and complex weapons, and were cheaper and quicker to install. At the end of the war it was abandoned and has since been removed by the development of Southsea promenade.

Southsea Castle (643 980)

This had been the principal defensive work of the district long before the 1859 Commission came on the scene. It had been built on the orders of Henry VIII in 1539 and was added to during the reign of Charles II in order to make it into a star fort, the fashionable trace of the day. From then on it was well armed at all times. When the Board of Ordnance decided to reduce the armament strength of coast works in 1716 it observed that Southsea had no less than 474 guns, which it proposed to reduce to 143. It is doubtful if all 474 were mounted or even serviceable.

The armament shrank as time went on; by 1805 it was down to eight 32-pounder and five 6-pounder guns.

The 1859 Report considered the castle to be a useful location and recommended it be improved by adding open batteries on each flank, and these were duly built, with a gorge wall on the land side loopholed for musketry. The new construction allowed for twenty-two rifled 9in or 10in on the seaward face, nine Armstrong guns for flank defence, four mortars, and, on the left flank of the west battery, a single 13.3in RML gun, a weapon thought to be capable of reaching well out into the anchorage and piercing any ship likely to appear there. Unfortunately for this good intention, the 13.3in never materialised. Although planned as a 13.3in 600-pounder, three guns were built to 13in calibre by the Elswick Ordnance Company in 1864, as well as a fourth, also 13in, by the Royal Gun Factory of Woolwich in the same year. Three of them split while being proved; one was repaired and sent to the Royal Military Repository, and the other serviceable gun remained in the Royal Arsenal. No service ammunition was ever made, and that was the end of the 13in idea. The eventual armament of Southsea's open batteries was the usual mixture of 7in 7 ton and 9in 12 ton RML guns installed in 1870, and shortly

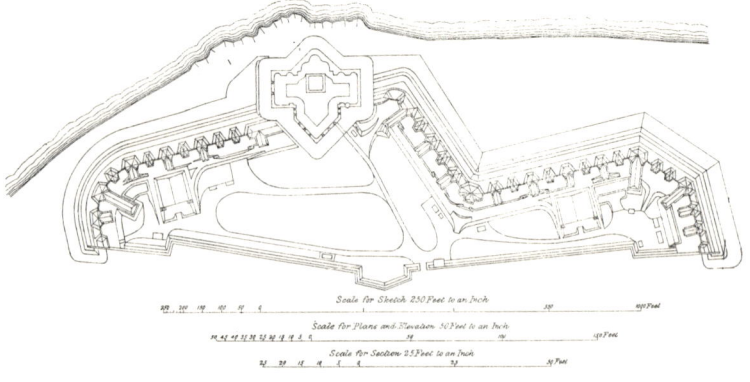

Ground plan of Southsea Battery drawn by Col Jervois in 1869. The square buildings on each flank, behind the embrasures, are the main magazines, while small expense magazines are between each pair of embrasures

THE PORTSMOUTH AND ISLE OF WIGHT DEFENCES 139

after that the position intended for the 13.3in weapon was occupied by a 12.5in 38 ton gun on a barbette platform.

Towards the turn of the century the usual re-armament with modern weapons took place and the auxiliary batteries were provided with 9.2in BL guns on barbette mountings, 6in on central pivot mountings and some 4.7in QF guns. These remained until after World War II and a coast artillery maintenance battery was stationed in the castle until 1956. The work is now maintained as a museum and pleasure garden by the local authority.

Fort Blockhouse (626 993)

One of the original defences of the principal entrance to Portsmouth Harbour, Blockhouse began as a tower erected in the reign of Edward VI to hold one end of a boom. It was subsequently improved and enlarged and became known by its present title some time in the eighteenth century. In 1805 it carried fifteen 36-pounder and fifteen 18-pounder guns and was obviously an important work. The 1859 Commission saw no reason to make any changes there, but neither did they recommend the provision of any modern weapons, and it seems that very little was done with the work to bring it up to date. In 1867 its armament still consisted of 32-pounder smooth-bores, and no heavy RML guns were ever installed.

By the time of World War I it had lost its value as a coastal defence work and was in the hands of the Royal Navy, who used it from then on as a submarine depot. Today it forms part of HMS *Dolphin*.

Fort Monckton (611 978)

Monckton was one of the many works erected during the Napoleonic Wars, its first appearance in the records being the 1805 return which shows twenty-four 36-pounder, twenty-three 18-pounder and twelve 12-pounder mounted there, which argues that it was of some importance in those days. This importance declined when the newer defences were built and Monckton was relegated to a beach defence role. The work is of bastioned trace, with two bastions commanding the sea front; it is enclosed by a dry ditch of elaborate trace with the remains of two 'redans' or triangular outworks and the whole was then surrounded by a considerable wet ditch, most of which has been canalised over the years until it is hardly recognisable as an obstacle.

By 1870 it had been provided with a number of 7in Armstrong guns but when these became obsolete the work was not re-armed and became simply a barrack and store. It later passed into the hands of the Royal Navy, in whose care it remains today.

Fort Gilkicker (607 975)

A battery had been built on Gilkicker Point in about 1796 and in 1859 it was recommended that this be strengthened to form part of the defences guarding the anchorage. Instead of simple strengthening, it was replaced entirely by a new casemated work of granite to carry 22 guns, with another 5 on the roof. Within the work was a barrack for 5 officers, 4 NCOs and 98 men. Work began in June 1863 but in the following year the contractor went bankrupt and all work stopped. The usual wrangle ensued, and it took eighteen months to sort out the legal aspects and advertise for a fresh tender. Eventually, in June 1865, a new contractor was appointed and work began afresh; but by this time the plans had been revised to allow for iron shields in the casemates and for the roof guns. It was completed in 1871, though the roof positions were never installed.

In 1872 the Director of Artillery asked for designs of traversing platform for 12in 35-ton RML guns to be installed here, but the work must have been low on the priority list, since a return of 1880 shows only four 9in 12-ton guns mounted. The 12in materialised in due course however, and were installed by 1885.

Thereafter there was no improvement in armament. When the RMLs fell obsolete, Gilkicker remained unarmed and eventually, like most of the defence works in the area, passed to the Royal Navy.

Eastney Batteries (665 986 and 670 988)

These, like Lumps Fort, appear to have been first built during the Napoleonic Wars, since the 1805 returns refer to 'Eastney Fort' and list three 32-pounder guns there. But also like Lumps, the 1859 Report refers to it as being in the process of construction, so that it looks like another case of a dilapidated work being used as the basis for new construction. The eventual form was two open batteries connected by a parapet concealing a sunken way, so as to command the entrance to Langstone Harbour and the waters of Spithead to the east of Horse Sand Fort. Each battery had ten embrasures and two barbette positions, but was never fully armed, the maximum number of guns provided being five 7in Armstrong and one 68-pounder to each battery. Their subsequent history is not recorded, but it seems probable that they were abandoned some time early in the century and are now within the grounds of the Royal Marine Barracks at Eastney.

Brown Down Battery (586 989)

This work, also dating from the 1800s, has never been of particular importance, although it acted as the connecting link between the inner and outer defences by virtue of being the end of the Stokes Bay Line of ditch from Gilkicker and its relationship to Fort Gomer. I can find no record of modern armament, and it appears that its function was merely to provide prepared platforms into which a mobile column of field artillery could deploy should a threat materialise. For many years its principal military function has been as part of a rifle range and training area, and today the work, scarcely recognisable, forms part of the Army Hovercraft Experimental Establishment.

The Land Defences

Fort Gomer (588 993)

This pre-dated the 1859 Commission, having been begun in

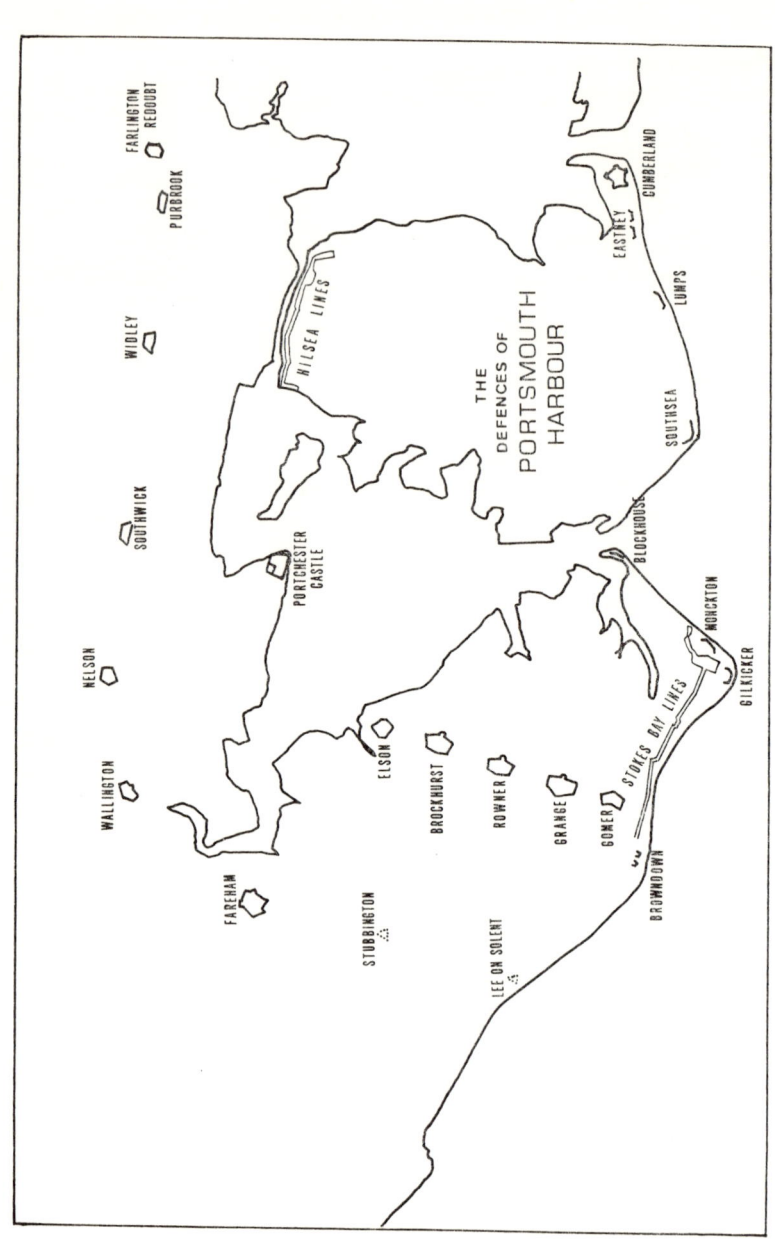

Map 3 The Portsmouth Harbour Defences

THE PORTSMOUTH AND ISLE OF WIGHT DEFENCES 143

1853 and completed in 1858. The armament was originally 32-pounder smooth-bore, but these were later changed to 40-pounder Armstrong, and a number of mobile guns were stationed here for the defence of the Stokes Bay Line. It is now occupied by the Royal Navy.

Fort Grange (591 002)

After Gomer and Elson forts had been approved in 1852, further consideration led to a decision to fill the gap between them by three more forts, and Grange is the most southerly of the three. Work began in 1858 and it was completed in 1863. Someone had blundered, however, since a report later said 'The work is surrounded with a wet ditch but with no provision for filling it with water.'

There is no record of what armament went into the work, but it was probably the customary 32-pounder smooth-bore, probably replaced by 64-pounder converted RML guns. Like all the other works of the outer line its defensive value declined in the closing years of the century and by 1910 it was the District Headquarters of the Royal Garrison Artillery. It is now occupied by the Department of the Environment and used as a store. They appear to have solved the ditch problem; it has recently been filled with earth.

Fort Rowner (594 011)

This was the second of the gap-fillers and was also begun in 1858. Built, like the other two, of brick, the Inspector of Works condemned the construction as being faulty and the contractor was fired in 1862, the work being taken over by the Royal Engineers and rebuilt using military labour. If nothing else, they at least made sure that the ditch would hold water, which was more than could be said for some of the original contractor's excuses.

Its subsequent career was undistinguished, serving as a barrack for a variety of units until being taken over by the Royal

Navy who now, according to the notice outside, run it as a Degaussing Establishment.

Fort Brockhurst (597 020)

As with its two companions, this brick fort was commenced in 1858 and was completed in 1863. From then on it was never armed but used solely as barrack and store accommodation until passing into naval occupancy.

Fort Elson (599 029)

This was planned at the same time as Gomer, to act as a land defence on the approach to Gosport and also to cover the upper reaches of Portsmouth Harbour. Construction began about 1855 and it was completed in 1860. As with the others of this line, its subsequent use was solely as a barrack and it was never armed. At present it is in naval hands.

Fort Fareham (572 049)

Fareham was to form the link between the Gosport Line, the Outer Line on Portsdown Hill and the advanced works in front of the Gosport Line. The other two forts of this advanced line were never built, but Fareham still had a tactical place without them, and so work began in October 1861. It was completed in December 1864 and was never armed. It was used for some years as barracks for siege artillery units based in the area before passing into naval hands.

Fort Wallington (588 069)

This is the left-hand end of the Portsdown Hill Line and was begun in September 1861 and completed in March 1865. It was to be armed with '17 guns on the ramparts, 6 mortars in casemates and 28 lighter guns' according to the 1869 report, though one is inclined to wonder how it was proposed to fire the mortars out of casemates. From examination some years ago, it appears to have had the racers laid for a number of 40-pounder RBL on the ramparts, but what calibre of mortars and lighter guns it was intended to provide is not known. In all probability the lighter weapons would have been 25-pounder RBL on travelling carriages which could either be used as moveable armament within the work or deployed in the surrounding area if necessary.

Fort Nelson (607 071)

Named after the nearby Nelson's Monument, this is a large work in stone and brick, surrounded by a deep ditch. Commenced in February 1862, work progressed slowly for no discoverable reason, and it was not finished until 1871. It was intended to mount 30 guns on the ramparts, nine mortars on the terreplein and 48 lighter guns, but no ordnance was ever mounted. In later years it was occupied by siege companies of the Royal Garrison Artillery and fell into disuse shortly after World War I. It then passed into naval ownership, although it appears at present to be empty.

Fort Southwick (628 068)

This is the major work of the Portsdown Hill Line, less heavily armed than others but with considerable barrack accommodation for the troops garrisoning the other works of the line. Built between 1861 and 1870 the planned armament was 31 guns on the ramparts, but they were never installed. It was subsequently used as a barrack and headquarter accommodation by the Royal Garrison Artillery and eventually became a naval establishment, since which it has been considerably rebuilt within the trace. For some reason it is sometimes referred to as Fort Paulsgrove.

Fort Widley (077 065)

This appears to have led a more active existence than its companions. Begun in late 1861 it was also a long time building, not being completed until 1871. It then appears to have actually been provided with armament. The design was originally for 29 guns on the ramparts, 10 mortars and 41 light guns, but this must have been considerably modified. In January 1883 a letter from the Officer Commanding, Southern District, to the Director of Artillery, refers to the laying of ground platforms for 6.6in howitzers in the Haxo Casemates. These weapons were mobile-siege guns, but numbers were provided as 'moveable armament of works' to be deployed on land faces as required. The Haxo casemate must also have been peculiar to Widley, as there is no trace of this form of emplacement in any other of the Portsdown Hill works.

Later in the same year the Commander Royal Engineers asked the Ordnance Select Committee for permission to fire a 7in Armstrong gun on a shortened platform in order to try the resistance of the racer beds. Permission was given, and presumably the racers were laid satisfactorily, since no adverse report appears in the records. This suggests that armament did not take place until 1883 since it is doubtful if the CRE would wait for longer than it took to set the concrete before checking whether the installation was effective.

After this mad burst of activity, Widley lapsed into the same coma as the rest of the line and had a similar history, passing into naval hands in the 1920s.

Fort Purbrook (679 064)

The last major work in the line, this was a large fort with a small outwork in front known as the 'Crookhorn Redoubt', this being sited so as to cover a small area which could not be seen from the fort proper. Together these two works were to mount 29 guns on their ramparts, 5 mortars and 62 smaller guns, notably protecting the flanks and rear. There is no record of any guns being provided, and it appears to have been used solely as a siege artillery barrack. It eventually passed into naval hands, and today, although still owned by them, is bolted and barred and appears to be empty.

Farlington Redoubt (686 064)

This was a small earthwork located to the east of Fort Purbrook and connected to it by a sunken way. It is doubtful whether it was ever armed, or even intended for permanent mounting of guns, being most probably no more than a prepared position for moveable armament so as to command a section of ground concealed from Fort Purbrook. It was never mentioned in subsequent records after being built in about 1868–70, and is now quite derelict and overgrown.

The Isle of Wight Defences (See Maps 2 and 4)

The position of the Isle of Wight made it both a natural choice for defensive positions and a natural target. By virtue of its command of the entrance to Portsmouth Harbour, across the Spithead anchorage, and its command of the other entrance to the Solent, the Needles Passage, it was an obvious place to install guns. But due to the equally obvious ease with which an enemy could land on the southern part of the island and take those guns in rear, it was also necessary to consider the defence of the island itself.

Prior to 1859 a certain amount of work had been done, particularly to guard the Needles Passage. Across the 'Bridge', as the narrow section opposite Sconce Point was then known, Hurst Castle, built in the time of Henry VIII had been provided with a number of earthen emplacements mounting 64-pounder guns, and the island side was defended by Fort Victoria at Sconce Point and Fort Albert further west. Victoria was, in the words of the Commissioners, 'not of the most approved construction' and indeed was little more than a brick wall with casemated guns and open batteries within. Albert was somewhat more impressive, standing in the sea a few yards from shore and with casemated batteries of 64-pounder guns, but it was also of brick and not representative of the latest thoughts on resistance to attack. Further to the east, Yarmouth had a four gun battery in what was

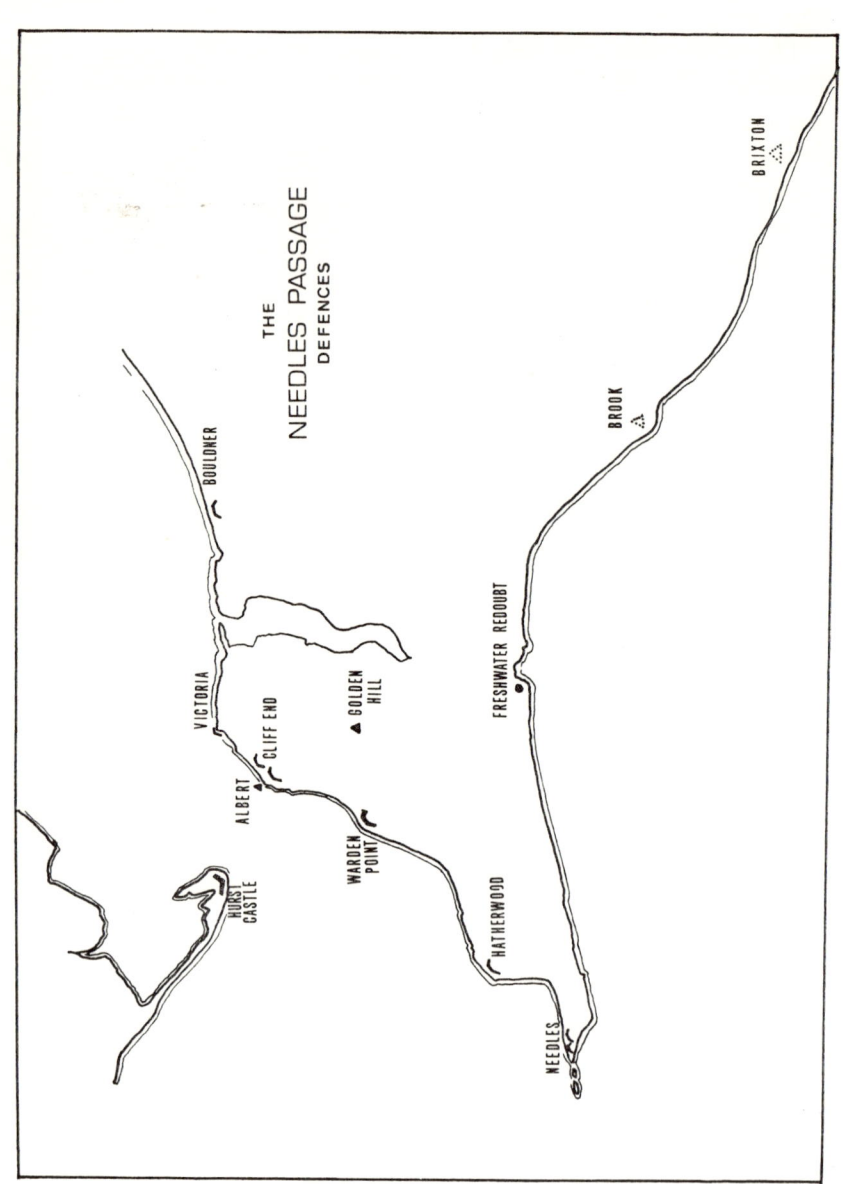

Map 4 The Needles Passage Defences

THE PORTSMOUTH AND ISLE OF WIGHT DEFENCES 149

left of its castle, and to the west of the 'Bridge' was Cliff End Fort, another elderly brick structure.

The eastern end, covering Spithead was in even worse array. There was nothing at all here, for the simple reason that no guns had hitherto been sufficiently powerful to have any effect on events in Portsmouth Roads. To guard against an enemy landing on the island there was merely an old bastioned fort at Sandown, which was by that time almost derelict. Here was virgin ground indeed, and the commissioners lost no time in designing a comprehensive scheme of defence which would cover almost any contingency.

The Needles Passage was the easiest problem, since it was no more than 3,000yd or so from the island shore to the furthest navigable part of the channel, and contemporary ordnance could cover this. The existing guns of Albert and Victoria were clearly insufficient and they were to be reinforced by open batteries on the cliff tops on each side. Another battery was to be built between Totland and Coldwell Bays on Warden Point, more on Hatherwood Point, and yet more at the Needles itself. Hurst Castle's armament was considered useless since the guns were almost at sea level and the gunners were exposed to view from passing ships 'within the ordinary range of grape shot', so it was recommended that a new casemated work should be built here. The four guns at Yarmouth were performing no useful function and were to be removed and Yarmouth no longer considered as a defensive work.

With all the armament thus clustered within two square miles, it was next necessary to defend them against attack from the rear, and to this effect a barrack fort was to be built somewhere between Totland and Freshwater to act as a base and support, with a redoubt on Freshwater Bay to prevent any attempt at landing there. On the south-western coast of the island it was observed that there were a number of 'chines' or ravines running through the cliffs which might afford a foothold, given good weather conditions, so towers were to be built at Brook and Brixton to act as supporting bases for a force of infantry and artillery who could be quickly deployed to frustrate any such attempts, and a battery placed on Atherfield Point to cover both Chayle and Brixton Bays. To link all these and provide the necessary mobility for the flying column, a road was to be built from Chayle to Brixton which would allow artillery to move and take position so as to be able to fire at any point on the coast line. It was also suggested that permanent emplacements for the field guns be made so as to command every likely landing place.

Having thus dealt with the west end of the island, the commissioners now turned to the eastern end. Here much greater areas of water had to be covered, and as we have already seen in discussing the Portsmouth defences, the principal deterrent in this area was to be the chain of sea forts. To support these works, shore batteries were to be built near Nettlestone Point and Appley House (close to St Helen's) each to have three tiers of casemates with mortars on the roof. The idea behind this form of construction was to ensure a heavy enough concentration of guns to deal with a concerted attack, while the guns on the upper tiers would have sufficient height to be able to command the decks of attacking vessels and rake them with grape shot.

Again, with this ordnance planned, it became necessary to protect the batteries from the possibility of a landing in Sandown Bay and an overland attack, and it was proposed to build a new fort at Sandown to replace the old work, though in order to provide some form of defence until the new work was built, the old fort was to be swept and dusted and armed with a few heavy guns. The new work was to be supported by flank batteries, while a fort in a commanding position on Bembridge Down would form a link between Sandown and St Helen's, and form the pivot of a possible defensive line. Two more works to complete the command of the bay were then to be built, one at Yaverland, and, on the other side of Sandown, one near Landguard, behind Shanklin.

The whole of the recommendations for the Island made a formidable list:

Cliff End Battery	20 guns
Warden Point Battery	6

Hatherwood Point Battery	6	
Needles Battery	6	
Hill Farm Battery	12	400 men
Hurst Castle	31	300
Sandown Bay	20	150
Yaverland	10	80
Bembridge Down	3	80
Sandown Barrack Battery	6	
Landguard	6	50
Atherfield Point	10	80
Brixton Tower	3	20
Brook Tower	3	20
Nettlestone Point	10	80
Appley House	10	80
Total	162 guns	1,340 men

The estimated cost of all this array was £325,000, but it is hard to avoid the conclusion that there has been some dissimulation here somewhere. It will be seen that there is no mention of the projected fort between Totland and Freshwater, or of the redoubt in Freshwater Bay, nor is there a costing for the military road between Chayle and Brixton. Furthermore, the imposing three-tiered works at Nettlestone and Appley House seem to have shrunk to ten-gun batteries in this table.

Not that it mattered very much, for the watchdogs of the public purse were sharpening their hatchets. Before submitting the report to Parliament, the work at Landguard was struck out, as were the three works at Brook, Brixton and Atherfield Point, and a work at Redcliffe, near Bembridge, which had been independently proposed by the War Office. Instead of the two works at Nettlestone and Appley House, a larger work at Puckpool, close to Ryde, was substituted. The military road was retained, though without the prepared emplacements, in the hope that the mobile column would be able to cover the coast without the need for the three supporting works.

The plan, as finally approved, went ahead with some speed. The new casemated work at Hurst Castle was given a high priority, and the new battery at Puckpool was also pressed forward with all speed, since this was to be principally armed with mortars and required less masonry work. The Needles Battery was ready by 1863 and the remainder of the work in this area was almost entirely completed by 1867. The basic plan was adhered to quite closely and few difficulties appeared during the construction, but as with every other area there were constant changes due to changes in armament and it is probably safe to say that before 1900 all the works were never correctly armed according to the latest intentions or free of workmen.

Fort Albert (628 890)

This was built in the 1850s to act, with Hurst Castle and Fort Victoria, to cover the Passage. Originally armed with 64-pounder guns it was more or less ignored in the construction programme of 1860, its place being taken by more up-to-date works. It appears to have been re-equipped with 7in RML guns in the early 1870s, probably as an afterthought when work on the rest of the island was more or less complete, but after this it lapsed into a sort of suspended animation for several years. When the School of Gunnery was formed at Golden Hill in 1888 Fort Albert was taken into use as an outstation and instructional battery, and a number of 6-pounder and 12-pounder QF guns were mounted there. At about this time too it was outfitted as a Brennan Torpedo Station. The Brennan torpedo was ideally suited to covering a narrow strait, since its range was governed by the amount of wire which could be carried on the torpedo reels, and nowhere else on the island would it have been of equal value. This installation remained in place until the late 1890s when the Brennan installations were all made obsolete. The light guns remained in place and the fort in use until the 1950s.

Bouldner Battery (387 906)

This is the only work in the Needles area which is an addition to the plans of the 1859 Report. With the adequate range of modern guns it was no longer necessary to concentrate all the armament in the immediate vicinity of Sconce Point—indeed it is doubtful whether a suitable site could have been found among the congestion which occupied all the usable areas, so that when, late in the 1890s it was decided to place some more modern weapons in a position to deal with any attempt to enter the Solent, a two-gun battery was built above Bouldner Cliff, east of Yarmouth. The construction is quite unlike any other work of the time, and consists of two pits widely separated and joined by a covered way, with accommodation and stores concealed by an earth glacis between the gunpits. There are magazines beneath with one ammunition lift supplying each pit. In each pit was a 6in BL gun on central pivot mounting. During World War II the pits were converted into a form of casemate by the addition of reinforced concrete overhead protection, probably to give some degree of protection against air attack.

The battery remained in service until 1956 and was then dismantled. It is now entirely derelict.

Cliff End Battery (330 890)

This was the principal defensive work proposed by the 1859 Report as 'earthen batteries on the heights behind Fort Albert'. The selected site was on the hill-crest, overlooking the old Cliff End Fort and Fort Victoria. Two batteries were built, the right-hand to contain eight 7in RML and the left-hand to contain twelve similar guns. The work was not completed until 1871 and the planned armament was by that time obsolescent, so that during its construction it had been redesigned as a single battery to mount six heavier weapons. In 1874 it was decided to mount 12.5in guns in the works, and these were installed and the battery functioning by 1880. These guns remained until World War I when they were replaced by 6in BL guns, and these remained the armament until after the end of World War II. Shortly after this the work was emptied, as the ground was suspect: the battery has since fallen into the sea due to cliff erosion. Only a few lumps of concrete remain on the beach below the position.

C.D.—K

Cliff End Fort (329 888)

This was an old work erected at the same time as Fort Albert, though not mentioned in the 1859 Report, since improvements had already been planned, money provided from the annual estimates, and work in hand. Originally a redbrick work, it was extensively reinforced with concrete during the 1860s and in 1875 was reported as ready to receive its armament of six 12in 35-ton guns. This, however, was not implemented, the War Office deciding to wait until the new 12.5in guns were available, and these were eventually installed in 1878. The first firing was done in April 1879 under the observation of the Committee on Heavy Gun Working, and in the course of two days' firing the committee observed that the racers had been badly laid, the loading stages could not be kept on their tracks and parts of the carriages were faulty; the net result was that the detachments were taking between five and ten minutes to get off one round. Various measures were taken to correct these faults, and in November the committee paid another visit to watch practice once more. This time the shock of discharge began to crack the emplacement concrete, and within five rounds the masonry was exposed. After sixteen rounds had been fired, practice was stopped since 'the whole of the foundations were much shaken'. As a result the work was emptied and in 1880–1 partly dismantled and rebuilt, this time ensuring that the concrete was properly set before allowing any firing.

By 1884 the 12.5in guns were back in place, but there is no record of any firing being done for some years. Early in the 1900s these guns were removed and replaced by 6in Mk 7 BL guns which remained in place until the 1950s.

Freshwater Redoubt (345 856)

This small outwork stands on the cliffs at the west end of Freshwater Bay, isolated by a deep ditch cut in the cliff top and entered by a narrow bridge. A large rampart with casemated stores surrounds a small terreplein in which living accommodation has subsequently been built.

The original armament was three 7in Armstrong guns on platforms overlooking the bay, intended to cope with the early stages of an attack until reinforcements could arrive from Golden Hill Fort. After the establishment of the District School of Gunnery, it became a practice battery and a fresh battery was built facing the sea, armed with two 12-pounder and three 6-pounder Nordenfeldt QF guns. It retained this role until 1956.

Golden Hill Fort (338 878)

This was planned as a defensible keep and barrack for the batteries defending the Needles area. Work began on excavating the ditch in 1863 and the fort was completed in 1867. The building is a hexagon, surrounded by a 31ft scarp and wet ditch. A drawbridge over the ditch leads into the work through a tunnel in the scarp. The interior was primarily intended for barrack accommodation for 8 officers and 128 men, with a small hospital with beds for 14 patients. The glacis was also prepared with positions for 18 light guns, but none was ever mounted and it was merely used as a barrack for the first few years of its life. Then in 1888 it was taken over as the Western District School of Gunnery, which role it retained until World War II. It then reverted to use as barracks for the duration of the war after which it was abandoned. It is at present used as a factory.

Hatherwood Point Battery (304 857)

This is another of the reinforcing works recommended in 1859. It was planned as a six gun barbette battery on the northeast side of Alum Bay, 254ft above sea level. Work began in 1865 and the emplacements were ready for arming in 1868, but by that time it had been decided to change the armament to four 9in and three 7in RML guns, thus requiring another emplacement to be built. Before work could begin on this, a fresh policy was declared; the armament would now be six 12.5in guns. Work began on rebuilding two emplacements, but before they were completed, and before work could begin on the other four, there was yet another change. 12.5in 38 ton guns were expensive (£3,205, plus £1,070 for the carriage), they were not in unlimited supply, and in the general rush to arm with 12.5in there seemed to be enough in the district already. What was needed here, it was decided, were shell guns which, from the high position, could rake the decks of warships with shrapnel. Accordingly, only two 12.5in were mounted, in the two eastern emplacements, the remainder having 40-pounder Armstrong guns installed, all of which was done by the summer of 1880.

It remained in that condition until the guns were scrapped in the 1920s, after which it was abandoned. At present the four 40-pounder emplacements exist in a derelict state, but one 12.5in emplacement and half the other have fallen into the sea due to cliff erosion. It is probable that this was the reason for the position being abandoned.

Hurst Castle (316 897)

Although not geographically on the Isle of Wight, this work is best considered here since it was entirely for defending the Needles Passage. It was originally built in 1541–4 on the orders of Henry VIII to mount thirty guns for the defence of Southampton against the French. The design was the usual one of circular keep with semi-circular barbette platforms and casemates. It featured in the Civil War and was, for a short time, the prison of Charles I. Then like most other defences, it lapsed into decrepitude. In 1779 Blomefield reported fourteen 18-pounder and eight 6-pounder guns installed but added 'the 6-pounders were formerly mounted on the battlements of the castle over the casemates, but have been removed on account of the decay of the platforms and the timber that supported the roof... There are five barrels of powder only in the magazine and the stores are decayed and incomplete.' A later survey, in 1787, reported the same number of guns but condemned them as being old and worn out.

This was hardly a work to strike terror into an attacker, but fortunately no attacker came. When the Crimean War caused some stirring in the defences, Hurst, so obviously ancient, was among the works selected to be improved, and in 1853 a number of open emplacements protected by earth parapets were built on each side of the Castle. As the 1859 Report pointed out, these would have been untenable against attack since the gunners were in view from the decks of passing ships, which, if enemy, could have sailed within case or grape-shot range and then cleared the platforms in short order. A casemated work was recommended.

As anyone who has ever sailed past Hurst will agree, a casemated work was built with a vengeance. It is the largest of its kind ever built in this country, an enormous single-storied work of granite with no less than 61 casemates, 37 to the west of the castle and 24 to the east. In addition it was proposed to put a barbette battery on the roof, though the gun strength of this was never defined. But, even allowing for 6 such guns each side, this would have given 73 guns, all of 7in calibre, which was overdoing it slightly. Before construction of the casemates was completed the barbettes on the roof were given up, but the alternative suggested was even more exotic—either three 2-gun turrets, or four platforms with 9ft parapets behind which 7in guns on Moncrieff mountings were to be installed. Eventually common sense (and no doubt money shortages) prevailed, and the idea of any sort of roof installation was abandoned. The work was completed as a single tier in 1870, and in 1871 the Elswick Ordnance Company were making the first 9in gun platforms for installation. Two were made and sent down for test, but before more could be done, in 1872 the guns were removed and the whole fort handed over to the Royal Engineers so that a contractor could remove parts of the masonry and install iron shields to each casemate. This took the remainder of the year and it was not until the spring of 1873 that the installation of the 9in guns was re-started. By April 1873 eighteen had been fitted, but a slight difficulty was that the carriages and slides were of Elswick design and did not resemble the service pattern. A question was raised as to whether it might not be possible to make some modification so as to reach a common standard throughout the service, and the reply is illuminating: 'the question is to be deferred until the change of armament now under consideration takes place.' So before all the sixty-one guns were in, plans were afoot for getting them out again.

Inevitably it was decided to install 12.5in guns, so the casemates were cleared once again. By this time thirty-three Elswick platforms had been delivered, and the contract was terminated, the equipment to be modified to approximate to the service pattern 'as opportunity offered' and put to use elsewhere. By 1879 a number of 12.5in were in place and a trial firing took place in May of that year.

It seems, though, that once again supply and finance caused second thoughts about installing sixty-one 12.5in guns there. A return of carriages dated December 1882 notes two 64-pounder guns on 11ft slides for a 3ft 6in parapet mounted here, and in the following year the Director of Artillery was enquiring when the graduated arcs for the new 10in guns would be ready. The final armament was a peculiar jumble; five 9in RML, two 64-pounder smoothbore; twenty-three 10in RML and ten 12.5in RML, an arrangement which still left twenty-one casemates unoccupied.

Having got all this in place, Hurst seems to have been left to wither away. There is no record of any subsequent armament being fitted and no sign of any modern emplacements. On reflection, the reason would appear to be a ballistic one; the Isle of Wight positions were provided with modern ordnance in later years which was quite sufficient to close the channel. Had Hurst been provided with, for example, a modern 9.2in gun, there was every risk that, firing from such a low site, a miss would have crossed the channel to impact on the island shore, and with the conglomeration of defences around Sconce Point might well have done more damage than an enemy ship could have achieved. When the RML guns became obsolete in the late 1890s and the island-side defences were improved, Hurst was abandoned as an armed work and reverted to use as an Admiralty signal station and a cross-observation and rangefinding post for the island batteries. Today the signal station still functions and the case-

THE PORTSMOUTH AND ISLE OF WIGHT DEFENCES 159

mates still stand, and there are plans afoot for refurbishing some of them, providing imitation guns, and opening them to the public.

Needles Battery (291 850)

Commenced in September 1861, this was a barbette battery of six 7in guns on the projecting point of the chalk ridge above the Needles Rocks. It was completed in June 1863 and armed in the following year, but the 1869 Report noted that it was intended to arm it with heavier guns in the near future. However, it seems that the stability of the platforms was in some doubt if heavier guns were fired from there, and nothing heavier was ever installed. Unfortunately it has not been possible to examine this work, since it forms part of a Ministry of Defence establishment and is inaccessible.

New Needles Battery (293 849)

This work, somewhat higher and further inland than the Needles Battery, replaced the latter work in the early 1890s. This relocation was due to a more favourable geological structure which could better withstand the discharge of heavy artillery without giving way and dumping the whole battery at the foot of the cliffs. By the turn of the century it was armed with 9.2in guns on barbette carriages and these remained in place until the 1950s.

In addition to its defensive role it became an instructional battery for Golden Hill, and it was here that the first anti-aircraft gun in British service was tested in 1913. This was a 1-pounder 'Pom-Pom' on a pedestal mounting which had been modified in the artificer's shop at Golden Hill to give the requisite high angle of elevation. The target for this test was a large kite towed by a destroyer.

At present, as with Needles Battery, New Needles is enclosed within a restricted area, and it has not been possible to examine the work.

Sconce Point Battery

This work is mentioned in some of the evidence presented to the 1859 Commission, and appears to have been an open battery dating from about 1800. It was apparently not considered to be worth rehabilitating since there is no official record of it and no traces can be found on the ground or detected on aerial photographs of the district. It is highly probable that cliff erosion has removed all trace of it.

Fort Victoria (337 898)

Although the 1859 Commission were not enthusiastic about this work and it was more or less replaced by new batteries on the heights above, it nevertheless managed to survive and become a functioning part of the defences. Built in the 1850s, it is of brick construction with concrete gunfloors and casemated in an early fashion, the casemates being provided with wide apertures for the guns and no form of shield. It was in active use in the middle 1860s since a number of trials of various suggested methods of rangefinding were carried out there, but it was not until about 1880, when the rest of the defences had been dealt with, that more modern armament, in the shape of a number of 10in RML guns, was installed.

The greatest disadvantage of Victoria was its low site, barely above the high water mark. The interior of the work can be seen into from passing ships, and hence it was relegated to a training role as an outstation of Golden Hill School of Gunnery.

At present the fort is undergoing renovation with the intention of turning it into a museum based on the central theme of the island's defences and showing the fort as it was in its hey-day.

Fort Warden or Warden Point Battery (323 876)

This work is properly known as Warden Point Battery, but some records refer to it, rather confusingly, as Fort Warden; the matter is not made any easier by the existence of a Warden

Battery in the Thames and Medway defence system which was sometimes called Warden Point Battery in official communications.

The work was begun in 1862 and completed in the following year, a battery of eight guns on barbette mountings some 2,500yd east of Hatherwood Point. The armament was intended to be entirely 9in RML but a report of practice of December 1872 indicates a mixture of 7in and 9in guns, four of each. These were soon removed and replaced by 12.5in guns by 1878.

One of these guns was later dismounted and the emplacement rebuilt to take the first 9in RML high angle gun, trials of which were conducted from 1885 to 1888, after which it was removed and the emplacement left empty. In the late 1890s the battery was completely rebuilt to accept modern 9.2in BL guns, and this remained the armament from then until 1956.

Bembridge Fort (626 859)

This was built between 1862 and 1867 on the summit of Bembridge Down to act as a barrack keep for the defences in Sandown Bay and also as a strongpoint to guard against a possible enemy landing in the Bembridge-Foreland-Whitecliff Bay area which could threaten the batteries to both north and south. A brick-built work surrounded by a large earthen rampart and ditch, it was armed with six 7in Armstrong guns, with positions prepared for a further four on the ramparts. In the 1890s the guns were removed and the Fort became purely a barrack and store and it was never re-armed. At present it is owned by a commercial undertaking.

Culver or Redcliffe Battery (638 855)

Redcliffe Battery was intended to assist Sandown and Yaverland Batteries in resisting any attempt at a landing in Sandown Bay. The work was not envisaged by the 1859 Commission, but had been independently proposed by the War Office and was originally turned down. Then, when acquisition of land in the area of Landguard for a proposed work there proved difficult, Redcliffe Battery was reinstated and was built a little to the west of Culver Cliff, 150ft above the sea. Work began in April 1861 and the battery was completed and ready for arming in September 1863. The original armament was four 7in Armstrong guns and these seem to have been left in place for some years, since there is no record of any heavy RML guns ever mounted there, and the remains of the emplacements are of the correct dimensions for these weapons.

By the time of World War I the Armstrongs had been retired, the emplacements filled in, and fresh concrete emplacements for a battery of 12-pounder QF guns had been built. During the 1920s the practice of testing equipment there grew up, until in the late 1930s it became the Coast Artillery Experimental Establishment. Among many other items, the first twin 6-pounder equipment was tested there in 1936.

During this period the original title was dropped and the work came to be known as Culver Cliff Battery. It was closed down in 1956 and today only the remains of the 12-pounder emplacements are to be seen, together with traces of the filled-in Armstrong pits.

Nodes Point Battery (636 898)

The 1859 plan called for a battery with keep in rear to oppose a landing between Bembridge and Nettlestone Point, but this plan was later abandoned in favour of an armoured fort standing about half a mile from shore on the edge of the shoals, which materialised at St Helen's Fort. Notwithstanding the ability of this work to prevent a landing, the idea of a battery on the point was still attractive and in 1862 a sum of money was inserted into the estimates to cover both St Helen's Fort and the land work. However all that was done was to purchase the land; there was no subsequent construction as a result of the appropriation, probably because the construction of St Helen's Fort absorbed all the allotted sum.

But when the Spithead defences needed modernising, the land

was finally put to use. With the era of powerful breech-loading guns capable of covering the Spithead anchorage from either shore it was no longer necessary to rely on the iron forts, and two batteries, one of 6in and one of 9.2in BL guns were installed here. The 6in were emplaced late in the 1890s and the 9.2in in about 1905. Both batteries remained in place and functioned until after World War II.

Puckpool Battery (614 922)

It will be recalled that the original recommendation of 1859 was for two batteries, one at Nettlestone Point and one at Appley House, mounting large numbers of guns and with mortars on their roofs. While this was approved, there was still a certain amount of doubt as to whether the best solution had actually been found. After re-examining the plans, it was decided in 1861 to relinquish the proposed works and build a heavy mortar battery at Puckpool Point, just east of Ryde.

This date and decision are not without interest; in that year Colonel Lefroy published a paper in the *Proceedings of the Royal Artillery Institution* (Vol III p231) on the use of high angle fire in breaching fortifications, and subsequent papers and observations by him, published in *Proceedings* and elsewhere, or submitted confidentially to the Ordnance Select Committee, show that he was greatly attracted by the idea of dropping shells on to the less well protected areas of targets, notably the decks of warships. The decision to build the mortar battery was taken and the sum of £67,000 inserted into the annual estimates for 1862 to cover the difference between the original plan (Nettlestone, Appley House and St Helen's Point) and the final plan (St Helen's Fort, Nodes Point and Puckpool). Work began in 1863 and it was completed in March 1865. Shortly thereafter twenty-one 13in mortars were mounted and platforms prepared on the ramparts for eleven light guns.

In spite of this, the Ordnance Select Committee still had reservations about the idea, and in 1863, while Puckpool was still in the excavation stage, they organised experimental firings

The 13in mortar mounted on a traversing platform, with loading derrick

with a 13in mortar to find out what would happen to a 'Warrior' target. The results were not impressive:

> As an experiment to ascertain whether, in the absence of suitable guns, mortars could be used with advantage against iron plated ships, the Committee consider that the results obtained are not sufficiently encouraging to warrant their being thus employed. The effect they produce is not serious ... and the fire is so extremely inaccurate that no reliance can be placed on their striking the target even at the limited range of 200 yards.

In spite of this the high-angle movement was gaining adherents, and they were not slow to point out that the object was not to assail the side of the ship—which was what the 'Warrior' target represented—but the thinner upper decks. Their hand was considerably strengthened by a report from Captain Cooper Key, now commanding HMS *Excellent*, the Royal Navy Gunnery

School, in which he referred to a highly successful experiment with a 13in mortar at ranges up to 1,800yd, his conclusion being that 'vessels could not remain at anchor under the fire of mortars ... unless their upper decks were rendered proof against shells.'

This by no means finished the arguing, but it was enough, it seems to ensure Puckpool being armed. The plan was changed in 1867, reducing the guns to five and increasing the mortar strength to thirty-eight pieces in a double line. But before this could be implemented, the failures to obtain suitable foundations for the iron forts on Sturbridge or Ryde sands became known, and the Puckpool arrangements were changed once more, and in 1868 it was modified to mount thirty mortars, four 12in 25-ton guns and one 7in Armstrong gun for flank defence.

The final result was a small barrack for four officers and sixty-seven men with a large terreplein for the mortars, in front of which were the emplacements for the five barbette-mounted guns, fronted in turn by an earth parapet and wet ditch. But the question of armament was still unsettled. It is doubtful if the 12in were ever installed, for in August 1871 the Director of Artillery complained that the planned 11in could not be installed here since the trials with the prototype gun were not completed. Eventually, in 1873, four 11in were installed.

After this Puckpool remained dormant for some years, although it appears that one unusual installation was made there during the 1880s. The extreme right-hand emplacement, originally the site of the flanking Armstrong gun, was rebuilt to accommodate an Armstrong-protected barbette mounting. The emplacement today holds a large concrete pivot block and a toothed training arc which do not correspond to any service mounting, but the general arrangement of which is quite certainly that of the Armstrong design.

The carriage was pivoted on the pedestal and traversed by a toothed pinion engaging in the arc. For loading, the weapon was swung through 90° and depressed so that loading could be performed under cover of the parapet. This type of mounting was never installed in Britain and was, indeed, only used for the 100-ton guns in Malta and Gibraltar in British service, although large numbers were supplied to various Australian defences. In 1883-4 the system was tested by the Ordnance Select Committee at Shoeburyness; they objected to the considerable size of the pit —35ft across—and the Inspector-General of Fortifications proposed a revised design to use a smaller pit of about 22ft diameter. The Puckpool installation is this size and would appear to have been a trial installation of the IGF's modified system. There is no record of the type of gun mounted, though the usual model provided by Armstrong's with this system was a 10in of 20 tons.

The remainder of the work was extensively rebuilt in 1898-1900 to take one 10in BL, two 9.2in BL and two 6in BL guns, and the emplacements are still in good condition, having remained in use until the 1950s.

Sandown Barrack Battery (590 830)

This was recommended in 1859 to be 'erected on a point below Sandown Barracks so as to flank the beach'. The work was begun in April 1861 and completed in September 1863 and shortly thereafter received its armament of four 7in Armstrong guns. It remained in commission until early in the present century but was never re-armed with modern ordnance and was abandoned shortly after World War I. The site is now a public green, and little is recognisable.

Sandown Fort (597 839)

This was intended to replace the existing ancient work in Sandown Bay and was begun as a casemated granite work for eighteen guns, with platforms for another ten guns on the terreplein. Work began in April 1861 but was delayed by the decision to incorporate iron shields and was not completed until 1866. The interior of the work was adapted to contain accommodation for four officers and sixty-seven men, while the original plan was modified to give sixteen casemates.

The original armament was a number of 7in 7-ton guns, but these were soon removed and replaced with 9in 12-ton, and by

1880 eight 10in 18-ton RML formed the heavy component, four in each face of the work, the remaining casemates carrying 9in RML guns. Early in the present century these were replaced by lighter weapons; a number of 3-pounder and 6-pounder QF guns were installed above the casemates. Today Sandown Fort is a zoo.

Yaverland Fort (612 849)

This was the last of the Sandown Bay works and was built on a spur of the downs about a mile east of Sandown Barrack Battery. It was a concrete work with the guns in barbette positions, with a small barrack accommodation. Commenced, like most of the island works, in April 1861, it was completed in September 1863 and then provided with eight 7in Armstrong RBL guns.

In the 1890s it was decided that Yaverland was capable of covering the whole of Sandown Bay if provided with modern ordnance, thus economising by leaving the other defences unchanged. The Armstrong guns, long obsolete in fact if not on paper, were removed and a battery of four 6in BL guns installed in four of the original emplacements after they had been suitably modified.

After the dissolution of coast artillery the fort remained in military hands for many years, being used by a variety of units, but it was eventually given up late in the 1960s and a holiday camp now occupies the site.

7
THE PLYMOUTH DEFENCES

Plymouth, by virtue of its excellent harbour and vital naval installations, had always been alert to possible attack. The first major work to be placed there was in the reign of Henry VIII when the Hoe was palisaded, with towers at each end. After the defeat of the Armada, Sir Francis Drake petitioned Queen Elizabeth for permission to build a fort, and work was begun on the site now occupied by the Royal Citadel. It apparently proceeded slowly and was never completely finished before being demolished in 1666 to make way for the Citadel. This was completed by 1671 as a bastioned star fort. It was always armed throughout its history of association with coast artillery, which ended with it being the home of the Coast Artillery School, and it is still occupied by a Royal Artillery unit.

In the time of Charles II a second tower was built across the water on what is now Mount Batten, a two-storied redoubt for ten guns. In subsequent years batteries were placed on the heights on each side of the Sound and on St Nicholas' Island (later known as Drake's Island) so as to cover the Sound and the entrance to the Hamoaze, the channel leading to the dockyard area of Devonport. As this latter installation increased in size it became necessary to provide some landward defence, and the Devonport Lines, the usual rampart and ditch, were begun in 1758 and improved upon from time to time.

When Thomas Blomefield inspected the area in August 1783 he found an impressive number of guns, but also found that their condition left a lot to be desired. The Citadel had 95 pieces ranging from 32-pounder to 4-pounder, another 159 pieces were

Page 169 (above) *The entrance to Crown Hill Fort Plymouth;* (below) *a high angle emplacement at Tregantle Down Battery, Plymouth, showing the remains of the racer ring. Loading was carried out from the parapet*

Page 170 *A 6in gun of Renney Battery, Plymouth, firing at practice in 1953*

arrayed in the various batteries flanking the Sound, and St Nicholas' Island had 29 guns and two brass mortars. But, added Blomefield, 'All the 32-pounder and many guns of other natures ... are exceedingly old and will, on examination, probably be found unserviceable.'

The Crimean War stimulus caused some further works to be started in 1857–8. The principal activity was the construction of a defensive line running across the peninsula between the St Germain River and the sea, from the village of Antony, so as to seal off the whole area and prevent an enemy gaining ground from which he could bombard Devonport or take the various defences on Maker Heights in the rear. It was a singularly inept plan, since it left the enormous expanse of Whitesand Bay within the defended zone and made no provision for covering it.

When the 1859 Commission came to study Plymouth, they divided the problem into two sections, the measures necessary to prevent a naval attack and the landward defences. Due to the geographical layout the sea defences could be separated into three distinct measures:

1. The defence of the entrance to the Hamoaze
2. The security of the Sound itself
3. The prevention of a fleet bombarding the dockyard.

The existing defences had changed little since Blomefield's day except that the number of guns had diminished. Drake's Island had twenty-two guns mounted, and together with the Citadel, Eastern and Western Kings Batteries and Mount Wise Battery the entrance to the Hamoaze was reasonably well covered. The batteries on Maker Heights were in no condition to materially protect the Sound, and that area depended upon a work on Picklecombe Point and two more across the Sound at Staddon Point. As a further measure of protection for the Sound, and to prevent a fleet from anchoring out of reach of these works, a new battery had been begun at Cawsand in 1858 but was not yet completed.

This left a number of holes, which the commissioners now

went about plugging. Firstly, to render the entrance to the Hamoaze as nearly impassable as they could, the Eastern and Western Kings and Drake's Island Batteries were to be strengthened, and a new battery built on Devil's Point, facing up the Hamoaze so as to take in rear any ship which managed to get that far. Across the narrow strait another battery would be built at the foot of Mount Edgcumb, on a site already occupied by a private saluting battery belonging to the Earl of Mount Edgcumb. The Picklecombe Point Battery was insufficient and was to be replaced by a new casemated work at the water's edge, which would be partnered by a similar work at the tip of Staddon Point. An open battery was to be built at Hooe Lake Point with a defended barrack above it, and finally an iron fort of immense strength was to be built close behind the breakwater at the entrance to the Sound.

This fairly took care of the Sound and the Hamoaze; with regard to the bombardment risk this became inseparable from various aspects of the land defence system, and the commissioners now went on to consider the whole problem. There were basically four areas from which the Dockyard could be put at risk:

1. The peninsula between the St Germains River and the sea, which the Commissioners called the 'Western Defences'.
2. The Peninsula between the Tamar and St Germains Rivers, the 'Saltash Position.'
3. The area inland of Plymouth between the Tamar and the Cattewater—the 'North-Eastern Position.'
4. The area between the Cattewater and the Sound—the 'Staddon Position'.

Command of these areas would automatically carry command of the adjacent water areas and thus ensure protection from bombardment by both land and naval forces.

In the western area the 'Antony Line' was under construction and this, it was felt, was well planned but needed further reinforcement. The various works on Maker Heights should be strengthened and a defensible barrack built there to act as a reserve depot for the various works and also as a keep and rallying point for troops who could be ferried across the Hamoaze in time of attack to rapidly reinforce the district. The only other addition necessary was a battery to cover Whitesand Bay and this was to be backed up by a work on Knatterbury Hill which would operate as a barrack for this work and for the new battery building at Cawsand.

The 'Saltash Position' was to be sealed off by three works joined by rampart and ditch with open batteries on the flanks. The ditch was to be tied in to the existing terrain, notably a ravine on the northern end and a cliff at the southern, so as to form an impassable barrier; but as an additional insurance two advance works were also planned about a mile forward of the line, at Elmgate and Burrell's Place.

The 'North-Eastern Position' already had the Devonport Lines, and there were also two batteries—'of field profile' as the report described them, or in other words simple earthworks—in advance of this line. Like most of this class of work they had, by 1859, been overtaken by building activity and they were quite impotent due to the houses surrounding them. Therefore the commissioners planned to move the defensive line further out and establish a line of works from the Tamar just north of the Royal Albert Bridge, via King's Tamerton, Barrington House, Quarry Pound, Mount View, Wellington Villas and the Borough Gaol, to come to an end at the Cat Down. There would also be a number of advanced works to secure certain heights from which the dockyard could be bombarded, and three works between the Devonport Line and the new northeastern Line, at East Down, Ash Park and Mount Pleasant, the latter to occupy the site of the existing field work.

Finally the Staddon area was reviewed. Two forts were to be built here to cover the area between the Cattewater and the existing battery on Staddon Heights. These would not only be able to act as land defences, but would also be able to command the waters of the Cattewater and Jennycliffe Bay, supporting the fire of the Citadel and Drake's Island batteries in these areas.

The plan so evolved was undoubtedly the most powerful, most complex and most expensive of all the various recommendations made by the commissioners. The final 'Table of Recommended Works' read as follows:

Sea Defences:

Picklecombe Point	40 guns	200 men	
Staddon Point	32	180	
Breakwater Fort	100	600	
Hooe Lake Point	10		
Drake's Island	30	180	
Eastern Kings	10		
Western Kings	15	50	
Mount-Edgcumb	10		
Whitesand Bay	10		
Knatterbury Hill	5	100	
Total	262 guns	1,310 men	£375,000

Saltash Position

Main work	30 guns	300 men	
St Stephens	20	200	
Left work	15		
South Pill	5	50	
Burrell's Place	30	300	
Elmgate	30	300	
Total	130 guns	1,150 men	£500,000

North-Eastern Defences

St Budeaux	40 guns	500 men	
Burrington House	20	200	
Quarry Pound	30	300	
Tor House	15	150	
Mount View	40	500	
Wellington Villas	15	150	
Borough Gaol	30	300	
Cat Down	15	150	
3 advanced works	25	300	
Total	230 guns	2,550 men	£1,200,000

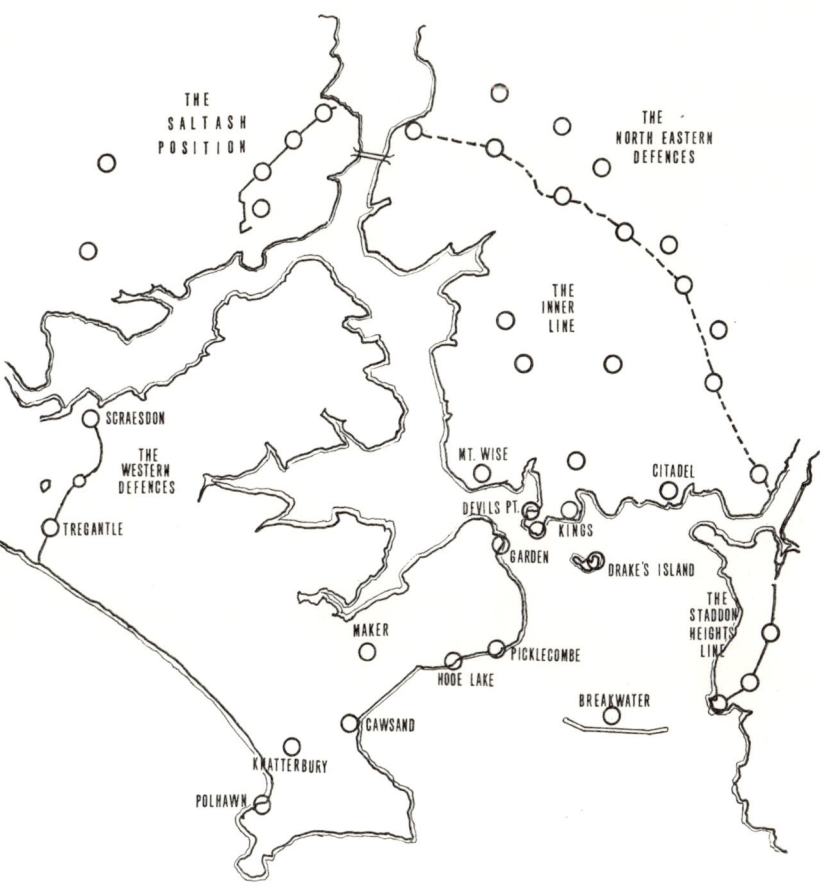

Map 5 Plymouth—the original defensive plan

Inner Line				
East Down		30 guns	500 men	
Mount Pleasant		10	100	
Ash Bank		30	500	
	Total	70 guns	1,100 men	£350,000
Staddon Heights				
Main work		30 guns	400 men	
Second work		20	200	
	Total	50 guns	600 men	£?00,000
Maker Heights				
Barracks and Improvements			300 men	£25,000
Antony Line (Western Defences)				
Improvements to work in progress				£20,000
Total for Defences		742 guns	7,010 men	£2,670,000

Taking into account sums which had already been approved for work which was in progress, the total to be spent on Plymouth was no less than £3,030,000, and it was estimated that in the event of an attack a garrison of 15,000 men would be needed.

There are one or two inconsistencies in the above table which defy rational explanation, since we have no record of how the commissioners did their costing. But it seems odd that the sea defences, 262 guns in works which include one iron fort and three casemated granite works in a total of ten positions, should only be estimated at £25,000 more than the inner line which was to comprise but three much simpler works mounting seventy guns between them. But, needless to say, this staggering proposition was severely pruned before it ever reached Parliament, though it was pruned in an unusually short-sighted way by removing the entire Saltash defences, all the inner line, part of the northeastern line and all the additions to the western line. This left one sector completely undefended and thus undermined the security of all the rest of the plan, but this revised scheme was accepted and passed.

As usual, when it came to actually surveying the area and

THE PLYMOUTH DEFENCES

locating the works on the ground there were a number of changes. One of the first difficulties came with the acquisition of the necessary land. The amount allotted for the purchase of land was £755,000, which fell short of the amount needed to provide all the contemplated works by some £150,000. But at the same time the military planners decided that with the range of artillery increasing almost daily, the contemplated northeastern line ought to be moved further out. The revised locations allowed the number to be reduced, and this, with the lower cost of land in the proposed areas, allowed a balance to be struck. Work began on most of the plan in 1861 but it moved slowly relative to the progress in other parts of the country. By the time the masonry was taking shape, the 'iron shield' controversy delayed further progress, and then the shields had to be incorporated in the designs. Plans were changed to try and effect economies, but even so, with the works finally built, the cupboard was so bare that there was no money left to provide the planned armament, and in 1866 a Special Committee observed that for all the work that had been done and money spent, a fleet could still bombard the dockyard from Whitesand Bay since there were no guns in the area capable of deterring them. A further sum of £422,320 was urged for the provision of armament, but it was refused, and the armament had to be paid for out of the army annual estimates, a slow business. In 1885 the Inspector-General of Artillery reported that the land defences were still unarmed, and, except for one or two weapons installed for trial purposes to test the mountings and other arrangements, unarmed they remained.

The final plan, ratified by the 1869 Commission, established new works on Staddon Point (Fort Bovisand) and Picklecombe Point; placed an iron fort behind the breakwater, and made some slight improvements in the Maker Heights area. Two very large forts, Staddon and Stamford, were built on the Staddon Heights, together with two small advanced works. The Whitesand Bay area got a casemated fort at Polhawn, but although land was purchased for the work on Knatterbury Hill the shortage of money caused the plan to be dropped and nothing was ever built there. Hooe Lake Point battery and its defended barrack fell by the wayside, victims of the shortage of funds, and the proposed Western Line got no further than the two forts at its ends, Scraesdon and Tregantle; although the intermediate work there had escaped the axe when the rampart and ditch were cancelled, finance again ruled it out. The northeastern line finally totalled eleven works with a sunken road connecting the works on the right flank.

In order to correct the deficiency of weapons covering Whitesand Bay this area was later selected as one of the first to have high angle guns installed, a battery of 9in RML being installed in about 1890, followed by batteries of 9.2in BL on high angle mountings in the early 1900s. With the general re-armament which followed the arrival of breech-loading new batteries were installed flanking the Sound, while some of the older works were provided with newer armament. Generally speaking, it can be said that the sea defences, particularly in the Sound, were given priority and were generally adequately armed at all times during their history, but the land defences were never properly equipped, and with the left flank open due to the abandonment of the 'Saltash Position', were a complete waste of effort and money.

Sea Defences

For ease of identification the sea defences are described in order of location, commencing in Whitesand Bay and moving clockwise round the Sound.

Tregantle Down Battery (389 531)

This was constructed between 1888–90 to mount four 9in RML guns on high angle mountings, and is the only work of this type known to still exist. The position is sunk behind a rise of ground to the north side of the military road to connect Tregantle Fort and Polhawn Battery. It consists of four pits, with a central magazine built into the earth mound; no accommodation was provided, the gunners being accommodated in the nearby

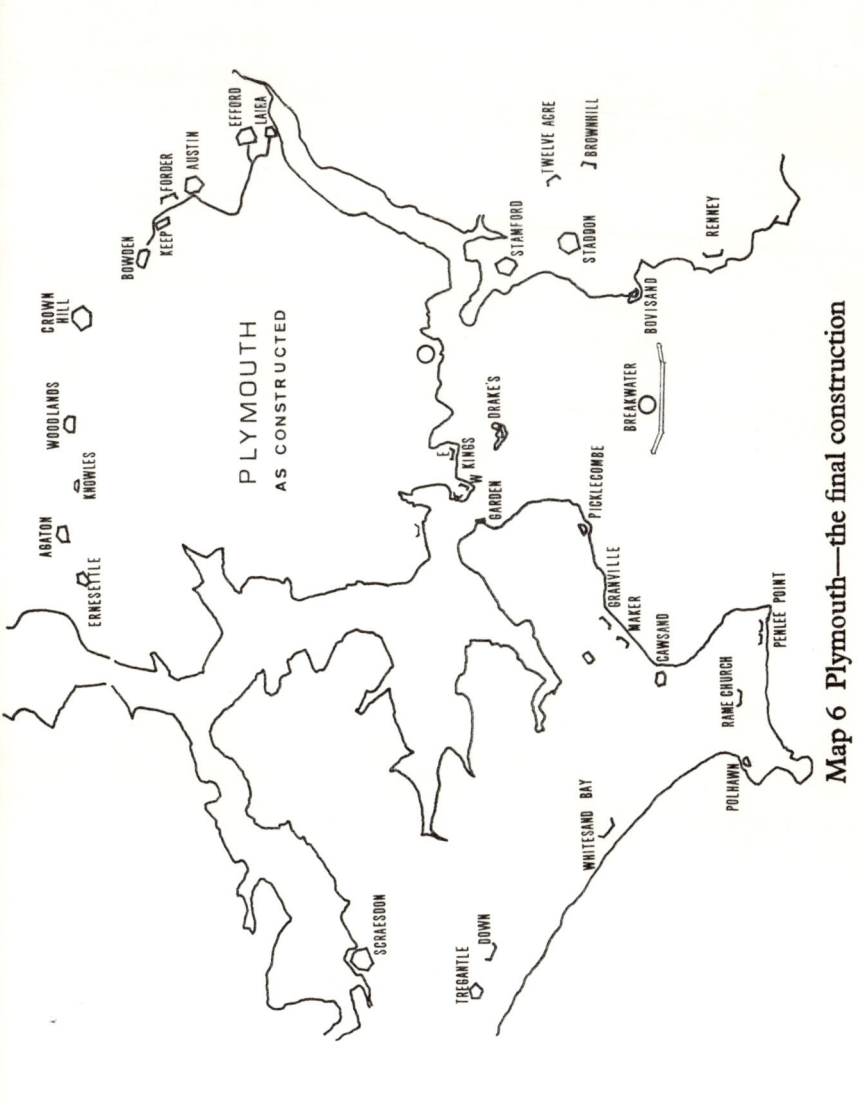

Map 6 Plymouth—the final construction

Tregantle Fort. The davits for hoisting the ammunition up the parapet curb are still in place, as are the toothed traversing rings. The battery is entirely abandoned and is in virtually the same condition now, except for the action of time, weather, and abundant undergrowth, as it was when the guns were declared obsolete and removed in 1922.

Whitesand Bay Battery (408 514)

This was also a later addition to the defences. The records are obscure, but it appears to have been built about 1890, contemporary with Tregantle Down, and was then known as Raleigh Battery, being armed with two 10in BL guns on barbette mountings, according to the Annual Report of the Ordnance Board of 1901. These weapons went out of service immediately after World War I in a rather peculiar sequence; the ammunition was declared obsolete in 1919, the mountings in 1922 and the guns in 1926. But the guns were withdrawn before the war, since an ordnance return for 1914 shows no 10in guns mounted in the Plymouth area at all. An Ordnance Board Minute of 1915 now refers to the work as 'Whitesand Bay Practice Battery', with an armament of 3-pounder QF guns, and it retained this role for the remainder of its existence, finally being given up in the 1950s.

Polhawn Battery (420 492)

This was the 1859 work to defend Whitesand Bay, and was built as a granite casemated work with seven 68-pounders in embrasures without shields. It was connected to Tregantle Fort by a military road (now public). Its principal defect was that its left end was open to attack by ships which would be outside the arc of fire of its guns, and for that reason the armament was never improved, its function being taken over by Tregantle Down and Raleigh Batteries. It was abandoned after World War I, and a local shopkeeper informed me that it had been bought in the early 1930s by a film company. It was later re-sold and is now a private residence, one of the few works in Britain so used.

Rame Church Battery (429 492)

The casual observer would be unlikely to associate this work with coast defence. It is some 400yd from the sea and sunk into a reverse slope so that there is about a hundred feet of crest in front of it. A large concrete wall surrounds the work, which is a rectangular area on two levels, gates in the wall giving access to both levels. The upper level now carries the remains of a number of World War II pre-fabricated huts in a dilapidated state, while the lower level consists of two 9.2in BL high angle gun pits separated by a mounded magazine. An engine house lies to the right rear of the area, and behind the gun pits are the remains of stores, accommodation and all the 'usual offices'. The whole work is abandoned and profusely overgrown.

Rame Church Battery was built in the late 1890s to accommodate the newly-introduced 9.2in high angle gun in order to supplement the 9in RMLs of Tregantle Down. It remained in service until shortly after the weapons were declared obsolete in 1929. The buildings on the upper level indicate its use as a camp during World War II, probably accommodation for an anti-aircraft battery lying between there and Penlee Point Battery, but the gun-floor is exactly as it was left when the guns were dismounted.

Penlee Point Battery (438 491)

This powerful work was built in about 1894–5 to mount three 6in and three 9.2in guns in two batteries. The 6in pits form the right hand battery and the 9.2in the left, a fence dividing the two. The usual accommodation, cookhouse, offices and so forth are in sunken ways at the rear. Beneath each battery is a magazine complex, the 6in being a single level with shell lifts to each pit, the 9.2in being an enormous two-level affair in two sections, one serving the two left-hand pits and the other the right-hand pit.

All the guns were in service during World War I, but the 6in were removed in the early 1930s and only the 9.2in battery was in use until 1956 when it was disarmed and abandoned.

Cawsand Battery (433 503)

This work was begun in 1858 and completed in 1863 and it is apparent from the structure that the plan and specification pre-dated the standard patterns produced as a result of the 1859 Commission. Instead of the usual granite or Portland stone, it is of a local stone and much less massively built than the general run of later works. The site was originally occupied in 1779 by three redoubts armed with 12-pounder smooth-bores, but these were entirely swept away in the building of the existing work.

It originally mounted nine 68-pounder guns behind earth parapets on the sea face and fourteen 7in and 8in Armstrong guns on the land face. It is rarely referred to in any records and was never re-armed with more modern weapons. At the present time it is a private residence.

Maker Heights

This area has, over the years, been a confusing muddle of redoubts and batteries, barracks and keeps, erected without much regard to what already existed and with works being abandoned, re-occupied and re-abandoned until it is almost impossible to categorise them. Records are of little help, referring indiscriminately to any one of a number of works by the same name at different periods. Unfortunately this area is now privately owned, and it has not been possible to walk over it as I have been able to do with most other areas, nor to obtain aerial photographs, so that certain problems are still unsolved.

The first positive identification is of a 'Maker Heights Battery' in 1805, mounting four 32-pounder guns, six 24-pounder and thirty-two 18-pounder, and this is probably the work referred to by Blomefield who inspected the district in 1783 but merely included the armament among the '153 pieces of ordnance mounted in the Lines of Plymouth Dock and the Batteries on the Heights of Maker and Staten [sic]'.

The 1859 Commission observed that there was a danger of an enemy landing and occupying the Maker Heights to bombard the dockyard, 'which would be so serious an event that we consider it advisable to repair and strengthen the existing old redoubts on Maker Heights as an additional precaution against the consequences of such a contingency.' They also recommended the building of a defensible barrack to act as a keep to the various works in the area. The barrack was duly built, though not armed, and one redoubt, identified only as 'Number Four' was brought into a defensible state and later provided with two 12.5in RML, which were certainly in place by January 1873. In about 1892 a new battery was built, well in front of the Heights, on the top of the cliffs overlooking the Sound, to take three 6in BL guns. This abandoned work still stands, with three platforms for barbette mountings and two magazines between them. The shell lifts for the magazines are of a very early hand-worked type, delivering the shell nose-first through a hatch in the floor of the emplacement, a pattern only seen in one other work, Coalhouse Fort, and one which enables the construction to be dated with some accuracy, since 6in installations from about 1895 onward used 'table lifts' which carried the shell horizontally.

Granville Battery (439 511)

This work is a few hundred yards north-east of the Maker Heights 6in battery just mentioned, and is a very much older work which was probably part of the Maker complex and appears to date from about 1852. The work is surrounded by a shallow dry ditch and is entered across a drawbridge. The masonry is of a local stone, exhibiting much rougher workmanship and finish than is generally found in defensive works. An unusual feature is the roof, pitched and tiled like a dwelling-house; indeed the whole work exhibits practically no defensive capability on the land side other than a few rifle slits and the ditch.

On entering the work, which is extremely derelict and much overgrown, on the left are the remains of a relatively modern concrete emplacement with a central magazine supplying ammunition by a simple davit hoist working down a rectangular shaft to the issue room below. The right of the work is so overgrown that it is impossible to say what the original platforms were, but it is probable that the armament was the usual 64-pounder SB or converted RML. There is no record of any heavy RML guns ever being mounted here, and indeed no reports of the 1860–90 period refer to the work at all. The concrete installation mounted three 12-pounder QF guns and from its general appearance would date from about 1893. These guns were in place throughout the time of World Wars I and II, when the work was known to its occupants as 'Rame Fort'. The guns were withdrawn shortly after the war and the work was abandoned.

Picklecombe Fort (455 515)

Picklecombe or Redding Point was the site of an earthen battery built some time early in the nineteenth century, but the 1859 Commissioners recommended the construction of a new work there which, with the aid of Bovisand and Breakwater Forts would completely blanket the Sound with fire. Due to limitations of the terrain it was necessary to put the work below the cliff at the water's edge, and hence it had to be a bombproof and casemated work of immense strength. The original plan was for a two-tier work carrying a mixture of 110-pounder, 68-pounder and 42-pounder guns, with an additional sixteen guns on the roof, all to be protected by iron shields, but this plan was modified in 1864 to provide for two tiers, each of twenty-one 9in or 10in guns, with no roof positions.

Work went exceptionally quickly, due no doubt to its important location, and by December 1871 the guns were being installed, 10in 18-ton on the lower tier and 9in 12-ton on the upper. By 1880 a slight change had been made, the flank guns on each tier now being 7in, and in November of that year the Watkin Position Finder was installed, one of the first such installations to be constructed. Two observing cells were built about 400yd on each side of the fort and connected to two look-out stations on the roof by electric telegraph.

With the arrival of modern weapons the RML guns were withdrawn and a number of 6in BL on central pivots were placed on the roof, protected by a concrete parapet. These were withdrawn some time during the 1920s, and after that time the fort remained unarmed, though retained for military use until 1956.

Garden Battery (456 532)

This was the work 'to occupy the position of the private saluting battery at Mount Edgcumb' and takes its name from its location on the water's edge below the ornamental French and Italian Gardens in the grounds of Mount Edgcumb House. It is a simple granite casemated work for seven guns behind iron shields. Begun in 1862 it was completed in the following year and was armed immediately with 68-pounder guns on wooden casemate carriages which, due to the dimensions of the casemates, had to be considerably cut and modified before they would fit inside and work. With the later general improvement in armament, two of these were removed and replaced with two 9in 12-ton RML on Elswick platforms in the middle 1870s.

No modern armament was ever installed. The RMLS remained until the early years of the century, after which it was disarmed and given up as a defensive work. At present it stands empty and is included in the List of the Ancient Monuments Commission as 'Mount Edgcumb Blockhouse'.

Mount Wise

A battery had been built here, within the Dockyard Lines, in very early days, and a record of 1779 indicates that it was provided with eight 32-pounder guns. In that year a new battery to the flank, known as Lower Mount Wise, was begun and completed in 1780, armed with six 24-pounder. These batteries were still in existence and armed in 1859 and the commissioners considered that this position would be of value for attacking any vessel passing through the Hamoaze. However no suggestions were made for improving the armament, probably because by that time the dockyard establishment had filled all the adjacent area and there would have been no room for a modern work to be built. With the improvements in other works completed, Mount Wise was disarmed and the batteries dismantled.

Devils Point Battery

This was recommended by the 1859 Report to take in rear any ship passing through the Hamoaze. It was never mentioned again and there is some doubt as to whether it was ever built. A map of Plymouth drawn about 1920 shows a 'battery' here, but beyond that nothing is known.

Eastern and Western Kings Batteries (466 535 and 461 532)

The batteries on these two points flanking Firestone Bay were built in 1779, Eastern Kings to take four 18-pounder and Western Kings to take ten 18-pounder, its heavier armament being due to its position closer to the entrance to the Hamoaze. This armament remained in place, a return of 1805 giving the same figures, until the time of the Royal Commission. In view of the useful positions, they recommended that these works should be extended, and within two years both batteries had been increased, Eastern by seven guns and Western by nine. Both extensions took the form of open earthworks, and the new approved armament was the 68-pounder gun.

When the other works flanking the sound were given newer guns, the somewhat vulnerable low site of these batteries led to the decision to abandon them, and they were consequently disarmed and abandoned some time in the 1880s. Today, I am told, some traces remain, but the site has been considerably encroached upon by dockyard installations over the years.

Drake's Island (468 528)

The position of St Nicholas or Drake's Island at the head of the Sound and outside the entrance to the Hamoaze, must have suggested its armament at an early date. Drake himself was Governor of the Island in 1584, and doubtless its defences date

Page 187 *Hubberstone Fort, Milford Haven. The defended barrack is at the top, with the shielded casemate near the sea*

Page 188 (above) *A 6in* BL *gun on the Elswick Ordnance Company pattern of disappearing mounting. An overhead shield gives additional protection;* (below) *one of the 6in disappearing mounting positions at Slouth Fort, Thames defences, as it is today*

from that time. Blomefield, in 1783, suggested reducing the armament to five 32-pounder guns but nobody seems to have taken much notice of him here, since its strength in 1805 was twenty-two 32-pounder and six 18-pounder, a reduction of but one 32-pounder and two brass mortars. The work at that time, so far as can be gathered, was an open battery with masonry embrasures. The 1859 Report noted that 'the situation of Drake's Island is particularly favourable for taking an important share of the defences of the harbour as well as the security of the Sound. We do not consider the existing battery of 22 guns is sufficient and cannot too strongly represent the necessity of strengthening the works on this island and arming them on every side as completely as the space and formation of the ground will allow'. If the commissioners had their way, Drake's Island was about to subside under the weight of ordnance, but the usual financial considerations intervened and the end result was a granite casemated work for twenty-one guns. As with most of the key positions in the Sound, this was put in hand immediately and by 1864 was in commission, armed with 68-pounder guns. These were soon withdrawn, the fort cleared and the contractors put in to install iron shields, after which 9in RML were provided. It seems that the full complement were never emplaced; an 1880 report gives nine and an 1884 report thirteen as the armament, and there is no record of more being supplied. In all probability the remaining casemates were occupied by the original 68-pounder guns. The installation of the RML guns was not without problems. In 1871 the Inspector of Artillery reported that the fitting of the luff tackle eyebolts, through which the traversing ropes ran, was faulty and the guns could not cover their full arc.

There is no record of later armament on Drake's Island, but it remained Crown property and inaccessible to the public. It has now passed into the hands of the National Trust.

Plymouth Citadel (481 531)

This has always been prominent in the history of Plymouth, but although always associated with the defences has actually been of minor importance. Before the advent of the Royal Commission it was, of course, the principal work, and its armament reflects this: in 1805 it was equipped with eleven 42-pounder, eight 32-pounder, twenty 24-pounder, seventeen 18-pounder, thirteen 9-pounder, three 6-pounder and three 18-pounder carronades. But when the newer works were built the Citadel's only role was to close the Cattewater entrance, and for this it was provided with 40-, 70- and 110-pounder Armstrong guns.

In spite of its lack of prominence it remained the Headquarters of the Coast Artillery of the district and after World War II became the home of the Coast Artillery School, and numerous weapons found their way there for instructional and trial purposes. Although still occupied by the Royal Regiment, parts of the Citadel, notably the ramparts, are open to the public and there is a fine array of muzzle-loading guns on garrison standing carriages still overlooking the Sound in much the same way as they must have done in Blomefield's day; though they seem to be in better condition than they were when he called.

Watch House (or Watch Tower) Battery (489 509)

This was built about 1895, shortly after Maker Heights battery and is of the same type, a concrete open work mounting a battery of 6in BL guns. On top of Staddon Point, 354ft above the sea, it is difficult to trace among the many other remains of military works which strew this area. The guns were in use during World War I but, like Maker Heights, were withdrawn in the 1930s and the work is now quite derelict.

Staddon Point Battery (488 507)

Staddon Point is another natural site for a defensive work, and today it resembles a masonry wedding cake, with work succeeding work up the side of the hill. The first work installed here was an open battery of ten 12-pounders, built in about 1770, just below the crest of the heights and known as Staddon Heights Battery. This was then superseded by a masonry work somewhat lower down, built in about 1850 and consisting of early pattern casemates in a hemispherical front, with a terreplein before it and a rampart wall. It is referred to variously as Staddon Height or Staddon Point Battery in the 1860s, and is notable for being one of the works provided with Anderson's Cupola for preparing the molten metal for Martin's Liquid Iron Shells, trials being reported in the Minutes of the Ordnance Select Committee for 1862.

The 1859 Report observed that, in common with the existing work on Picklecombe Point, it was well chosen 'but the works themselves are of insufficient extent, and from their construction are entirely unfit to resist the concentrated horizontal fire of shells that could be brought to bear on them from large ships of war'. Since the ground precluded any extension, the only alternatives were to either dismantle it and rebuild, or build a new work elsewhere, and the latter course was chosen, Bovisand Fort being the result. Staddon Point was not abandoned though, but was linked by a covered way with Fort Bovisand and acted as a barrack for that work. It was also surrounded by a deep dry ditch which enclosed both it and Bovisand, and flanking caponiers were installed. It was later armed with a battery of four 12-pounder QF guns in the terreplein as an anti-torpedo-boat measure, and these remained in place until after World War II.

Fort Bovisand (487 507)

Of all the casemated works of the 1859 Commission, this is probably the best preserved. This is due to a combination of fortuitous circumstances; firstly it was continuously occupied by coast artillery units from its construction until 1956; after that it was locked up and its construction and remoteness deterred most of the usual wreckers; finally it was leased from the Crown by the Fort Bovisand Underwater Centre, whose Director, Lt Cmdr Alan Bax, is interested and concerned enough to ensure that the work is maintained substantially in its original form. The structure is entirely sound and complete, the casemates retain their armour, mantlet bars and other fittings, and above each shield can be seen painted the nomenclature of the gun originally installed there. In a recent letter Lt Cmdr Bax has assured me that any visitor who wishes to inspect the work will be welcomed, and for anyone who wants to see a casemated fort as originally built, this is about the only opportunity to do so.

As mentioned above, this work was intended to replace Staddon Point Battery, and was designed in 1860 as a granite casemated work of two tiers to house fifty 68-pounder and 110-pounder guns behind iron shields, with a detached magazine structure in the rear. Work began in 1861 but due to the financial difficulties arising in this district, and due to second thoughts about the magazine arrangements, the plan was changed in 1864 so that a lesser number of heavier guns would be mounted, with magazines in a basement beneath. The final plan was for twenty-four guns in a single tier, and it was completed to this in 1870. Shortly thereafter provision was made for a single 7in, 7 ton, Pattern 1 Moncrieff disappearing mounting to be installed, a pit being prepared in late 1871, the gun erected in the following year, and two test shots eventually being fired in September 1873. However there is no trace today of the pit, and it must have been filled in many years ago.

The principal armament was twenty-three 9in RML and one 10in, and these were installed by September 1872 when the Committee on Traversing Gear attended to watch a trial of a new type of gear fitted to one of the 9in gun platforms. But this armament lacked the power considered to be necessary for this work, and by 1880 the proportion had been changed to nine 9in and fourteen 10in. In the same year work began on installing the Watkin Position Finder in a similar fashion to the installation at Picklecombe, an observing cell about 400yd on each flank, connected to look-out posts on top of the casemates by an electric telegraph system.

With the demise of the RML guns Bovisand appears to have become redundant as a defensive work, there being no record of subsequent re-armament. However, it remained in artillery hands, and the addition of a variety of concrete structures above the casemates indicates its use as part of a fortress plotting and rangefinding system during both wars. Its other function was as a store and target depot, since it was provided with a small dock and jetty from which launches could set forth towing targets for the various service and training batteries in the area.

Renney Battery (494 491)

This is of similar layout and vintage to Penlee Point Battery, having been built at the same time with the intention of co-operating with each other to close the entrance to the Sound with modern armament. Mounting three 6in and three 9.2in BL guns, it was later augmented by a twin 6-pounder battery for close defence. A service battery throughout both World Wars, it later became the principal practice battery for the Coast Artillery School when that establishment moved into Plymouth Citadel in 1946. The armament was removed in 1956 but the area of the work is still in the hands of the Ministry of Defence.

Plymouth Breakwater Fort (471 505)

Due to the fact that neither the contemporary guns nor their immediately contemplated replacements could close the Sound from positions on land, the 1859 Report was 'therefore of the opinion that a powerful casemated work of such a form as to bring fire to bear in every direction, more especially to seaward, should be constructed immediately behind the breakwater, near its centre'. Plans were drawn up accordingly and a small stump of rock, Shovel Rock, selected as the foundation. The original plan, approved in 1860, was for a four-tiered granite work, each floor being protected by bomb-proof arches, mounting forty guns all protected by iron shields. The foundations were begun in the following year, but before the main structure was commenced, the results of the various iron shield tests at Shoeburyness indicated that a completely iron structure was the only type of work capable of resisting heavy gunfire, and the plan was changed to a two-tiered iron fort, the lower level being the magazine and store level and the upper tier mounting eighteen heavy guns.

The fort is oval in form, 144ft long and 114ft wide, and stands about 100yd behind the centre of the Breakwater with its lower floor about 16ft above the high water level. This floor rests on a masonry foundation which is sunk into the rock for a depth of some 36ft below low water level. The erection of the iron section was begun in 1867, but in the following year work was halted while an experimental casemate representing the proposed design was built at Shoeburyness and subjected to firing trials. It withstood thirty-seven shots from a 12in 25 ton RML, a 10in 18 ton RML and a 15in American Rodman RML, all at 200yd. It was, naturally enough, in a somewhat second-hand condition after that, but experts pronounced it still defensible. Nevertheless some minor changes were made to the design and layout of the armour before work recommenced on the building of the fort.

The work was finished in 1870, but while it was in the design and construction stage the muzzle-pivoting carriage had been proposed, and the Inspector-General of Fortifications had the casemate ports designed and built to suit. The Director of Artillery, on the other hand, had not been impressed with the idea, and had ruled against the adoption of this type of carriage. Nonetheless the fort was completed with small ports, and in 1870 the Director of Artillery was confronted with a problem. As mentioned previously, he passed it to the inevitable special committee who, after deliberation, suggested that the holes in the ports be enlarged to suit the conventional carriages. I have been unable to discover the Inspector-General's reply to this, but it was probably acrimonious; he could hardly have been blamed had he invited the special committee down to Plymouth and given them a hacksaw apiece. The armour wall consisted of four thicknesses of 5in plate, separated by iron concrete, and the prospect of attempting to enlarge them in situ was uninviting. However, at this time, Fort Cunningham, Bermuda, was in course of construction, also with small ports, and the Inspector-General bided his time without any attempts to enlarge the ports. Then in July 1872 he came back to the Director of Artillery to say that he now had *two* forts with small ports and what did the Director think of that . . . or words to that effect.

This had the desired result, and the development of muzzle-pivoting—or small port—carriages was tackled with some urgency. Cunningham had priority and it was not until September 1879 that the first 12.5in 38 ton gun and small port carriage was actually installed in the Plymouth fort, and even then—'through an oversight'—it had not been fitted with sights. By the following year fourteen 12.5in and four 10in RML guns had been installed and the fort was finally a viable defensive work—nineteen years after its commencement. Soon after this it was equipped with position finders in concrete cells on the high ground near Bovisand and Picklecombe Forts, connected by submarine cable.

Its subsequent history is something of an anti-climax. Its reason for existence vanished with the building of Penlee Point and Renney Batteries, since these, with their 9.2in guns, could deal with anything in the Sound and for a long way outside it. When the RML era came to a close the armament was withdrawn and the fort came into use as an observation and signal post. It is now in naval hands, used as a signal station. The basic work is unaltered and the signal station is an addition built on the roof.

The Land Defences

1 The Western Position

This was originally intended to be a continuous ditch running from Antony village to the sea, with two major works, an intermediate work and an advanced work. All except the two forts were struck out on financial grounds, and there is room for suspecting that, had work not already begun on these, they too might have gone the same way, leaving this sector as unprotected as the Saltash Position.

Scraesdon Fort (392 549)

This is the northern work, northwest of the village of Antony (or Anthony, as it was known then). The land forms a high spur between the St Germains river and a small tributary valley, and the fort was built on this naturally defensible point, the steep slopes to the north and west forming a natural scarp for the work and a ditch being dug around the remainder. Due to the lie of the land this ditch reaches quite staggering depths on the southern face, and would-be explorers are cautioned that an unwary approach through the undergrowth which surrounds it could lead to a fall of over eighty feet in some parts.

The work was designed in 1859 to mount twenty-seven guns on the ramparts, mainly facing up the St Germains river and across it, ie to north and northwest. It is roughly rectangular and exceptionally large, the longer (east–west) dimension being about 250yd. The design is simple, no more than a rectangle of casemate accommodation within the rampart, with caponiers flanking the entrance. The terreplein is now covered with a jumble of World War II pre-fabricated huts, some in various stages of decomposition, some in good repair, for the Fort is still Crown property and frequently used as an exercise area by a variety of military units. The gun platforms on the ramparts are for the most part designed for 68-pounders on traversing platforms, but at the western corners are pits with high parapets and sweeper plates which were apparently prepared for Moncrieff carriages, though none were ever installed. Indeed there is no record of any guns ever being mounted here, and the work seems to have spent its entire life as a barrack for a variety of units, interspersed with long dormant periods under the eye of a caretaker.

Tregantle Fort (388 533)

The southern end of the 'Antony Line', this work was considerably different to Scraesdon. It is roughly octagonal in form, but the basic trace is blurred by numerous outworks, notably a small redan on the south face, reached from the caponier level. The connecting passage has a door leading to the intervening ditch which is guarded by a 'chicane', not, as in the modern idiom, a collection of oil drums and straw bales, but a form of drawbridge over a deep pit inside the outer door. With this outer door closed, the drawbridge was hauled up to form a flush-fitting second door closing the passage into the work, and leaving the pit to welcome any stormers who managed to force the outer door from the ditch. Tregantle is the only work in which I have found one of these medieval devices in complete order.

Inside the main work are two levels of terreplein, the lower containing barrack accommodation for 1,000 men and the upper a number of gun embrasures and Haxo Casemates. The embrasure positions are for 68-pounders, while the Haxo Casemates appear to have been prepared for siege howitzers. On the right of the main gate is a self-defensible keep with its own ditch and drawbridge, equipped with casemates and musketry slits so as to sweep the whole of the upper terreplein with fire, and with its own caponiers guarding its ditch. This keep is derelict and locked; inside is the principal water tower for the present installation, since, like Scraesdon, Tregantle is still Crown property and is maintained by a resident staff as a training establishment.

The planned armament was thirty-five guns, plus an undetermined number of light guns for defence of the keep and ditch. In all probability none of the planned ordnance ever got there, but a 32-pounder smoothbore breech-loader was tried there in 1866 as a case-shot weapon for use in the caponiers, so at least the fort heard the report of a gun once during its life.

Tregantle is said to have cost £189,119, and its first use was as barrack accommodation by a coast artillery brigade of one officer and fifty men. By 1882 it was occupied by six garrison artillery gunners, who must have felt lonely with the other 994 bed-spaces empty. In the early 1900s it passed from artillery ownership, becoming an infantry batallion headquarters, during which period extensive rifle ranges were constructed between the fort and the sea, and from then on it was used as a musketry training school. The work was more or less abandoned after World War I, some parts being used as stores in connection with the rifle ranges which were still in use. In 1938 it was re-opened as the Territorial Army 'Passive Air Defence' School, teaching fire-fighting, gas precautions, rescue work and other air raid precautionary techniques. In the following year, on the outbreak of war, it became the Army Gas School, until 1942 when this area was taken over by the United States Army and the fort used by them for accommodation. After 1945 it returned to the care of the British Army, with whom it now remains.

2 The Northeastern Line

None of the works on the northeastern line were ever armed, except for occasional tests of gun mountings. They all spent most of their lives as barracks for a variety of military units and were mostly abandoned after World War I. Some were taken back into use during World War II as stores depots and accommodation. After this they were again abandoned, but at present every one is occupied, due to the outward expansion of the City of Plymouth. For the most part they were simple structures of rampart wall, gorge wall, ditch and casemate accommodation, with guns on the ramparts and in Haxo Casemates—where guns were provided. I have, therefore, in the interest of economy of space, kept their descriptions to a minimum.

Ernesettle Battery (448 592)

Well described by the 1869 Report as 'the left anchor of the defences' this is on a spur overlooking the Tamar. It was built in 1868 as a casemated barrack for 60 men, to mount 15 guns and 6 mortars in open battery. It is today occupied by a Royal Naval Ammunition Depot.

Agaton Fort (455 595)

This work is on a hill, 280ft above sea level and 800yd east of Ernesettle. Pentagonal in shape, it consisted of casemated accommodation and a terreplein surrounded by ramparts and ditch, closed by a gorge wall. The centre of the work has been entirely flattened and new buildings erected to house a Ministry of Transport Heavy Vehicle Testing Station, but the casemates, ramparts and ditch are still well preserved. The ditch is flanked by caponiers. The original armament was '20 guns in open battery including one in Haxo Casemate on the left flank, and six mortars in two nests at the foot of the exterior slope'. This seems to have been modified, since there are five Haxo casemates remaining, and there may possibly have been more. Eight open positions, all for 68-pounder guns, have been traced, and an overgrown depression on the east side, between ramparts and ditch, is probably the site of the 'nests' for the mortars.

Knowles Battery (463 596)

Another 800yd step on the perimeter line brings one to Knowles Battery, a work sited so as to deny occupation of the small knoll on which it stands and from which, in less populous days, it must have been possible to see down the valley and into the dockyard area. This danger was deemed sufficient to warrant a work here, although it is quite close to both Agaton and Woodlands Forts. It has not been possible to enter this work, it now being occupied by a Secondary Modern School, but the gorge wall is well preserved and the work seems to be largely in its original condition. It was intended for twelve guns in open battery plus one in a Haxo Casemate.

Woodland Fort (470 593)

Like the majority of its companions, this consists of rampart and ditch facing north, with bombproof accommodation in the rampart and a gorge wall. It was intended to mount sixteen guns in open battery, plus two in casemates on the flanks. Today the gorge wall and part of the ramparts have gone, and the casemated accommodation is now occupied by a local public library and community centre. Above, the ramparts are overgrown by a thicket of brambles, but it is possible to see that the flank guns were in Haxo casemates and some of the armament was intended to be Moncrieff mountings behind high parapets.

Crown Hill Fort (487 592)

To quote the 1869 Report, this is 'The Key of the North-Eastern Defences.' It is in advance of the general line, forming the cornerstone where the line bends round to the south-east. It is a very large seven-sided fort, bastioned at each corner, ditched, with extensive caponiers and counterscarp galleries, the most ambitious work of the entire line. The interior contained barrack accommodation, while the ramparts were to be provided with twenty-eight guns in open battery, four in Haxo casemates, and six mortars.

Since its building, completed in 1868, Crown Hill has been continuously garrisoned, and is today the Headquarters of Plymouth Garrison, and maintained in perfect condition, though unfortunately, of course, not open to public inspection.

Bowden Fort (496 583)

On the same plan as the other minor works, Bowden consisted of a rampart containing bomb-proof casemated accommodation and an external ditch, closed by a gorge wall and drawbridge. The original armament was to be twelve guns on open platforms and three mortars.

Egg Buckland Keep (500 581)

This work was intended as a defensible barrack to provide accommodation for the men intended to man the smaller works at the end of the line and for a mobile column. It must be the last building ever erected in England to be officially termed as a 'keep'. Due to the later buildings around it, it is not possible to gain access all round, but what is visible—the front face—indicates a rectangular work surrounded by a ditch with access by drawbridge. Caponiers flank the ditch and cover the entrance. There is no record of any intention to arm it with artillery. At present it is occupied by a commercial undertaking and is not open to inspection.

Forder Battery (501 581)

This was located on a spur of ground about 400yd east of Egg Buckland Keep and was a simple earth rampart open battery without gorge wall or accommodation, the gorge being commanded by the Keep. The armament was to be sixteen guns with expense magazines in traverses between the gun embrasures. Today hardly any trace of the work remains, the site having been levelled and occupied by a television re-transmission station.

Fort Austin (506 576)

This is some 800yd from Egg Buckland Keep and lies just off Fort Austin Avenue, at the commencement of a sunken military road which runs for the remainder of the line and connects this work with Fort Efford and Laira Battery. Its plan is similar to that of the other works in the line, ramparts and casemates with ditch and gorge wall, though this has a rather imposing gatehouse-cum-keep in the gorge wall. The ditch has been merged with the military road and the original front entrance is now half-way up the front face of the work and bricked up. The intended armament was 15 guns and 5 mortars.

Fort Efford (513 566)

This is at the end of a short cul-de-sac leading from the military road and is of the usual rampart and gorge wall design. However the work is rather more complex than others of the line, with a number of interior buildings which appear to have been originally intended as stores and accommodation. The casemates have a magazine level beneath and lifts for moving ammunition up to the Haxo casemates and platforms on the ramparts. The original intention was to place twenty-one guns on the terreplein and ramparts, three in Haxo casemates, and five in casemates on the right flank to cover the gap to Laira Battery. This seems to have been one of the few works garrisoned by a siege artillery unit after its erection, since a Minute of the Ordnance Select Committee in 1888 refers to a 'six-inch to one mile range map' being used here. This tends to suggest some form of armament, probably the moveable armament of a siege battery, and not the originally intended form of fixed armament.

During the period between 1930 and 1950 this work was used as an ammunition storage depot and a light tramway track was laid in the terreplein and the casemates and accommodation converted into storage space.

Laira Battery (514 563)

The final work in the northeastern line, this overlooks the head of the Cattewater and the River Plym. Connected by the military road to Fort Austin, it was a small rampart and gorge wall work with ten guns in emplacements and three in casemates. These latter were originally intended to be in Haxo casemates, but they were eventually placed in the normal form of casemates, joined together, but built on top of the rampart and mounded over to give the effect of a three-bay Haxo, a most unusual construction and one not seen anywhere else. Expense magazines were provided on the ramparts, with casemates beneath, and magazines below ground level supplying ammunition via lifts. The work was abandoned for many years, but is now occupied by a transport company.

3 The Staddon Line

As originally planned, this was to have a large work on the summit of the heights and a second work to the south-west, overlooking the gully leading inland from Bovisand Bay. These were to be linked by a line of rampart and ditch running from the sea at West Hooe, past the two works, and connecting with the ditch surrounding Staddon Point Battery. However the plan was changed in order to provide a work which could not only defend the land front but which could also command Jennycliff Bay in the Sound and the anchorage within the Cattewater at Clovelly Bay. The line of ramparts was given up, and finally two small outworks were authorised in its place.

Fort Stamford (493 527)

This is on the high ground near Turnchapel, overlooking both the Sound and the Cattewater; it is of unusual construction. The gorge face (the north-western face) appears to be the usual granite gorge wall with accommodation within and entrance via a drawbridge over the ditch. On entering, however, it is seen that the inner side of the wall is mounded and the accommodation is virtually underground. This mounding and rampart continues round the fort, with an additional occupied mound dividing the terreplein. The magazines are in the mound and ammunition was supplied to the ramparts by simple davit hoists outside the magazine doors. The whole work can thus be said to be completely bomb-proof.

The original intention was to mount seven 9in RML on the front overlooking the Sound and another thirteen on the land front, with pits for six mortars. From the appearance of the gun platforms on the ramparts, this may well have been done, but an 1884 report notes that there were then two 10in 18-ton RML on the sea face.

No modern armament was ever installed, but the fort remained in military hands until after World War II.

Fort Staddon (496 517)

This occupies the site originally proposed by the 1859 Commission on the highest point of the area. It was intended solely as a land defensive work and was to be armed with sixteen guns on the ramparts, six in Haxo casemates and six mortars in covered casemates, with twelve more guns in the keep. As with the rest of the land defences though, the guns never appeared. The work was retained in use as a barrack and store and is at present occupied by a Ministry of Defence radio station.

Brownhill Battery

The official location of this by the 1869 Commission was 'on the high ground in rear of the salient of the scarp of Staddon Fort' which is a little cryptic. Extensive walking about in likely places has failed to show any sign of it however. It was planned as a simple open work to mount fourteen guns, and was definitely built as an 1879 report refers to it as Brownhill Fort and refers to its use as a guncotton store for the submarine defences. It appears that it was demolished some time between the two wars.

Twelve Acre Break Battery

The second outwork of Fort Staddon, this was no more than an emplacement for three guns with an expense magazine. As with Brownhill Battery a good deal of shoe-leather has been expended hunting for the work without success. There is no subsequent mention in any record after the 1869 Report, and there must be some doubt as to whether it got built at all. If it was, it must have been demolished many years ago.

8
THE MILFORD HAVEN DEFENCES

The first move to erect defences in this area was in about 1590 when two blockhouses were built under the orders of Henry VIII to cover the entrance to the Haven. Shortly after this a plan was put forward to construct works on Dale Point, Thorn Island and Stack Rock, but nothing further was done. If they did nothing else, these proposals made during the sixteenth century highlighted the obvious defensive locations which were put to use in later years.

In 1756 with the danger of invasion in the air, many plans were proposed, but the only result was the commencement of work at Paterchurch which, when the danger passed, was abandoned without being completed. But some time later, during the Napoleonic Wars, a Naval dockyard was established at Milford Haven and two batteries, one at Hakin Point and one on the other side of the town, were constructed so as to protect the dockyard.

In 1814 the yard was moved further up the inlet and re-established at Pembroke Dock, and a number of defence schemes were then discussed which culminated in the building of Pater Battery, for twenty-three guns, at Pembroke Dock in 1840. This was followed by the building of a defensible barrack on the hill overlooking the dockyard and two Martello Towers, one at the south-west and one at the north-east corners of the yard area. The towers mounted four 12-pounder brass howitzers, two on each floor, and a 32-pounder of 56cwt on a traversing platform on the roof. So far this had been a Royal Naval responsibility, but in 1855 the defences were taken over by the Army and Pater Battery renovated.

At the same time as this building was taking place at Pembroke, other defences in the Haven had been authorised. In 1850 work began on a tower on Stack Rock; two years later a battery was built on Thorn Island and work began on more batteries at Dale Point and West Blockhouse Point. But in December 1858 the patchy state of the defences led to expressions of concern from the Admiralty, and a special committee, which included Captain Cooper Key and Major Jervois RE, was set up by the Secretary of State for War to report on the defence of the area. By this time West Blockhouse Point had a six-gun battery, Dale Point nine guns, Thorn Island nine guns and Stack Rock Tower three guns, in addition to the works immediately adjacent to the Dockyard. This was held to be insufficient, and the special committee recommended that Stack Rock Tower be strengthened and new works built around the haven at Hakin, Chapel Bay, South Hook Point and Popton Point, with a boom obstacle between Hakin and Popton. This plan was approved, £190,000 voted, and work put in hand in 1859, but before very much was done the larger question of national defence arose and the 1859 Commission was created and came to take a second look at the area and its problems.

By and large they endorsed the earlier plans, though increasing the strength of the proposed works. Instead of merely improving Stack Rock, they recommended that a two-tier casemated work should be built to augment the existing Tower, while the other proposed works should also become casemated batteries with defensible barracks in rear. Having rubber-stamped, as it were, the earlier plans, the commissioners now turned to look at the land side defences. It will serve no useful purpose here to go too deeply into their proposals since, as will be seen, the majority came to nothing, but the basic idea was to ring the area with land defences in much the same way as had been proposed for Portsmouth and Plymouth.

Three defensive lines were proposed; to the north of the Haven a line of six small forts running roughly on an arc from

Neyland Ferry to St Ishmaels: to the south of the dockyard five works in an arc from Carew to Hundleton: and as a further defence against a landing on the south coast of the peninsula, a line of works beginning at Tenby and running along the coast to Trewent. The following list shows the full extent of the project:

The Haven
    Four new works and improvements,
        already sanctioned—   £190,000

The Northern Line:

Scoveston		20 guns	300 men	
Waterston		6	50	
Honeyborough		6	50	
Barn Lake		6	50	
Newton		10	100	
Burton		10	100	
	Total	58 guns	650 men	£250,000

The Southern Line:

Pennar Farm		15 guns	150 men	
Bush Corner		20	300	
Ferry Hill		15	200	
Advanced Work		6		
Intermediate Work		6		
	Total	62 guns	650 men	£250,000

The Tenby Line:

Tenby		15 guns	150 men	
Caldy Island		10	100	
Lydstep		6	50	
Freshwater East		6	50	
Freshwater West		6	50	
	Total	43 guns	400 men	£100,000

All of which added up to a total of £790,000 and was estimated to demand a garrison of between seven and eight thousand men when fully manned for war.

To call this plan ambitious would be an understatement, and although Pembroke was a relatively important naval installation, to the legislators in London it was, to use a phrase employed many years later in a different context, 'a far-off country of which we know little.' In the circumstances it is hardly surprising that the most energetic swings of the economy axe were made in this direction. The entire Southern line was cut out, and all the Northern Line except one work. In view of these deletions, the planners looked afresh at the Tenby line and came to the conclusion that without the other portions of the defences there seemed little point in keeping this; but since the legislators had allowed it to go through, they proceeded with a portion of the line, though moving very slowly and eventually giving most of it up. The work at Tenby was built, and land purchased for some of the other works; plans were drawn up for batteries at Lydstep and Freshwater East, and were approved, and it was intended to draw up plans for other works. But in the event none of these came to fruition, the land was sold, and only the work at Tenby left, little use any longer except to deter a possible landing in the harbour there.

Eventually the plans were settled and the works took shape. It seems that advantage was taken of the appropriations unused on the Tenby Line to make some improvements in the works already existing on Thorn Island and at Dale Point. They were converted from open batteries to casemated granite works, though not of the same magnitude nor to the same design as the other works built; indeed, Dale is so different in appearance from the usual run of 1860s construction that it resembles a restored castle rather than a utilitarian fort.

With subsequent improvements the Haven remained fortified until 1956, though little further was done in the way of new works. Most of the older works were abandoned and sold in the 1930s, and since 1956 they have often changed hands again due to the large amount of redevelopment in progress in the area.

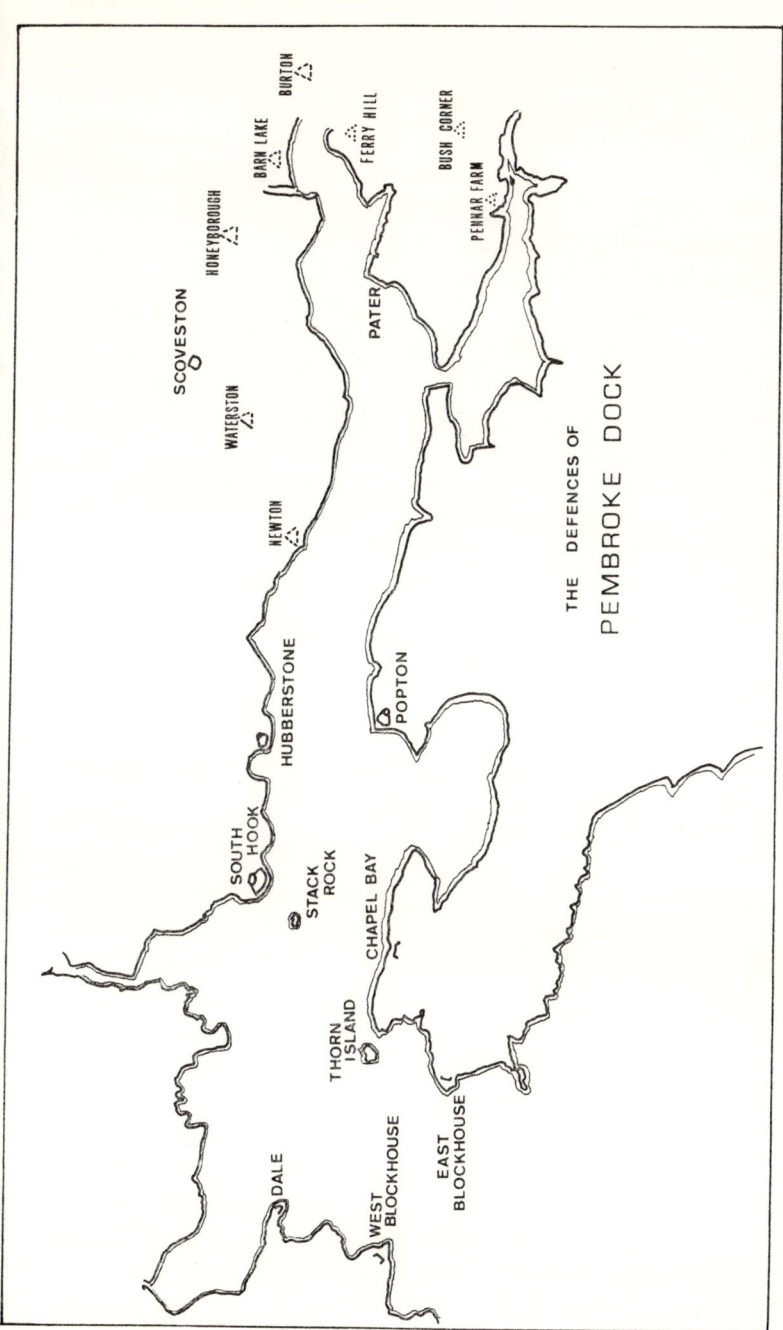

Map 7 The Pembroke and Milford Haven Defences

The Land Defences

Only one of the projected land defences was built.

Fort Scoveston (945 066)

This was originally intended to be the central work in the line covering the northern land approach to the Haven. When the government examined the plans before submitting them to Parliament, the entire line was struck out, but after some debate, Scoveston was allowed to stand since its central position covered the likely approaches to both Neyland and Milford Haven. It was accordingly sanctioned, and work began in August 1861. The work is hexagonal with sides of 130yd length, and surrounded by a dry ditch with access via a drawbridge; it was planned to mount thirty-two guns on the ramparts. Inside the work was accommodation for a 128-man garrison, a magazine, stores, and bomb-proof casemates. Completed in April 1864 it was never armed, and from then on was used as barrack accommodation, though most of the time it stood empty under a caretaker's eye. Eventually, after World War I it was abandoned, and after lying empty for some years was sold in October 1932. During World War II an anti-aircraft gun battery was sited there, but then it was abandoned once more and now stands derelict.

The Sea Defences

St Catherine's Island Fort, Tenby (136 002)

As with Scoveston, St Catherine's Island was the only work of its planned line to reach completion. But this southern line of defence was a long time gestating, and it was 1867 before a decision was taken to build here and purchase land for the remainder of the works. This work was begun in January 1868, hardly the best time of year to start such a project on that coast. The site selected was a small rock eminence a few hundred yards from shore and connected to the mainland by a ridge of rock and sand at low water. It was a simple rectangular work perched on the rock, to mount six guns in casemates behind iron shields and five more in barbette mountings on the roof. While still in the building stage the barbette guns were cancelled and the provision of five 9in guns on Moncrieff carriages considered, but with the difficulties over the 9in Moncrieff design, eventually the design settled at six 7in RML guns in casemates.

Completed in about 1877 it was manned for some years thereafter, a report of 1884 remarking on the breaking of the magazine lamps by concussion when the guns were fired at practice. It stood empty for many years until abandoned and sold in the 1930s. I recall that when I was in the area in 1959, 'Gun Fort House' as it was then called was advertised for sale for £10,000, the cost of construction having been £16,260. It had been converted into a private residence and occupied for some years. It is now a zoo.

We can now consider the actual Haven defences, beginning at the west of the entrance and moving clockwise around the Haven.

West Blockhouse Battery (817 037)

A work was originally placed here in Henry VIII's time, but had been in a ruinous state for many years when a fresh work was built in 1852. A six-gun open battery, it was apparently serviceable when examined in 1859, and the Commission did not recommend any changes there. Nonetheless, periodic improvement took place; in 1881 a number of 80-pounder converted rifled guns were mounted, and these were sufficiently powerful to cover the Haven entrance. In about 1897 these were withdrawn (although they were not to be declared obsolete until 1921) and in 1904 four 6in BL were installed. These remained in place until after World War II when the work was finally abandoned.

Dale Fort (824 051)

Dale Battery had been completed and provided with nine 68-pounder guns by 1857 and although the Royal Commission made no recommendations about strengthening or extending it, some rebuilding was subsequently done to improve its defences and enhance its status from 'battery' to 'Fort'.

Probably the most interesting period of its history was in the early 1890s when it was the site of trials of the Zalinski Pneumatic Dynamite Torpedo Gun. This was a 10in calibre compressed air gun which projected a fin-stabilised shell filled with dynamite. It was developed by an American called Mefford and then taken over and improved by a Lieutenant Zalinski of the US Artillery. One or two were installed in the coast defences of the New York area in the late 1880s as well as being fitted into a special cruiser, the USS *Vesuvius*, and the British Army decided that the weapon ought to be investigated. After trials at Shoeburyness, it was installed here in 1892 and numerous trials were fired in 1893 against a paddle steamer borrowed from the Admiralty. After considering the results, the Ordnance Committee turned the weapon down on the grounds that the complication of air compressing machinery was not worth the effort, since the performance was not as good as that of conventional guns. It was removed from Dale and returned to the USA.

After this burst of activity Dale went to sleep. The RML guns remained there until some time after World War I, after which they were removed and the fort sold. It is now a residential field centre specialising in the maritime sciences.

South Hook Fort (870 055)

This was planned as a twenty gun open battery with a defensible barrack carrying guns on the roof in the rear. When the work began in December 1859 the plans were slightly changed by the 1859 Commission to provide two separate batteries, one of fifteen and one of five guns, protected by earthworks, with guns mounted in embrasures, and all connected by a covered way running along the rear. The defensible barrack, for 180 officers and men, was built on a slightly modified plan to present a curved face to the north and thus close approach from that direction. As can be seen from the plan, the work was ditched on both sides, and this also shows the layout of the open batteries,

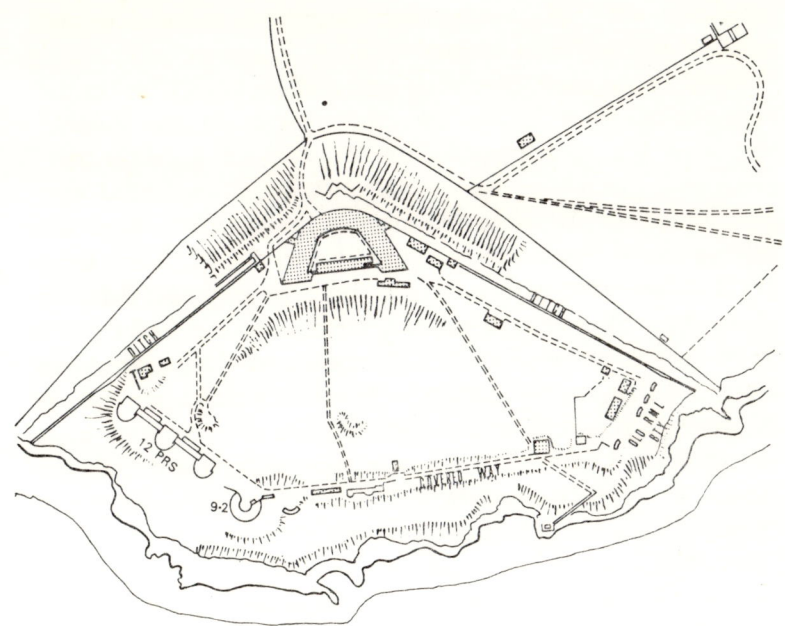

South Hook Fort, Milford Haven. Based on the plan in the sale catalogue of 1932. The defensible barrack is protected by a ditch and scarp. The new battery on the left of the plan replaced the former open battery of RML *guns, but the old work on the other flank was merely abandoned*

although it is based on the plan of the work as it was when sold. The gun positions were some 100ft above the water level, and approach from the sea was efficiently deterred by the cliffs, which, it was considered, could be scarped when needed, to further secure this approach.

The batteries were ready in April 1861, but the barrack was not completed until March 1865. The armament appears to have been late in arriving, since in 1870 it was still being debated whether the mountings were to have hydraulic recoil buffers or not. A combination of 7in and 9in RMLs was installed in 1871.

These guns remained in place until the late 1890s when they were removed and the right flank battery rebuilt to take a 9.2in BL gun and three 12-pounder QF guns. These remained in place until the early 1930s when they were removed and the fort then abandoned as a defensive work, being auctioned off in August 1936.

Stack Rock Fort (864 049)

This prominent rock in the middle of the Haven was an obvious choice for a battery, particularly in the days of short range weapons; a three-gun tower was built there in 1850–2. The Special Commission recommended strengthening it, and the 1859 Commission amended their plan to make it a casemated work containing two tiers of nineteen casemates, with sixteen guns on the terreplein, a total of fifty-four guns. On this plan work began in 1859 and the foundations were completed in 1861. By this time the iron shield idea was in the air, and instead of the original all-masonry construction, the design was changed to use granite piers with iron shields between them, together with an increase in wall thickness and other measures to strengthen the construction. Work was then resumed, a fresh contractor making a start by completing the basement floor and magazines, but in 1863 he was brought to a halt while fresh plans were considered. With the increased power of some of the guns then in the design stage it seemed that the original 54 gun concept was unnecessarily lavish, not to say expensive, and a revised plan was produced having sixteen guns in a single tier in the front face and seven smaller guns on two floors in the gorge, facing into the Haven. The upper tier was to be used for accommodation, and surmounting this were to be three turrets each mounting two 12in 25 ton guns. The interior of the work was to provide accommodation for 4 officers and 152 men, together with a 12-bed hospital.

Work began once more under yet another contractor in June 1864. Due to the location, necessitating shipping every workman, stone, iron plate, nail, window pane or whatever out across the waters of the Haven, work proceeded slowly and it was not completed until 1871. By the following year sixteen 10in guns were in place in the casemates, rope mantlets were being fitted to the shields, and the seven 7in guns for the gorge were installed. Like every other work with similar plans the roof turrets got no further than the planning stage.

In 1874 it was proposed to remove the 10in and install 12.5in guns in their place, but an examination of the Fort showed that the existing 10in had a maximum elevation of $2\frac{1}{4}°$ and a maximum depression of $6\frac{3}{4}°$, and the increased size of the 12.5in guns vis-a-vis the size of the casemate shield ports would have restricted the fire of the heavier guns to an even smaller amount. One solution was a proposal to cut away the masonry of the gun floors so as to lower them by nine inches, but this gave only a marginal improvement and the idea was dropped.

When modern armament became available, the same sort of problem militated against installation here. The work was considerably restricted by its site and there could be no question of fitting a modern weapon into the casemates. So the RMLs remained in place until they were declared obsolete in 1922, the only concession to breech-loading being the addition of some 12-pounder QF on the roof in the early 1900s. When the RML guns were finally scrapped, they were merely dismounted and left, some being dumped into the sea where they were visible at low water for several years until the action of the tides rolled them into deeper water.

After the end of World War I the work was abandoned and it was finally sold at auction in October 1932. The work originally cost £96,840 to build, and a pencilled note on the sale catalogue indicates that it was knocked down to a bid of £60.

Hubberstone Fort (891 055)

This is the work at Hakin Point (or Signal Staff Point) recommended by the Special Committee in 1858. Their plan called for a thirty-two gun battery, consisting of twelve guns in casemates behind masonry embrasures, ten on the terreplein above and ten in an open battery on the flank. This was approved by the Royal Commission and work began on the open battery early in 1860. It was completed by November of that year and armed soon after, though due to the terrain it finished up as a nine gun installation. With the completion of this part, which served to place some instant defence in the area, work began on the casemated battery. This contract was for the masonry only, since although iron shields were agreed, the design had not then been settled. Eventually the shields were produced and fitted and the casemates handed over for arming in October 1863. At the same time other contracts had been let and the defended barrack, terreplein battery and ditch were completed early in 1865.

As finally built it comprised an eleven-gun casemate, eight on the terreplein and nine in the east flank open battery, and the aerial photograph, taken in the early 1960s, reveals traces of all three. At the top of the site is the defensible barrack, roughly semi-circular, and with the gorge closed by a high wall. Below this wall, on the sloping ground, are traces of the terreplein battery. From the right hand corner of the barrack a sunken way runs around the terreplein down to the casemates, and to the right of the casemates, extending to the outer ditch, is the remains of the flank open battery. The ditch in front of the barrack is protected by caponiers and a counter-scarp gallery, entrance to the work being by a drawbridge. In later years the ditch was filled in on the left extremity of the casemates, allowing a gate to be placed in the wall and giving access from the casemate gun floor level to an adjacent road.

In August 1868 plans were approved for alteration of the magazine arrangements and also for a proposal to remove the eight guns from the terreplein and replace them with eight guns on Moncrieff carriages in pits built on top of the casemates. Although Moncrieff carriages were frequently suggested for works at this time, this is one of the few where they were actually adopted, and by January 1872 the pits were ready for the guns. They had been formed by increasing the depth of masonry on the roof and the casemate block, thus strengthening the protection there, and they can be seen in the aerial photograph as semi-circular recesses in the casemate roof.

One is at a loss to explain this incredible installation which, together with a similar arrangement across the Haven at Popton

Fort, is the most unusual and ridiculous application of the disappearing carriage ever attempted. The object behind the disappearing carriage is to place the guns so that their position is completely concealed except for the short time of exposure for firing, and to mount them thus on the roof of a prominent casemate was simply to draw attention to their location and provide the enemy with a convenient and permanent aiming mark. Moreover the work was ineptly done, for in 1884 the Superintendent, Royal Carriage Department, reported that the guns could not be depressed for more than 5° because the parapets were too high, and thus there was a considerable space of dead water in front of the fort which could not be reached by the guns.

While this work was in train, the main armament was also installed in the casemates, and judging by existing reports it must have been done exceptionally quickly. On 22 August 1871 the Officer Commanding answered a query as to armament by saying that no guns were yet mounted in the casemates. On 4 September the Inspector of Artillery was complaining that the guns could not be traversed fully because of the positioning of the traversing tackle ringbolts. In view of the work involved, shifting eleven 12-ton guns and their carriages and slides into the casemate and mounting them all within the space of twelve days was a creditable performance.

By 1881 the open battery on the flank had been re-armed with 10in RML on barbette mountings and with that the fort's armament was complete. It was never provided with modern weapons. Some time early in the century the casemate guns were taken out and the casemates bricked up, and shortly after World War I it was abandoned. It was sold for £1,050 in 1932, having cost £87,894 to build.

Pater Battery (956 040; SW Tower 955 036; NE Tower 964 038)

This open battery was built in 1840 in front of the original dockyard. In 1845 it was augmented by two towers and a defensive barrack on the land side. When inspected in 1858 the battery mounted nineteen guns, one tower one gun and the other tower three guns. With the construction of the new works the battery was no longer considered important, and late in the nineteenth century it was disarmed and in 1903 dismantled to make way for extensions to the dockyard. The two towers are Ancient Monuments and are under the care of the Department of the Environment, while the defensible barrack has also passed from military ownership and is now the home of a golf club.

Popton Fort (894 038)

This work, on the south side of the Haven, lies opposite Hubberstone Fort and the original intention was to suspend a boom between the two to prevent the passage of ships toward the dockyard. Although money was appropriated for this obstacle it was never installed. Popton Fort was a casemated granite work very similar in layout to Hubberstone, a defended barrack in rear and a casemated battery overlooking the Haven. Originally intended for forty-five guns, the plans were modified to take eleven 9in in casemates with twenty guns in open battery on the terreplein. Work seems to have gone more quickly here than at Hubberstone, in spite of difficulty in obtaining secure foundations since the 9in were in the casemates by 1868. As with Hubberstone, plans were then drawn up for placing six Moncrieff mountings with 7in guns on top of the casemates, and this was completed by 1872.

The barrack keep was finally built to a different design to that of Hubberstone, being in the form of an irregular hexagon, flanked by musketry from six bastions. It contained accommodation for 10 officers and 260 men, plus a sick-bay for 4 patients, all in buildings constructed of iron framing with a concrete roof capable of supporting light guns.

Erected at a cost of £90,227 its subsequent history was much the same as that of Hubberstone. The armament was never brought up to modern standards and it was sold at auction in 1932 for £300. In 1959 it was bought by the BP Oil Company and now lies within the area of their Ocean Terminal. At the time of its purchase it was considerably overgrown and dilapidated but the company have restored the work to its original appearance and use the barrack keep as an office building, while the pumping facilities are out of sight on the casemate gun floors. I am informed that the result is very pleasing; the Company obtained period gas-light fittings, converted them to electric operation, and installed them on the exterior of the work.

Chapel Bay Battery (861 035)

This was built opposite Stack Rock and intended to cooperate with that work and with South Hook. The original recommendation was for a ten gun battery but this was later changed to a rectangular defensible barrack for sixty-five men, with a six gun barbette battery overlooking the Haven and mounting 10in 18-ton RML guns. Work on this did not begin until 1870 but it was completed and armed by 1877. This remained the armament until 1900 when it was extensively rebuilt to take one 9.2in, two 6in and two 12-pounder guns, the 9.2in being on a barbette mounting. Thus revitalised, the work remained in service until the end of World War I when it was dismantled and sold in 1932. It is now completely derelict.

Thorn Island Fort (864 038)

This was originally a small open battery built in 1852 and although no additions were recommended in 1859, it appears to have been improved to the extent of providing a masonry work to house a small garrison and by 1880 it was provided with nine 7in RML guns. In spite of being passed over, the sum of £85,000 was spent in re-modelling it.

Thereafter it was never re-armed, was abandoned after World War I, and in 1932 was sold at auction.

East Blockhouse Battery (844 028)

Arriving back at the right-hand side of the entrance, East Blockhouse was designed to work in conjunction with West Blockhouse on the other side of the channel. As with its partner it was built in 1852 as an open battery with six guns, and no recommendations for improvement were made in 1859. But it was improved, firstly by installing 80-pounder converted RML guns and later by extending it to give a strength of twelve guns. Then, in the 1890s it was remodelled and two 9.2in barbette guns were installed. These replaced the older works and remained in place until the middle 1930s when they were removed and replaced by the latest marks of 6in guns. After World War II the battery was dismantled and abandoned, but the site is still occupied by the Ministry of Defence.

9
THE LESSER FORTRESSES

The three ports forming the subject of this short chapter were all, at one time or another, considered as fortresses, though their importance later declined to the status of 'defended ports'. However, some of their installations are not without interest.

Dover

In the days of the 1859 Commission Dover had a great deal more significance than it has today, for until 1919 it was a naval base and dockyard. Before that, of course, its proximity to France led to its being fortified in one way or another from the earliest days. The principal fortification from the historical point of view is, of course, Dover Castle, the 'Key of England', though its role was primarily to defend the area and deny the road to London to anyone who landed there. Its first application in the coast defence role appears to have been under Henry VIII, who also built Archcliffe Fort on the other side of the harbour, and from this time onward a proportion of the Castle armament was always allotted to sea defence. At the time of the First Dutch War (1652) the armament was listed rather exotically as 'four culverins, twenty-eight demi-culverins, and eighteen sakers' but these were later changed for something more prosaic and their numbers augmented, until in 1716 there were ninety-eight guns of various calibres mounted, which the Board of Ordnance proposed to reduce to thirty-six. By this time however the coast defences had moved out of the castle and closer to the sea.

Earthen batteries—the Western Outworks—were built on the ridge of high ground across the valley, and eventually the Citadel was established there, replacing the Castle as the primary military work in the area. Late in the sixteenth century Archcliffe Fort was improved, and by 1805 the armament returns for Dover show a number of works in use:

Dover Castle: twenty 32-pounder, eight 24-pounder, sixty-four 18-pounder, six 12-pounder plus a number of carronades for local defence
Drop Redoubt: thirteen 24-pounder
Guildford Battery: four 32-pounder and carronades
Moat Bulwark: three 32-pounder
Amherst Battery: four 32-pounder
Townshend Battery: two 24-pounder
Archcliffe Fort: five 32-pounder, six 12-pounder, two 18-pounder carronade.

The 1859 Commissioners seem to have been less concerned about Dover than one might have expected, but since the enlargement of the harbour was under way, and since the occupation of Dover by an enemy would obviously be a considerable threat, 'Your Commissioners are of opinion that no other course is open but to complete the works in progress and to give the defences such additional strength as may be considered necessary to render them secure.' The works in progress were, in fact, not very much more than bringing some of the older batteries up to a better standard, and the only new work which was proposed was Castle Hill Fort, which was built during the 1860s on the same ridge as the Castle, some 700yd away out to the north-east. This was primarily a land defence work to protect the harbour though it had a secondary coast defence capability. It was an irregular pentagon, bastioned at the corners, containing large casemated accommodation and stores and with guns on the ramparts. A wet ditch surrounded the work, and an extension ditch ran to the south-east to a small redoubt. The work was armed with 9in RML guns after its completion but was later superseded by more modern installations, and after 1900 played no part in

THE LESSER FORTRESSES

the defences, although it has been in continuous military occupation since it was built.

But Dover takes a unique place in the story of coast defence for one particular feature; the Dover Turret. I have been unable to trace the first germ of this idea, but it seems to have begun in 1873 when the Admiralty demanded a gun capable of defeating 20in of armour at 1,000yd, and began designing a suitable turret ship to carry four of them. A design of 14in RML gun was prepared, capable of being bored out to larger calibres, and it was proposed to try this in 14in, 15in and finally 16in calibre to determine which best met the requirement. The Secretary of State for War gave the authority for the gun, costing £8,000, to be made in 1874. It was completed as a 14.5in and fired preliminary trials in 1876. It was then bored out to 15in calibre for more trials and then bored again to 16in. The barrel liner cracked after 166 shots had been fired at the various calibres, but the gun was then 'chambered', ie the chamber section at the breech was enlarged to 18in calibre to allow a heavier charge to be fired. With a 1,700lb shell and a 425lb gunpowder charge, it produced a muzzle velocity of 1,700ft per sec and a muzzle energy of 29,600ft tons, sending its shot through 56in of iron and teak at 200yd, which should dispose of any lingering doubts about the power of muzzle-loading guns.

The Admiralty expressed themselves satisfied with this and the manufacture of service guns was put in hand; each gun now cost £10,084 and each round of ammunition £26.12.0d (£26.60). So far it had been purely a naval gun, but some time in 1877 the Admiralty expressed their opinion that something more powerful was needed in Dover and the plan of installing a turret, similar to the naval pattern, with two of these 16in 80-ton guns inside it, was born. The selected site was the tip of the Admiralty Pier, and by 1879 designs of turret and gun mounting were in hand. After a brief flirtation with the idea of a muzzle-pivoting design, a straightforward carriage and slide were adopted, but with the provision of steam power for all operations of loading, ammunition supply, elevation and training of the turret. These designs were all approved in July 1879.

By late 1882 the guns had been moved to Dover on lighters and installed in the turret, the steam engines installed, and on January 1883 the Superintendent RCD reported that all was in place and working. He asked for a firing trial to settle various small adjustments, but the Inspector-General of Fortifications 'called attention to the expressions of anxiety lest the shock of discharge should, by bringing down portions of the cliff, endanger the houses below.' The subsequent discussions went on for six months, the inevitable special committee being formed, but in the end a firing trial was authorised and on 16 July 1883 four rounds were fired, with no ill-effects.

The trial revealed numerous small defects and work now began on rectifying them, but a notable lack of urgency now descended and it was not until 22 March 1886 that the Director of Fortifications and Works reported that the turret was ready to be handed over to the Royal Artillery to take its place in the defences. It was duly taken over on 21 April 1886, but there were still 'several minor deficiencies' and it was not until August of that year that everything about the turret was serviceable and in working order.

For the next few years the turret was an object of pride,

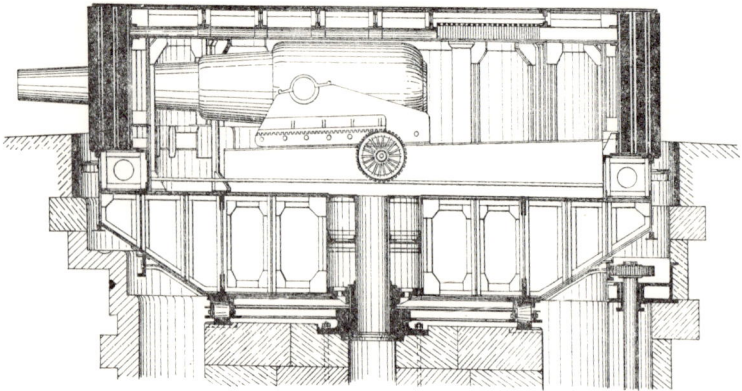

The Dover Turret, showing the method of mounting it on rollers on top of a cylinder of masonry. Traversing was done by the shaft and gear on the right, which engaged in a rack on the turret structure

mounting the heaviest land service ordnance in the kingdom and provided with the most up-to-date and efficient machinery. The pier end had been enlarged, with new foundations running down seven fathoms below the low water mark, with the guns 95ft above, 33ft above high water. A massive masonry cylinder carried a steel racer on which the turret revolved on a roller race. The total revolving weight, including the iron framework, three layers of 7in-thick armour with two intermediate layers of 2in-thick armour, plus the guns and their mountings, was 895 tons. The outside diameter of the turret was 37ft. The steam engines—the main engine of 300hp for revolving the turret, and an auxiliary of 30hp for loading and hoisting ammunition—were down the shaft, some 30ft below the guns. The magazines were in the pier structure at the same level.

There is no record of the guns ever being fired again, and once the novelty wore off they were virtually mothballed. The turret came back into official recognition in 1898 when the Ordnance Board briefly considered the idea of taking out the 16in RML guns and replacing them with two 9.2in BL, but this idea was never followed up. In October 1902 the 16in RMLs were declared obsolete, and that, it was felt, was that. Officially the Dover Turret ceased to exist, and even such an impeccable authority as General Headlam in his *History of the Royal Artillery* observed that 'in 1905 the great 100-ton guns still took part in annual practice at Malta and Gibraltar, although the Dover Turret had gone'.

But it hadn't gone. The guns were run in and greased, and a wooden floor built over them. The turret was encased in brickwork and an asphalt roof, and a door in the brickwork gave entrance to what was now a gloomy store-room with a low ceiling. The Admiralty pier was extended, two wars came and went, and so far as can be ascertained the store-room was used for rope, blocks, and the bits and pieces necessary on a pier. Then in 1968 someone went for a length of rope or whatever and one of the floorboards felt suspiciously unsafe beneath his feet. He called a carpenter who decided to remove a few planks and replace them. Having removed them, the carpenter was curious as to what lay in the gloom below, probably suspecting it to be a large hole with the waters of Dover Harbour at the bottom. He called for a torch; and discovered two 16in 80-ton RML guns, sitting quietly on their platforms, exactly as they had been run in and left sixty-six years before.

Subsequent examination showed that the guns and their mountings and all the apparatus of the turret were in remarkably good condition and at present work is in progress restoring it so that it may be opened for public inspection at some future date.

The Citadel Ridge behind Archcliffe Fort held a proliferation of defensive works and barracks, of which three were basically coast defence works; Citadel Battery, Drop Battery and Drop Redoubt at the eastern end of the ridge. These were all armed in the Napoleonic Wars and their armament brought up to date in the 1860s by installing numerous 7in Armstrong guns. The Citadel Battery was later improved when in 1902 two 9.2in BL guns were installed, to remain in place until the 1950s. At the same time as this installation, a new work to the east of the Castle, Langdon Battery, was built to take four 10in BL guns, though the armament actually installed was two 10in and two 9.2in, which remained until the 1920s when the 10in were scrapped and another two 9.2in replaced them.

World War I, with the activity of the famous Dover Patrol and the port's vast importance as one of the principal supply routes for the British Expeditionary Force, led to some strengthening of the defences. The heavy gun strength was satisfactory, but the likelihood of light German craft trying a tip-and-run raid on the busy harbour led to the provision of numbers of light guns on the piers and breakwater; firstly the Pier Extension Battery on the end of the extended Admiralty Pier; then the Eastern Arm Battery of 6-pounder guns on the Eastern breakwater, and finally the South Breakwater Battery of three 12-pounder QF guns on the west end of the detached breakwater, all of which remained in place throughout both wars.

World War II brought about a massive increase in gun strength. This was less a defensive measure as an offensive one against Axis shipping trying to run through the Straits by hugging the French Coast. When France collapsed in 1940 the immediate thought was to provide defence, but when the Germans moved long range guns into the Cap Gris Nez area and began to bombard British shipping, and also parts of Kent, consideration was rapidly given to offensive weapons. The first to be moved in were two naval 14in manned by Royal Marines, and in September 1940 the decision was taken to erect five new batteries of guns on long-range mountings. The first to be ready, in February 1941, was Fan Bay Battery of three 6in guns on mountings allowing them to reach as far as 25,000yd. In October 1941 they were joined by South Foreland Battery of four 9.2in with a range of 31,000yd, while in 1942 Lydden Spout Battery of three 6in, Hougham Battery of four 8in and Wanstone Battery of two 15in were all installed, the last-named being completed in June 1942.

The speed of installation of these works is in considerable contrast to the leisurely pace with which Dover Turret had been completed, and the comparison is not inapt, since Hougham and Wanstone Batteries were in shielded barbettes which, to the untrained eye, looked very much like turrets, although they dispensed with the complicated underpinnings. The 15in were of the pattern developed in the 1930s for arming Singapore and these two guns were the only 15in ever erected outside Singapore. The 8in were basically naval mountings rapidly modified by Vickers-Armstrong and installed in concrete barbette positions.

Dover was also the location of the only super-long-range gun ever employed by Britain. The Germans had brought up, to positions behind Cap Gris Nez, two 21cm, K12 high velocity super-long-range guns, and in October 1940 the Director of Naval Ordnance suggested producing a similar gun for retaliatory fire, capable of shooting up to sixty nautical miles (121,600yd). Without going into involved ballistics, it can be briefly said that for a given calibre, the longer the gun, the greater the velocity and range, but the size of gun which could be manufactured in England at that time was governed by the gunmaking machinery available. The greatest length that could be produced was the standard 16in naval gun barrel, 61ft 11.3in long, and an 8in calibre liner of this length was produced, to be fitted into a 13.5in barrel so that an 8in shell would be fired by a 13.5in cartridge. The liner was deeply rifled with a small number of grooves, and the shell made with ribs to engage in the rifling, almost a reversion to the pattern used with the old RML guns.

The first of these '13.5/8in Hypervelocity' guns was built and emplaced on an experimental mounting on the Isle of Grain for its first trials in June 1942, and a second gun was later built and installed on a 13.5in barbette carriage, at Dover in the Royal Marine battery alongside the two 14in. It was fired from there in March 1943 and achieved a range of almost 100,000yd (56.8 miles), being aimed towards Harwich so that the fall of the shell could be observed from the experimental range at Shoeburyness. Numerous problems became apparent, the principal one being that the rate of wear was so phenomenal that the gun was unlikely to last for more than 28 shots before being worn out. In view of this it was never used against Occupied France and was later dismantled. Although unsuccessful as an offensive weapon, it provided a great deal of information on high velocity ballistics which was of considerable use in later years.

Portland

The principal value of Portland was as a 'harbour of refuge' and little had been done in the way of fortification other than to provide a minimal amount of protection for vessels which might seek shelter there in time of war. Henry VIII had built one of his artillery castles there, but this had fallen into disuse as a coast defence work; when Blomefield inspected in 1783 he found 'a battery of three 18-pounder guns, the carriages of which are totally rotten: the guns also are very old and will probably be found unserviceable when properly examined.' He noted the existence of some open batteries on the cliffs, but the guns for these were stored in the castle. When the 1859 Commission came to examine the area there were no naval establishments there and 'we are informed that there is no present intention of constructing any', but 'its situation and capabilities will render it of special value to this country in time of war; it is therefore absolutely necessary that it should be so effectually defended as to ensure its use to ourselves and deny its possession to an enemy.' Consequently they proposed some formidable works; the 1850s had seen the approval of a scheme to isolate the harbour from the promontory of Portland Bill by the excavation of an enormous ditch across its width from east to west. This had a two-fold benefit in that it defended the harbour and also formed a source of material for the new breakwater then being built. The presence of the convict prison solved the labour question. Behind, ie to the north of this ditch, a rampart was to be thrown up and under this bomb-proof barracks would be built. The north and east flanks of this area were barred by unscaleable cliffs, so that when completed the work would form an immense fifty-six acre citadel which came to be known as Verne Fort. Earthen open batteries were built on three sides of this area.

To cover the harbour a small battery was in the course of construction on the inner pier head, and it was now proposed to augment this with a large casemated work on the end of the breakwater, as and when that structure reached its ultimate planned extent. Open batteries were to be built on either side of the promontory, one on Durdale (or Disdale—the spelling varies in different reports) Point, and one on Blacknor Point. Durdale would prevent a fleet anchoring to the east to bombard the harbour, and Blacknor would cover the West Bay area. In addition the commissioners now proposed to improve the armament of the earthen batteries in Verne Fort with sea defence guns so that they could cross fire with these two batteries. Finally to guard the northern side of the harbour, a work, principally of open batteries, would be built on The Nothe, a small promontory separating Weymouth from Portland harbour.

Work began on The Nothe even before the report was published, but instead of open batteries it was built as a ten gun casemated work, iron shielded, with two light guns on the land flank. The work was let out to contract, but the contractor ran into difficulties in 1862 and it was taken over by the Royal Engineers and completed using military and convict labour. By 1872 it was armed with four 9in and six 10in RML guns, the land face guns never being installed. In the 1890s, with the improvement in other works, it became redundant as a defensive work and was converted to use as an infantry barrack.

Verne Fort, or Citadel, was built largely by convicts and was originally armed with 9in RML in the open batteries. This was later improved by the provision of two 12.5in RML bearing on the approach to the harbour. This too was given up as a defensive work in the 1900s but remained in military hands for many years before being taken over by the Prison Commissioners, who doubtless felt they had a good claim on it. It is still in their care.

The two open batteries at the ends of the ditch, Blacknor and, as it finally became known, East Weare, were both provided with the usual 9in RML guns in the early 1870s, but when re-armament was in progress in the 1890s, Blacknor received 6in BL and East Weare a battery each of 6in and 9.2in. These gave good command of the southern approaches to the harbour, but to close the northern approach and deny the whole of Weymouth Bay to an enemy, a new barbette battery of 9.2in was built near Osmington Mills, known as Upton Battery. All three of these up-dated works remained in commission until after World War II.

The Pier Head Battery, in process of building in 1859, was eventually provided with 7in RML guns, and then, late in the 1880s, with 12-pounder QF, more suited to the close-in protection of the harbour entrance.

The crowning glory of Portland's defences was, of course, the Breakwater Fort. This was originally intended as a casemated granite work to be placed on the end of the breakwater itself, but questions arose as to the breakwater's ability to take the weight, and it was built as a separate structure at the end of the breakwater. By this time the iron fort idea had taken hold, and the final plan called for a 116ft diameter iron fort resting on foundations some thirty feet below low water level. The usual ring of masonry was built and capped with concrete, and a granite substructure built, rising to 23ft above high water. The iron fort was then built on top, using the same system of construction as Spitbank: two rings of iron box girders, one forming the floor and one the roof skeleton, supported by iron pillars between the casemate ports. The walls were of three thicknesses of 6½in plate, backed by armour bars, and the roof was also of iron armour. Into this went fourteen 12.5in guns, installed in 1874-5. In 1884 steam power was provided, at a cost of £1,600 per gun, for the supply of ammunition and operation of the guns. In the early 1900s it was improved by the addition of heavy modern armament (two 9.2in were installed) but it appears that this installation was never entirely satisfactory and they were removed shortly after the end of World War I. 12-pounder QF guns were installed in about 1912 to act in cooperation with the Pier Head Battery, but these were later withdrawn and the work passed into the hands of the Admiralty.

Harwich

The Harwich area was for many years classed as a fortress, and the principal work, Landguard Fort, has a long history. Construction here, on the point opposite Harwich, began in 1628 to replace a temporary earth battery which had been built on the point after the recommendation of a Commission set up by James I. The resulting work was of earth ramparts, with a bastioned trace of almost 1,000yd length. When completed it was armed with 'two demi-cannon, twenty-eight culverins, one basilisk, seventeen demi-culverins and ten sakers.' But when the Engineer to the Board of Ordnance inspected the work in 1700 he reported it as being in 'the most miserable condition of any Fort in Europe' and as a result the work was razed and a new fort begun in 1715. By the end of the eighteenth century this was an important work, and when Blomefield visited in 1779 he found 115 guns mounted. When the 1850s brought about renewed interest in coast defence, Landguard had only twelve guns serviceable, and it was consequently re-armed with five 10in and five 12.5in RML and two 64-pounder converted guns in the 1870s.

These went to the scrapyard in the early 1900s, but by then the importance of Harwich had declined and the replacements were two 6in BL and two 4.7in QF. The two 6in were on disappearing mountings, Harwich being almost the home of the disappearing carriage in England. With the rising presence of Germany across the water, two more 6in on central pivot mounting and one 10in on barbette mounting were installed in about 1910. After the war the 10in and the disappearing carriage guns were removed, and the fort remained armed with 6in and 4.7in until 1956.

On the other side of the estuary, in Harwich itself, apart from one of Henry VIII's artillery castles much dilapidated, Blomefield had noted a 'stockaded battery' which he considered not essential to the defence of the harbour, and since it had neither magazines nor store houses, he had the guns removed to Landguard. This left the south side defenceless and in about 1880 a major work, Beacon Hill Battery, was built. This was one of the first to be furnished with the hydropneumatic disappearing carriage guns, both 9.2in and 10in being installed there. These remained in use until after World War I when they were replaced by four 6in on barbette mountings. The second work in Harwich was not built until World War II; this was Angel Gate Battery, a small work with two 6-pounder QF guns and a searchlight at the tip of the peninsula to prevent light craft from slipping into the harbour.

Inside the haven, at Shotley Point, a number of works had existed since the Napoleonic Wars, notably two Martello Towers; but these were supplemented in the 1860s by Shotley Battery mounting fourteen 7in RML guns in embrasures. The work was still in existence in 1904, but became redundant shortly afterwards and was abandoned as a defence, the site being later incorporated into a naval shore establishment.

Two more defence works have existed in the Harwich area; during World War I a defensive minefield was laid outside the entrance to the harbour and a battery of 4.7in guns—inevitably called 'Minefield Battery'—was sited to cover it and thus deter minesweeping operations. I have, unfortunately been unable to determine the exact location of this work; it did not survive the end of the war and is not marked on any of the **War Department Lands** Maps which I have examined. The other work, Brackenbury Battery, was built just north of Felixstowe in 1940 to mount two 6in guns and was abandoned when the war ended. It is rather unusual in being one of the few emergency works of that time which was actually given a name.

EPILOGUE

From the post-Crimean programme to the dissolution of coast artillery was just 100 years, and, as the reader has now seen, this was the only period subsequent to the invention of the cannon that the coast defences of England and Wales were really a viable force and a technically effective deterrent. The question which now remains is 'Was it worth it?' Did the defences into which so much money, time and labour were poured actually perform the task for which they were intended? This, of course, is almost impossible to answer satisfactorily. From today's viewpoint, the answer appears to be in the negative and gives rise to the 'Palmerston's Folly' attitude. But does anyone criticise a householder for insuring his home against fire for thirty years during which time he never has a fire? If I fit my house with expensive burglar-proof locks and never have a burglary did I waste money, or, unknown to me, was a potential burglar deterred? One can never answer this sort of hypothetical question. But on the basis of the political scene at various periods, and of potential threats, it seems likely that the presence of strong defences—for with all their minor defects the defences were usually adequate—may have been a factor which made a potential enemy think twice. The few times that the defences were called upon, they acquitted themselves well; but in the last analysis a strong and alert navy was the best form of defence. And the navy were the first to admit that without defended dockyards and depots to shelter them a strong and alert fleet could not be maintained. So if the defences had done nothing but induce a feeling of security in the navy, so as to allow them to sail the seas with the assurance that their bases were safe, then they proved their worth.

It is almost impossible to compute the cost of the coast defences during this 100 years, due to the complexity of the accounting systems used, as previously observed. We have already seen that between 1859 and 1890 some £17 million had been spent, and after that the various appropriations and estimates, and the expenditure during the two world wars must have been easily the same again. Add to that the annual bill for upkeep of the works, maintenance of armament, feeding, clothing, housing and paying the soldiers, the ammunition bill, and many other charges which must have accrued, it is doubtless safe to say that the total period saw £50 million absorbed. It sounds fearsome, but by today's standards? According to *Whitaker's Almanac* before me, such a sum paid the annual salary for the Home Office staff for 1970–1, and who is prepared to stand up and say which represents the better bargain? And in case anyone should think Britain foolishly alone in this sort of business, it might as well be pointed out that every nation with a seaboard spent similar sums on their defences. In 1886 the Endicott Board in the United States of America called for an expenditure of $126,377,800 (approximately £30 million at the contemporary rate of exchange) for seacoast defences; and, while the cost has never been publicly revealed, the German fortification of Heligoland and the Russian works at Kronstadt, to give but two examples which spring readily to mind, must have soaked up similar sums.

On balance then, let us be fair. The fortress builders did the best they could, basing their decisions on what they saw before them. That the majority of their works were never called upon to fire in anger might be attributed to the deterrent value of the forts or it might be that nobody intended to attack those localities at all. But the threat of a powerful gun expertly manned and firmly anchored in concrete is one which the sailor has, throughout the ages, regarded with some respect. 'No sailor but a fool would attack a fortress', 'Jacky' Fisher is said to have remarked. Perhaps our enemies were less foolish than we thought. Or perhaps the warning ' A Fierce Dog is on the Premises' kept them away.

APPENDICES

List of Coast Defence Works

This list tabulates, in alphabetical order, every coast defence work of significance erected on the coast of England and Wales; by 'significance' is meant that the work was a viable means of defence after 1850. Earlier earthen batteries have not been included unless they were subsequently re-armed and brought into use during that period. The dates of building are as accurate as possible; the date of abandonment is the year in which the work ceased to be considered for its defensive role as originally cast. It does not necessarily mean that the work was abandoned by the War Department at that time. In many cases this date of abandonment is an approximation; thus, the emergency batteries are all shown as having been abandoned in 1946 when, in fact, the work of dismantling them began late in 1944 and continued into 1947 in some cases.

The entries in the 'remarks' column indicate the current state of the work according to the latest information available to me. The entry 'emergency' indicates a beach battery or other emergency work erected in World War II and demolished immediately thereafter; 'private' means that the work is in private hands, either owned or leased from the Ministry of Defence; 'MoD' indicates that the work is either occupied by or is situated on land owned and occupied by the Ministry of Defence; 'access' indicates that it is possible to gain access to the work, either because it stands on open ground or is open to the public.

LIST OF COAST DEFENCE WORKS

Work	Location	Built	Abandoned	Principal Armament	Remarks
ABBOTSBURY	Dorset	1940	1946	4in QF	Emergency
AGATON Fort	Plymouth	1868	1946	Not armed	Private
ALBEMARLE Bty	Sheerness	1900	1956	4.7in QF	MoD
ALBERT Fort	Isle of Wight	1850	1950s	Brennan Torp	Private
ALDEBURGH	Suffolk	1940	1946	6in BL	Emergency
AMHERST Bty	Dover	1800	1900	32-pounder SB	MoD
ANGEL GATE Bty	Harwich	1940	1956	6-pounder QF	Private
APPLEDORE	Devon	1940	1946	4.7in QF	Emergency
ARCHCLIFFE Fort	Dover	16th C	1956	10in RML	MoD
AUSTIN Fort	Plymouth	1865	1920s	Not armed	Private
AVONMOUTH	Glos	1940	1946	6in BL	Emergency
BARNSTAPLE	Devon	1940	1946	4in QF	Emergency
BARTONS POINT Bty	Sheppey	1900	1956	9.2in BL	Derelict
BARRY ISLAND	Glamorgan	1940	1946	6in BL	Emergency
BEACON HILL Bty	Harwich	1880	1956	10in BL	MoD
BEMBRIDGE Fort	Isle of Wight	1867	1946	7in RBL	Private
BETHLEHEM	Kent	1940	1946	6in BL	Emergency
BEXHILL	Sussex	1940	1946	4in QF	Emergency
BLACKNOR Bty	Portland	1900	1956	6in BL	
BLOCKHOUSE Fort	Plymouth	1545	1910	32-pounder SB	MoD
BLYTH	Northumberland	1940	1946	6in BL	Emergency
BOGNOR REGIS	Sussex	1940	1946	5.5in BL	Emergency
BOSTON	Lincs	1940	1946	6in BL	Emergency
BOULDNER Bty	Isle of Wight	1922	1956	6in BL	Derelict; Access
BOVISAND Fort	Plymouth	1870	1956	10in RML	Private
BOWDEN Fort	Plymouth	1868	1930s	Not armed	Private
BRACKENBURY Bty	Felixstowe	1940	1946	6in BL	Emergency
BREANDOWN Fort	Weston-super-Mare	1860	1920s	7in RML	Derelict; Access
BRIGHTLINGSEA	Essex	1940	1946	4.7in QF	Emergency
BRIGHTON	Sussex	1940	1946	6in BL	Emergency

C.D.—P

Work	Location	Built	Abandoned	Principal Armament	Remarks
BRIXHAM	Devon	1940	1946	4.7in QF	Emergency
BROCKHURST Fort	Portsmouth	1863	1920	Not armed	MoD
BROWNDOWN Bty	Portsmouth	1800	1920	Moveable	MoD
BROWN HILL Bty	Plymouth	1865	1900	Moveable	Demolished
BULL SAND Fort	Humber	1916	1950s	4.7in QF	Derelict
BURNHAM-ON-SEA	Essex	1940	1946	6in BL	Emergency
CAERNARVON	Caerns	1940	1946	4in QF	Emergency
CAPEL Bty	Dover	1941		Radar	Derelict
CASTLE HILL Fort	Dover	1865	1956	9in RML	MoD
CAWSAND Bty	Plymouth	1863	1926	7in RBL	Private
CHAPEL BAY Bty	Pembroke	1877	1932	9.2in BL	Derelict
CITADEL Bty	Dover	1900	1956	9.2in BL	MoD
CLACTON	Essex	1940	1946	6in BL	Emergency
CLEY	Norfolk	1940	1946	6in BL	Emergency
CLIFF END Bty	Isle of Wight	1871	1946	12.5in RML	Demolished
CLIFF END Fort	Isle of Wight	1850	1956	12.5in RML	Holiday Camp
CLIFFE Bty	Thames	1865	1947	12in RML	Derelict; Access
CLIFFORDS Fort	Tyne	16th C	1956	6in BL	Derelict
COALHOUSE Fort	Thames	1867	1946	12.5in RML	Derelict; Access
COATHAM Bty	Tees	1918	1956	9.2in BL	Derelict; Access
COVEHITHE	Suffolk	1940	1946	6in BL	Emergency
CROMER	Norfolk	1940	1946	6in BL	Emergency
CROOKHORN Redoubt	Portsmouth	1865	1920	Not armed	
CROSBY Bty	Mersey	1900	1949	6in BL	Derelict; Access
CROWN HILL Fort	Plymouth	1868	1900	Not armed	MoD
CULVER CLIFF Bty	Isle of Wight	1863	1956	7in RBL	See Redcliffe
CUMBERLAND Fort	Portsmouth	1746	1924	6in BL	MoD
DALE Fort	Pembroke	1857	1920	7in RML	Private
DARNET Fort	Medway	1865	1920	9in RML	Derelict
DARTMOUTH	Devon	1940	1946	4.7in QF	Emergency

Name	Location	Date	Armament	Status
DAWLISH	Devon	1940	4in QF	Emergency
DEAD MAN'S Bty	Thames	1915	6in BL	Derelict
DEAL	Kent	1940	6in BL	Emergency
DEVIL'S POINT Bty	Plymouth	1865		MoD
DOVER TURRET	Dover	1880	16in RML	Preserved
DRAKE'S ISLAND Bty	Plymouth	1865	9in RML	National Trust
DROP By	Dover	1800	7in RBL	MoD
DROP Redoubt	Dover	1800	7in RML	MoD
DUMPTON POINT	Kent	1940	5.5in BL	Emergency
DUNGENESS	Kent	1940	6in BL	Emergency
DUNWICH	Suffolk	1940	4in QF	Emergency
DYMCHURCH	Kent	1940	6in BL	Emergency
EAST BLOCKHOUSE Bty	Pembroke	1852	9.2in BL	MoD
EASTBOURNE	Sussex	1940	6in BL	Emergency
EASTERN ARM Bty	Dover	1915	6-pounder QF	Demolished
EASTNEY Bty	Portsmouth	1800	7in RBL	MoD
EASTERN KINGS Bty	Plymouth	1779	68-pounder	MoD; Demolished
EAST TILBURY Bty	Thames	1892	10in BL	Private
EAST WEARE Bty	Portland	1865	9.2in BL	Derelict; Access
EFFORD Fort	Plymouth	1865	Not armed	Private
EGG BUCKLAND Keep	Plymouth	1865	Not armed	Private
ELSON Fort	Portsmouth	1860	Not armed	MoD
ERNESETTLE Bty	Plymouth	1868	Not armed	MoD
EXMOUTH	Devon	1940	4.7in QF	Emergency
FAN BAY Bty	Dover	1941	6in BL	Demolished
FAREHAM Fort	Portsmouth	1864	Not armed	MoD
FARLINGTON Redoubt	Portsmouth	1865	Not armed	Demolished
FILEY	Yorks	1940	6in BL	Emergency
FISHGUARD	Pembs	1940	6in BL	Emergency
FLATHOLME Bty	Severn	1860	7in RML	Derelict; Access
FLEETWOOD	Lancs	1940	4in BL	Emergency
FLETCHER Bty	Sheppey	1918	9.2in BL	Derelict; Access
FOLKESTONE	Kent	1940	6in BL	Emergency

Work	Location	Built	Abandoned	Principal Armament	Remarks
FORDER Bty	Plymouth	1865	1900	Not armed	Demolished
FOWEY	Cornwall	1940	1946	4.7in QF	Emergency
FRESHWATER Redoubt	Isle of Wight	1800	1956	12-pounder QF	
FRIARS BAY Bty	Newhaven	1941	1946	Radar	Derelict
FRINTON	Essex	1940	1946	6in BL	Emergency
GARDEN Bty	Plymouth	1863	1900	9in RML	Preserved
GARRISON POINT Fort	Medway	1667	1956	12.5in RML	MoD
GILKICKER Fort	Portsmouth	1796	1910	12in RML	MoD
GODWIN Fort	Humber	1900	1956	9.2in BL	Derelict
GOLDEN HILL Fort	Isle of Wight	1867	1946	Not armed	Private
GOMER Fort	Portsmouth	1858	1920	Not armed	MoD
GRAIN Bty	Medway	1865	1956	9in RML	Demolished
GRAIN Fort	Medway	1865	1956	9.2in BL	Demolished
GRAIN Tower	Medway	1800	1946	6-pounder QF	Signal Station
GRANGE Fort	Portsmouth	1863	1920	Not armed	DoE
GRANVILLE Bty	Plymouth	1852	1946	12-pounder QF	Derelict; Access
GREATSTONE	Kent	1940	1946	6in BL	Emergency
GREAT YARMOUTH	Norfolk	1940	1946	6in BL	Emergency
GREEN Bty	Humber	1900	1930	9.2in BL	Demolished
GRIMSBY	Lincs	1940	1946	6in BL	Emergency
HAILE SAND Fort	Humber	1916	1949	4in QF	Derelict
HAPPISBURGH	Norfolk	1940	1946	6in BL	Emergency
HARTLEY Bty	Tyne	1919	1926	12in BL Turret	Demolished
HART WARREN Bty	Tees	1917	1930	9.2in BL	Derelict
HASTINGS	Sussex	1940	1946	6in BL	Emergency
HATHERWOOD POINT Bty	Isle of Wight	1868	1925	12.5in RML	Derelict; Access
HAWKINS Bty	Plymouth	1900	1930	9.2in BL H/A	Demolished
HAYLE	Cornwall	1940	1946	4in QF	Emergency
HAYLE Bty	Plymouth	1900	1956	12-pounder QF	Derelict
HENGISTBURY HEAD	Hants	1940	1946	4in QF	Emergency

HERNE BAY	Kent	1940	1946	6in BL	Emergency
HEUGH Bty	Hartlepool	1900	1920	6in BL	Demolished
HIGH CAPE	Norfolk	1940	1946	6in BL	Emergency
HILPSFORD Bty	Barrow-in-Furness	1900	1946	6in BL	Derelict
HOLYHEAD	Anglesey	1940	1946	6in BL	Emergency
HORSE SAND Fort	Portsmouth	1870	1956	12in BL	MoD
HOO Fort	Medway	1865	1920	9in RML	Derelict
HORNSEA	Yorks	1940	1946	4.7in QF	Emergency
HOUGHAM Bty	Dover	1941	1956	8in BL	Demolished
HUBBERSTONE Fort	Pembroke	1865	1932	10in RML	Private
HUNSTANTON	Norfolk	1940	1946	6in BL	Emergency
HURST CASTLE	Needles Passage	1541	1900	12.5in RML	Preserved
HYTHE	Kent	1940	1946	6in BL	Emergency
ILFRACOMBE	Devon	1940	1946	4in QF	Emergency
JOSS BAY	Kent	1940	1946	5.5in BL	Emergency
JURY'S GAP	Kent	1940	1946	6in BL	Emergency
KESSINGLAND	Suffolk	1940	1946	6in BL	Emergency
KILNSEA Bty	Humber	1900	1946	9.2in BL	Derelict
KINGSDOWN	Kent	1940	1946	6in BL	Emergency
KINGSGATE	Kent	1940	1946	4in QF	Emergency
KING'S LYNN	Norfolk	1940	1946	6in BL	Emergency
KITCHENER Bty	Tyne	1919	1926	12in Turret	Demolished
KNOWLES Bty	Plymouth	1869	1920	Not armed	Private
LAIRA Bty	Plymouth	1865	1920	Not armed	Private
LANDGUARD Fort	Harwich	1628	1956	10in BL	MoD
LANGDON Bty	Dover	1900	1956	10in BL	MoD
LANGNEY Redoubt	Eastbourne	1800	1900	7in RBL	Preserved
LAVERNOCK Bty	Cardiff	1860	1946	6in BL	Demolished
LIGHTHOUSE Bty	Hartlepool	1900	1920	6in BL	Demolished
LITTLEHAMPTON	Sussex	1940	1946	6in BL	Emergency
LITTLESTONE	Kent	1940	1946	6in BL	Emergency
LLANELLY	Carmarthen	1940	1946	4in QF	Emergency
LOOE	Cornwall	1940	1946	4in QF	Emergency

Work	Location	Built	Abandoned	Principal Armament	Remarks
LOWER HOPE POINT Bty	Thames	1898	1920	12-pounder QF	Demolished
LOWESTOFT	Suffolk	1940	1946	6in BL	Emergency
LUMPS Fort	Portsmouth	1858	1920	7in RML	Demolished
LYDDEN SPOUT Bty	Dover	1941	1956	6in BL	Demolished
LYME REGIS	Dorset	1940	1946	4.7in QF	Emergency
LYTHAM	Lancs	1940	1946	4in QF	Emergency
MABLETHORP	Lincs	1940	1946	6in BL	Emergency
MAKER Redoubt	Plymouth	1800	1910	12.5in RML	Private
MAKER HEIGHTS Bty	Plymouth	1900	1956	6in BL	Derelict; Access
MARGATE	Kent	1940	1946	6in BL	Emergency
MARSDEN Bty	Tyne	1919	1926	12in BL Turret	Demolished
MARTELLO Bty	Sheerness	1900	1956	4.7in QF	MoD
MARYPORT	Cumberland	1940	1946	4in QF	Emergency
MERSEA	Essex	1940	1946	4.7in QF	Emergency
MILL POINT	Kent	1940	1946	5.5in BL	Emergency
MINEFIELD Bty	Harwich	1915	1920	4.7in QF	Demolished
MINEHEAD	Somerset	1940	1946	4in QF	Emergency
MINSMERE	Suffolk	1940	1946	6in BL	Emergency
MONCKTON Fort	Portsmouth	1800	1900	7in RBL	MoD
MONCRIEFF Bty	Hythe	1802	1880	24-pounder SB	Demolished
MOUNT WISE Bty	Plymouth	1779	1890	32-pounder SB	Demolished
MUMBLES Bty	Swansea	1860	1900	80-pounder RML	Demolished
NELLS POINT Bty	Severn	1892	1920	4.7in QF	Demolished
NELSON Fort	Portsmouth	1871	1920	Not armed	MoD
NEEDLES Bty	Isle of Wight	1863	1900	7in RBL	MoD
NEWHAVEN Fort	Sussex	1855	1956	6in BL	MoD
NEW NEEDLES Bty	Isle of Wight	1892	1956	9.2in BL	MoD
NEWPORT	Mon	1940	1946	12-pounder QF	Emergency
NEW TAVERN Fort	Thames	1700	1920	12in RML	Demolished
NEWQUAY	Cornwall	1940	1946	4in QF	Emergency

Name	Location	Year	Armament	Status
NODES POINT Bty	Isle of Wight	1892	9.2in BL	Holiday Camp
NO MAN'S LAND Fort	Portsmouth	1871	12in BL	MoD
NORMAN'S BAY	Sussex	1940	4.7in QF	Emergency
NOTHE Fort	Portland	1865	10in RML	
PADSTOW	Cornwall	1940	4in QF	Emergency
PALLISER Bty	Tees	1940	Also known as Hart Warren Bty (q.v.)	
PAR SANDS	Cornwall	1940	4in QF	Emergency
PASLEY Bty	Tees		Also known as Coatham Bty (q.v.)	
PATER Bty	Pembroke	1840	32-pounder SB	Demolished
PAULL POINT Bty	Humber	1800	4in BL	
PERCH ROCK Bty	Mersey	1860	7in RBL	Private; Access
PENLEE POINT Bty	Plymouth	1900	9.2in BL	Derelict; Access
PENZANCE	Cornwall	1940	4in QF	Emergency
PETT LEVEL	Sussex	1940	6in BL	Emergency
PEVENSEY	Sussex	1940	5.5in BL	Emergency
PICKLECOMBE Fort	Plymouth	1870	10in RML	Private
PIER EXTENSION Bty	Dover	1914	12-pounder QF	Demolished
PIER HEAD Bty	Portland	1860	12-pounder QF	Demolished
PLYMOUTH BREAKWATER Fort		1870	12.5in RML	MoD
PLYMOUTH CITADEL		1671	110-pounder RML	MoD
POLHAWN Bty	Plymouth	1865	68-pounder RML	Private
POOLE	Dorset	1940	4.7in QF	Emergency
POPTON Fort	Pembroke	1868	10in RML	Private
PORTISHEAD Bty	Severn	1946	6in BL	Demolished
PORTLAND BREAKWATER Fort		1850	9.2in BL	Signal Station
PORT TALBOT	Glamorgan	1874	4in QF	Emergency
PRESTON	Lancs	1940	4in QF	Emergency
PUCKPOOL Bty	Isle of Wight	1940	9.2in BL	Derelict; Access
PURBROOK Fort	Portsmouth	1870	Not armed	MoD
RALEIGH Bty	Plymouth	1870	10in BL	Private
RAME CHURCH Bty	Plymouth	1900	9.2in BL H/A	Derelict; Access
RAMSGATE	Kent	1900	6in BL	Emergency
REDCLIFFE Bty	Isle of Wight	1940	7in RBL	Derelict; Access

Work	Location	Built	Abandoned	Principal Armament	Remarks
RENNEY Bty	Plymouth	1900	1956	9.2in BL	MoD
ROBERTS Bty	Tyne	1919	1926	12in BL Turret	Demolished
ROWNER Fort	Portsmouth	1865	1920	Not armed	MoD
RUDDER ROCK Bty	Steepholme Is Severn	1860	1898	7in RML	Derelict; Access
St ANTHONY'S Bty	Falmouth	1895	1949	6in BL	Derelict
St CATHERINE'S Is. Fort	Tenby	1877	1920	7in RBL	Private
St HELEN'S Fort	Isle of Wight	1868	1900	12.5in RML	Signal Station
St MARGARET'S BAY	Kent	1940	1946	5.5in BL	Emergency
SALCOMBE	Devon	1940	1946	4in QF	Emergency
SANDOWN BARRACK Bty	Isle of Wight	1863	1932	7in RBL	Demolished
SANDOWN Fort	Isle of Wight	1866	1946	10in RML	Private
SANDWICH BAY	Kent	1940	1946	6in BL	Emergency
SCARBOROUGH	Yorks	1940	1946	6in BL	Emergency
SCARS ELBOW Bty	Thames	1940	1956	6-pounder QF	Derelict
SCRAESDON Fort	Plymouth	1865	1920	Not armed	MoD
SCONCE POINT Bty	Isle of Wight	1800	1870		Demolished
SCOVESTON Fort	Pembroke	1865	1930	Not armed	
SEAFORD	Sussex	1940	1946	6in BL	Emergency
SEAFORTH Bty	Mersey	1860	1900	12.5in RML	
SEAHAM HARBOUR	Durham	1940	1946	6in BL	Emergency
SEATON	Devon	1940	1946	4in QF	Emergency
SEATON CAREW	Durham	1940	1946	6in BL	Emergency
SHELLNESS	Kent	1940	1946	6in BL	Emergency
SHERINGHAM	Norfolk	1940	1946	6in BL	Emergency
SHOEBURYNESS	Essex	1940	1946	6in BL	Emergency
SHOREHAM-BY-SEA	Sussex	1940	1946	6in BL	Emergency
SHORNMEAD Fort	Thames	1869	1946	11in RML	MoD
SHOTLEY Bty	Harwich	1860	1905	7in RML	MoD
SHOULDER OF MUTTON Bty	Dover	1800	1880	7in RBL	Demolished
SIDMOUTH	Devon	1940	1946	4in QF	Emergency

Name	Location	Date	Armament	Status
SKEGNESS	Lincs	1940	6in BL	Emergency
SLOUGH Fort	Thames	1865	9.2in BL	Private
SOUTH BREAKWATER Bty	Dover	1915	12-pounder QF	Demolished
SOUTH FORELAND Bty	Dover	1942	9.2in BL	MoD
SOUTH GARE Bty	Tees	1900	4.7in QF	Derelict
SOUTH HOOK Fort	Pembroke	1865	9.2in BL	Private
SOUTHSEA CASTLE	Portsmouth	1539	9.2in BL	
SOUTHWICK Fort	Portsmouth	1870	Not armed	MoD
SOUTHWOLD	Suffolk	1940	6in BL	Emergency
SPANISH Bty	Tyne	1892	6in BL	Derelict
SPITBANK Fort	Portsmouth	1870	12in BL	MoD
SPURN POINT Bty	Humber	1900	4.7in QF	Derelict
STACK ROCK Fort	Pembroke	1871	10in RML	Private
STADDON Fort	Plymouth	1865	Not armed	MoD
STADDON POINT Bty	Plymouth	1770	12-pounder QF	Private
STALLINGBOROUGH	Lincs	1940	4.7in QF	Emergency
STAMFORD Fort	Plymouth	1865	10in RML	Private
SUNDERLAND	Durham	1940	6in BL	Emergency
SUTHERLAND Fort	Hythe	1800	24-pounder SB	Demolished
SWANAGE	Dorset	1940	4in QF	Emergency
SWANSEA	Glamorgan	1940	6in BL	Emergency
TEIGNMOUTH	Devon	1940	4.7in QF	Emergency
THORN ISLAND Fort	Pembroke	1852	7in RBL	Hotel
THORPENESS	Suffolk	1940	6in BL	Emergency
TILBURY Fort	Thames	1667	11in RML	DoE; Access
TORQUAY	Devon	1940	4.7in QF	Emergency
TREGANTLE DOWN Bty	Plymouth	1890	9in RML H/A	Derelict; Access
TREGANTLE Fort	Plymouth	1865	32-pounder SB	MoD
TWELVE ACRE BREAK Bty	Plymouth	1865	Moveable?	Demolished
TWISS Bty	Shorncliffe	1803	24-pounder SB	Demolished
TYNEMOUTH CASTLE Bty	Tyne	16th C	9.2in BL	Preserved
UPTON Bty	Portland	1900	9.2in BL	Derelict

Work	Location	Built	Abandoned	Principal Armament	Remarks
VERNE HILL Fort	Portland	1860	1900	12.5in RML	Prison
VICTORIA Fort	Isle of Wight	1850	1946	10in RML	Preserved; Access
WALLINGTON Fort	Portsmouth	1865	1920	40-pounder RBL	
WALNEY Bty	Barrow-in-Furness	1900	1946	6in BL	Demolished
WANSTONE Bty	Dover	1942	1956	15in BL	Demolished
WARDEN Bty	Medway	1900	1923	6in BL	Derelict
WARDEN POINT Bty	Isle of Wight	1863	1956	9.2in BL	Holiday Camp
WATCH HOUSE Bty	Plymouth	1895	1930	6in BL	Derelict; Access
WESTERN KINGS Bty	Plymouth	1779	1880	68-pounder RML	MoD
WEST BAY	Dorset	1940	1946	5.5in BL	Emergency
WEST BLOCKHOUSE Bty	Pembroke	1852	1956	6in BL	Landmark Trust
WHITBY	Yorks	1940	1946	6in BL	Emergency
WHITESAND BAY Bty	Plymouth	1890	1956	10in BL	Holiday Camp
WHITEHAVEN	Cumberland	1940	1946	4in BL	Emergency
WIDLEY Fort	Portsmouth	1871	1920	Not armed	MoD
WINTERTON	Norfolk	1940	1946	4in BL	Emergency
WINCHELSEA	Sussex	1940	1946	6in BL	Emergency
WOODLAND Fort	Plymouth	1865	1920	7in RBL	Community Centre
WORKINGTON	Cumberland	1940	1946	4in QF	Emergency
WORTHING	Sussex	1940	1946	6in BL	Emergency
YAVERLAND Bty	Isle of Wight	1863	1956	6in BL	Holiday Camp

APPENDIX

Details of Armament

The details given here are necessarily brief, since a full technical description of every mark of each gun would occupy several pages and would be totally devoid of interest to the majority of readers. What I have aimed to do here is to list the principal weapons used by coast artillery throughout the last hundred years, giving their important features, and, in the case of the older weapons, one or two dimensions which will enable them to be identified if found. Due to the vast proliferation of carriages, slides and mountings on which the weapons were installed at various times, it has not been possible to condense the data to manageable size, and therefore brief notes are all that are given on that aspect.

Smooth-bore Ordnance

32-pounder	There were sixteen different types of 32-pounder gun, ranging from 5ft 4in long at 25cwt, to 9ft 7in long at 63cwt, with calibre ranging from 6.3in to 6.41in, in service. The most common in land service was the 58cwt model of 9ft 6in, introduced in 1847. This was of cast iron, and 6.375in calibre.
68-pounder	The land service 68-pounder was introduced in 1841, weighed 112cwt, was 10ft 10in long, and had a calibre of 8.12in.
13in mortar	This was of 36cwt, 3ft 4in long and of cast iron.

Converted Smooth-bore

These were old smooth-bore guns converted to rifled muzzle-loaders by the insertion of rifled liners on Palliser's System.

64-pounder/8in	This was an 8in SB converted to 64-pounder RML. Length 122.75in. Calibre 6.29in. Weight 71cwt. Length of bore 103.27in. Officially

64/32-pounder	known as 'Ordnance Converted, Rifled, 64-pounder 71cwt Mk I', it was introduced in 1869 and declared obsolete in April 1908. This was the 32-pounder 58cwt converted to 64-pounder RML. Length 114in, weight 58 cwt, calibre 6.3in. Length of bore 108.45in. Introduced 1870, obsolete 1908.
80/68-pounder	Conversion of a 68-pounder of 95cwt. Length 136.55in, weight 100cwt, calibre 6.29in. Length of bore 113.25in. Known as the 80-pounder of five tons. Introduced 1872, obsolete February 1921.

Rifled Breech-loading (Armstrong) Guns

Few Armstrong guns were used as guns of position within works, usually on land faces where they could fire shell to deal with personnel, their performance being insufficient to attack armour. The designs were originally naval broadside or pivot guns given up by the navy in exchange for RML guns and transferred to land service.

7in 82cwt	Also known as the 110-pounder. Introduced 29 June 1861 as a sea service gun. Length 120in. Greatest diameter 27.7in. 76 grooves. 883 of these guns were manufactured. The projectile charge was 11lb of gunpowder. Muzzle velocity was 1,100ft/sec, and penetration of iron was 5in at 1,000yd, an obviously insufficient performance.
40-pounder of 35cwt	Introduced 2 May 1862, this was 121in long, had a greatest diameter of 16.4in, calibre 4.75in and was rifled with 56 grooves. 819 were made. The common shell weighed 38lb 5oz and was propelled by 5lb of gunpowder. Gun declared obsolete in December 1920.
40-pounder of 32cwt	Also known as the 'OP' (Old Pattern) 40-pounder. Introduced 25 January 1861. Length

120in, calibre 4.75in, greatest diameter 16.44 in, rifled with 56 grooves. Ammunition as for the 35cwt gun. Obsolete December 1920.

The mountings for these guns were generally wooden traversing slides and carriages, a few being fitted to wrought iron slides in later years.

Rifled Muzzle-loading Guns

64-pounder — In addition to the converted guns, there were three marks of 64-pounder RML. The first appeared in 1865 and the others in 1868. The Mk I was 119.5in long with a 98in bore calibre 6.3in and with three rifling grooves. This gun proposed by Sir William Armstrong, was the first RML to enter British service. The other two marks differed only in details of assembly. All were declared obsolete in April 1908.

The mountings were of the traversing slide and carriage pattern, wood or wrought iron, or a Moncrieff disappearing carriage introduced in 1873. The 64-pounder fired a 64lb common shell at 1,260ft/sec, using a 10lb gunpowder cartridge.

7in — There were two types of 7in RML, the 7 ton designed for land service in 1868 and the $6\frac{1}{2}$ ton sea service introduced in 1866. Numbers of the latter were transferred to land service in the late 1880s and they can be identified by their having a 'heel scale' of degrees marked off on the cascable, the metal loop at the breech end. Of the 7 ton model, the weapon used in most forts, the Mark III was the standard issue, only two of the earlier marks ever being made. The Mk III was 148in long with a 126 in bore, and the greatest external diameter was

31in at the breech end. The Mk III 6½ ton gun was 133in long with a 111in bore.

The 7 ton fired a 112lb Palliser shot at 1,560 ft/sec with a 30lb gunpowder charge, and could penetrate 8in of iron at 1,000yd. There were numerous patterns of mounting of the traversing slide type, differing in the type of pivot, height of gun etc, in order to suit different types of embrasure. There were also two patterns of Moncrieff carriage.

All 7in equipment was made obsolete in 1922.

8in

The 8in of 9 tons was originally a naval gun but a few were issued to land service in the 1870s. Introduced in 1866 it was 144in long with a 118in bore and a greatest diameter of 35in. It was rifled with four grooves.

The projectile was a 176lb Palliser shell, propelled by a 35lb powder charge at 1,390ft/sec, and this could pierce 8.25in of iron at 1,000 yd. One pattern of carriage and two of traversing slide were provided, one slide for casemates and one for open embrasures. All 8in equipment was declared obsolete in 1923.

9in

There were five marks of 9in 12 ton gun, introduced from 1865 to 1872. The basic data is the same for all: length 156in, bore 125in, diameter 39in, rifled with 6 grooves. The Mk I is recognisable by having five stepped diameters to the external contour of the barrel, while later marks have but three.

The high angle guns were the Mks 6, 6A, 6B or 6C, which were re-worked earlier marks having new barrel liners with 27 grooves. The Mk 6 was introduced in 1889, the others in 1892–3.

The 9in 12 ton gun fired a 256lb Palliser shell at 1,440ft/sec, using a 50lb gunpowder charge, and could penetrate 9·6in of armour at 1,000yd.

The mountings were of the traversing slide and carriage type, differing in pivot location, gun height and so forth. There was also a Moncrieff carriage for a 12ft 6in parapet, only two of which were made. The high angle mountings ran to four marks, of which two were purely experimental, and the others differed only in details of construction. These carriages allowed firing bewteen 20 and 70 degrees elevation. All 9in equipment was made obsolete in 1922.

10in

Two marks of 10in 18 ton gun were introduced in 1868 and 1869, differing only in details of their construction. Length 170in, bore 145.5in, diameter 45in, rifled with 7 grooves. The gun fired a 400lb Palliser shell at 1,380ft/sec with a 70lb gunpowder charge and could penetrate 12in of iron at 1,000yd. There were also six marks of high angle 10in, converted from 9in 12 ton by boring out and inserting a 32-grooved liner. The finished weapon was thus interchangeable with the high angle 9in models.

The standard mountings were traversing slide and carriage type and were of complicated nomenclature, 'low' and 'high' platforms being used with 'high' or 'low' carriages. The object was to obtain a low centre of gravity in order to better control recoil, but the idea was not particularly successful and was not adopted with other guns. There was also a 'small port' muzzle-pivoting carriage for use in the iron forts.

All 10in equipment was made obsolete in February 1922.

11in	The 11in of 25 tons was a naval design introduced in 1871, and the choice of calibre was due to a very tight naval specification controlling weight and length. 11in was selected as calibre giving the best performance within the allowed limits. Shortly afterwards further development resulted in the 12in gun, still within the prescribed limits, and only small numbers of the 11in were made, some of which found their way into land service. The gun was 180in long with a bore of 145in, diameter 53in, and rifled with 9 grooves. The mounting was a traversing slide and carriage. The gun fired a 548lb Palliser shell at 1,360 ft/sec using an 85lb gunpowder cartridge, and could pierce 13.1in of iron at 1,000yd. It was made obsolete in October 1904.
12in	Nominally of 25 tons, the Mark I of 1871 was actually $23\frac{1}{2}$ tons and only four were made, all of which went to the navy. The Mark II actually was 25 tons, and about 24 were built, most of which also went to the navy. Length 182.5in, bore 145in, diameter 53.5in, 9 rifled grooves. Declared obsolete in August 1904.

The 35 ton gun was designed for sea service but some were later transferred to land service. It was originally intended as a naval turret gun, and was known as the 'Woolwich Infant'. Introduced in 1871 it was declared obsolete in 1904. Length 195in, bore 162.5in, 9 grooves, diameter 56in. Fired a 714lb Palliser shot at 1,390ft/sec with a 140lb cartridge, and could penetrate 15in of iron at 1,000yd.

The mountings were a variety of traversing slide and carriage patterns, varying in pivot placement and height.

APPENDIX

12.5in

The 12.5in of 38 tons, introduced in 1875, became the most popular coast defence heavy gun. Length 230in, bore 198in, diameter 57.5 in, rifled with 9 grooves. The projectile was an 818lb Palliser shell and the cartridge was 200lb of gunpowder, giving a velocity of 1,575 ft/sec and a penetration of 18in of iron at 1,000yd.

The mountings were all of the traversing slide and carriage type, differing in pivot placement and gun height; there was also a special pattern for Spithead Forts in which the rear trucks were a foot further back than normal in order to try and reduce the liability to jump when fired.

16in

Only two of these 80 ton guns entered land service, both of which went into the Dover Turret, where they still are. Introduced in 1882 it was declared obsolete in October 1902. Length 26ft 9in, bore 288in, diameter 72in, rifled with 33 grooves. The gun cost £10,084 and fired a 1,700lb armour-piercing steel shell by means of a 450lb gunpowder charge, giving a velocity of 1,540ft/sec and a penetration of 23in at 1,000yd.

The mounting was special to the gun and formed part of the turret structure; it was basically a carriage and slide.

Breech-loading Ordnance

Calibre	Weight	Mounting	Projectile (weight in lb)	Velocity (in ft/sec)	Range (in yd)
QF GUNS					
3-pounder (1.85in)	5cwt	Pedestal	3	1,825	5,000
6-pounder (2.244in)	6cwt	Pedestal or twin	6	1,725	5,500
12-pounder (3.0in)	12cwt	Pedestal	12	2,200	9,000
4in	42cwt	Pedestal	28	2,600	14,300
4.7in	41cwt	Pedestal	45	2,125	13,000
5.25in	86cwt	Turret	80	2,800	25,200
6in	7 tons	Central pivot	100	2,150	15,700
BL GUNS					
4in	42cwt	Central pivot	31	2,800	17,000
5.5in	6 tons	Pedestal	82	2,800	17,300
6in	7 tons	Barbette, central pivot or disappearing	100	2,560	20,200
7.5in	14 tons	Barbette	200	2,800	23,400
8in	17 tons	Central pivot	256	2,725	29,200
9.2in	28 tons	Barbette, high angle or disappearing	380	2,825	34,000
10in	29 tons	Barbette or disappearing	500	2,040	18,900
12in	43 tons	Yoke (Spitbank)	714	1,914	8,000
	46 tons	Turret (Tynemouth)	714	2,350	27,100
13.5in	76 tons	Barbette or disappearing	1,250	2,550	34,000
15in	100 tons	Barbette	1,938	2,400	36,900

The weight is, in all cases, the weight of the gun and breech mechanism only and does not include the weight of the mounting. The figures for velocity and range are based on the last mark of weapon introduced; early marks would not attain this performance.

BIBLIOGRAPHY

Headlam, Major-General Sir John, *History of the Royal Artillery.* 1935.
Lloyd E. W. and Hadcock A. G., *Artillery, Its Present Position.* Portsmouth, 1893.
Journal of the Army Historical Society.
Journal of the Royal Artillery.
Maurice-Jones, Col. K. W., *History of Coast Artillery in the British Army.* Royal Artillery Institution, 1959.
Proceedings of the Department of the Director of Artillery.
Proceedings of the Ordnance Select Committee, 1860–1868.
Proceedings of the Royal Artillery Institute.
Sutcliffe, Sheila, *Martello Towers.* Newton Abbot, 1972.
Treatise on Ammunition. 1887.
Treatise on the Construction of Service Ordnance. 1879.
Treatise on Military Carriages. 1888.
Treatise on Service Ordnance. 1893.
Willock, Col. R., *Bulwark of Empire.* Princeton NJ, 1962.

ACKNOWLEDGEMENTS

It only remains for me to pay tribute to some of the people who have, without exception, been of the utmost assistance to me in my search for information. Many I cannot name, since I never knew their names—casual meetings with local inhabitants who have frequently produced some piece of historical information or who have put me on the trail of an elusive work. But of those I do know, I hereby acknowledge my indebtedness and the order of listing is purely adventitious and no measure of their relative value:

Captain G. Dudley, Harbourmaster of the Milford Haven Conservancy Board, for keeping me up to date with happenings in his parish.

Major Richard Bartelot and the Library Staff of the Royal Artillery Institution, who have ferreted out all sorts of documents and answered my long-range queries with unfailing goodwill and alacrity.

Lt-Cmdr Alan Bax of the Bovisand Underwater Centre for allowing me to clamber all over the place.

Lt-Col Ken Melley, RA, of the Royal School of Artillery for innumerable reminiscences of his Coast Artillery days, which gave me much valuable data.

Mr Len Cramp of Yarmouth, Isle of Wight, for explaining the project at Fort Victoria, and for other information on the Isle of Wight defences.

The City Engineer's Department of Plymouth for admitting me to Fort Austin and for providing the talisman which got me into Fort Efford.

ACKNOWLEDGEMENTS

The Manchester Public Library for being one of the few places with a complete copy of the 1859 Report, and for providing me with copies of parts thereof.

Aerofilms Limited for diligently searching their files to find aerial cover of various areas and for kindly allowing some to be used for illustrations.

Miss Willis of the Pembrokeshire Record Office in Haverfordwest for unearthing the original sale documents of the Milford Haven Forts and for granting me permission to use some of the plans therein.

D. C. Emerson, Director of Studies of the Dale Fort Field Study Centre for answering many questions when he was in the throes of preparing his PhD thesis.

The Portsmouth News for searching the files to find me photographs of the Portsdown and Spithead Forts.

George Z. Trebinski for valiantly braving the winter gales on a motor-cycle in order to examine and photograph some of the Isle of Wight forts.

Mr M. W. D. Brace, of Thomas Chapel, Kilgetty, for much information on Stack Rock and other works in the Milford Haven area.

Mr T. A. Heatley, CEng, MICE, FIMunE, Borough Surveyor of Tynemouth for kindly supplying me with information relating to the Tyne defences.

And finally, my wife, for tolerating my eccentricities, surviving my absences, and listening with every appearance of comprehension while I 'talked-out' some of the more knotty problems.

INDEX

References to illustrations are in bold

Admiralty: rejects iron armour, 27
Agaton, Fort, **119**, 198
Albert, Fort, **52**, 152
Alum Bay, 155
American Civil War, lessons from, 50
Anderson's Cupola, 43, **191**
Angel Gate Battery, 232
Antony line, Plymouth Defences, 172, 195
Archcliffe Fort, Dover, 222, 226
Armament: estimates of cost (1859), 25
Armoured forts, 64, 66
Armstrong gun: features, 35; defects, 37
Armstrong, Mitchell & Co, and disappearing mounting, 76, 78
Armstrong, Sir William, 35
Armstrong's Protected Barbette System, **52**, 70, 165
Army Gas School, 197
Arrol-Withers mounting, 91
Austin, Fort, 201
Auto-sights, 83

Barbette mounting, **33**, 80
Barracks Act (1890), 87

Barton's Point Battery, 117
Beacon Hill Battery, 232
Bembridge Down Fort, **51**, 161
Blacknor Point Battery, 229, 230
Blockhouse, Fort, 139
Blomefield, Thomas: Inspector of Royal Artillery, 17; Reports on Drake's Island, 189; Dover, 17; Harwich, 231, 232; Hythe, 17, 18; Hurst Castle, 156; Maker, 182; Plymouth, 168; Portland, 17, 228; Upnor, 17
Bouldner Battery, 152
Bovisand Fort, **102**, 191
Bowden Fort, 200
Boxer, Colonel, Superintendent Royal Laboratory, 43
Brackenbury Battery, 233
Brancaster, 13
Breech-loading gun introduced, 69
Brennan controlled torpedo, 97–8, 152
Brockhurst, Fort, 144
Brown Down Battery, 141
Brownhill Battery, 203

Campbell, Sir Frederick, and breech-loading, 71

Canister shot, 43
Canvey Island, 97
Casemate trials, Shoeburyness, 30, **31**, 102
Casemate defects, 57
Castle Hill Fort, 222
Cattewater, Plymouth, 202
Cawsand Battery, 182
Chapel Bay Battery, 219
Chatham Dockyard, Dutch attack upon, 16
Cheyney Rock Battery, 117
Chicane, at Tregantle Fort, 196
Citadel Battery, 226
Clarke, Major G. S., criticises fortification theory, 46
Clarke, Sir George, Superintendent Royal Carriage Dept, 78
Cliff End Battery, 153
Cliff End Fort, 154
Cliffe Fort, **34**, 108
Coalhouse Fort, 99
Coast Artillery Experimental Establishment, 162
Coast Artillery School, Plymouth Citadel, 190
Committees: on the Armament of Home Ports, 89; on the Arming of Spithead Forts, 131; on Heavy Guns, 133, 154; on Iron Plate, 29; on Muzzle Pivoting Carriages, 59; on Ordnance, 71; Ordnance Select, 61; on Traversing Gear, 192
Common shell, 44
Cooling Castle, Kent, 14
Cordite, introduction of, 81
Cost of defensive works outside Britain, 68
Cost of ordnance and emplacements analysed, 56
Count of the Saxon Shore appointed, 14
Crimean War, 18
Crookhorn Redoubt, 146

Crown Hill Fort, **169**, 199
Culver (Redcliffe) Battery, 161
Cumberland, Fort, 135

Dale Fort, 211
Darnet Fort, 115
Dead Man's Battery, 105
Demolition, Army School of, and Shornmead Fort, 107
Depression position finder, 83, 184, 192
Depression rangefinder, 82,
De Russy, Colonel, USA: invents disappearing carriage, 60
Devil's Point Battery, 186
Diocletian reviews coast defences, 14
Disappearing carriages, disadvantages of, 78
Dolphin, HMS, 139
Dover: armament during World War II, 92, 227–8; Citadel, 226; early defences, 15, 221–2; general, 221–8; 1859 recommendations, 222; report by Blomefield, 17; Turret, 223–5, **224**
Drake, Sir Francis, and Plymouth fortification, 168, 186
Drake's Island, 186
Drop Battery, 226
Drop Redoubt, 222, 226
Durdale (or Disdale) Point, Portland, 229
Dutch attack on Medway, 16, 116
Dynamite Gun, Zalinski's, 212

East Blockhouse Battery, 219
Eastern Arm Battery, 226
Eastern Kings Battery, 186
Eastney Batteries, 141
East Tilbury Battery, 104
East Weare Battery, 230
Efford, Fort, **120**, 210
Egg Buckland Keep, 200
Elson, Fort, 144

INDEX

Elswick Ordnance Company, 76, 157
Emergency Batteries, 91
Ernesettle Battery, **119**, 198
Excellent, HMS: RN Gunnery Establishment, 164
'Expenditure on Fortification and Armament', return of, 87

Fan Bay Battery, 227
Fareham, Fort, 144
Farlington Redoubt, 147
Ferguson, James (Treasury member of Royal Commission), 20
Fire control, 81–3
Fletcher Battery, 118
Floating Batteries at Kinburn, 18, 27
Forder Battery, 200
Fortification: terms defined, 45–9
Freshwater Redoubt, 154

Garden Battery, Mount Edgcumb, 185
Garrison Point Fort, 115
German high velocity guns in France, 227
Gilkicker, Fort, 140
Golden Hill Fort, 155
Gomer Fort, 141
Gordon, General, as CRE Sheerness, 99
Grain Battery, 114
Grain Fort, **48**, 112
Grain Tower, 114
Grange Fort, 143
Granville Battery, 183
Gravesend (New Tavern) Fort, 105

Harwich defences, 231–3
Hatherwood Point Battery, 155
Hawkshaw, Sir John, builder of Spitbank Forts, 127
Haxo Casemate, 47, **120**
Henry VIII and coast defence, 15

Hercules, HMS, trials against disappearing gun, 77
High angle guns, 84, **85**, 109, 178, 181
Hoo Fort, 115
Horse Sand Fort, 64, **65**, 131
Hubberstone Fort, **187**, 215
Humber, construction of works during World War I, 89
Hurst Castle, **101**, 156
Hydropneumatic disappearing carriage, 76, **188**
Hypervelocity gun at Dover, 227–8
Hythe, reported on by Blomefield, 17–18

Imperial Defence Act (1888), 86
Inglis, Lt Col, designs small-port carriage, 60
Inspector-General of Fortification, and high angle guns, 84
Ironclad construction, 28
Iron plate trails, 29
Isle of Wight defences, 147–67

Jennycliffe Bay, Plymouth, 202
Jervois, Sir W. F. Drummond: and fort planning, 46, 206; and muzzle-pivoting carriages, 59, 104

Key, Captain Astley Cooper, RN, 20, 164, 206
Kinburn, floating batteries at, 18, 27
Knowles Battery, 199

La Gloire, 19
Laira Battery, 202
Landguard Fort, 231
Langdon Battery, 226
Lefroy, Lt Col J. H., RA, 20, 83, 163
Lower Hope Point Battery, 110

Lower Mount Wise Battery, 185
Lumps Fort, 136
Lydden Spout Battery, 227
Lyddite, introduction of, 81

Maker Heights Battery, 182
Maker, various works at, 182
Mantlets, protecting casemate ports, 58
Martello Towers: at Pembroke, 205; at Shotley, 232
Martin's Liquid Iron shell, 43, 191
Medway Defences, proposals, 94
Medway, Dutch attack on, 16, 116
Mefford, inventor of dynamite gun, 212
Mile Town, Sheerness, 94, 96
Milford Haven Defences; general, 205–20; land defences, 210; sea defences, 210–20; table of proposals, 207
Minefield Battery, 232
Monckton, Fort, 139
Moncrieff, Captain, and disappearing carriage design, 61–3
Moncrieff carriage, **61**
Mortar, 13in, **164**
Mount Edgcumb Blockhouse, 185
Mount Wise Battery, 185
Muzzle-pivoting carriages, 58, **59**

Naval Defence Act (1889), 87
Naval Works Act (1895), 88
Needles Battery, 159
Needles Passage defences, 148–9
Nelson, Fort, 145
New Needles Battery, 159
New Tavern Fort, 105
Noble, Lieut W. H., on 'racking' and 'punching', 41
Nodes Point Battery, 162
No Man's Land Fort, 64, **65**, 133
Northeastern line, Plymouth, 198
Nothe Fort, 229

Ordnance:
Breech-loading—6in, 72, **170**, 188; 8in, 227; 9.2in, **33**, 72, 80; 10in, 71; 13.5/8in, 227–8; 15in, 227; others, and tabulated data for all, 254
Quick firing—4.7in, **73**; other types tabulated, 254
Rifled, converted—64-pounder/8in, 247; 64/32-pounder, 248; 80/68-pounder, 248
Rifled breech-loading—7in (110-pounder), 248; 40-pounder, 248
Rifled muzzle-loading—64-pounder, 249; 68-pounder, 33, 37, 247; 7in, 50, **56**, 249; 8in, 250; 9in, 38, 50, **85**, 250; 10in, 251; 11in, 252; 12in, 252; 12.5in, 253; 13in, 138; 16in, 223, 253; 17.72in, 69
Smooth-bore—32-pounder, 247; 13in mortar, **164**, 247
Ordnance Select Committee:
on High Angle firing, 163
on Moncrieff's Proposals, 61

Palliser, Major, 18th Hussars: invents gun liner, 39; invents piercing projectile, 42
Palmerston, Lord, directs formation of Royal Commission, 19
Passive Air Defence School, 197
Pater Battery, 205, 217
Paulsgrove (Southwick) Fort, 145
Penlee Point Battery, **33,** 181
Performance of guns, tabulated, 247–54
Peto, Sir Samuel Morton, MP, publishes pamphlet, 26
Picklecombe experiment, 73–5
Picklecombe Fort, **53, 54,** 184
Pier Extension Battery, 226
Pier Head Battery, 230
Plymouth Breakwater Fort, 64, 193

INDEX

Plymouth Citadel, **120**, 168, 189
Plymouth Defences: general, 168–204; land defences 195–204; sea defences, 178–95; table of recommendations, 174
Polhawn Battery, 180
Pom-Pom, 1 pounder, trials of as anti-aircraft gun, 159
Popton Fort, 218
Portchester, Roman fort, 13, 14
Portland Bill, trials of disappearing gun at, 77
Portland Breakwater Fort, 64, 230–1
Portland Defences: general, 228–31; report by Blomefield, 17
Portsmouth Defences: armament at various dates, table, 75; general 121–47; land defences, 141–7; recommendations, 122–6
Projectiles: material, 41; shape, 40, 42
Puckpool Battery, **51**, 163
'Punching' theory of armour attack, 40
Purbrook, Fort, 146

Queenborough Lines, Sheerness, 72
Quick-firing guns, 72, 254

'Racking' theory of armour attack, 40
Raleigh Battery, 180
Rame Church Battery, 181
Rame Fort (Granville Battery), 184
Redcliffe (Culver) Battery, 161
Redding Point (Picklecombe Point), 184
Red hot shot, 43
Redoubt No 4, Maker Heights, 183
Renney Battery, **170**, 193
Rifled breech-loading (RBL) guns; features, 35; defects, 37
Rifled, converted (Palliser) guns, 39
Rifled muzzle-loading (RML) guns, 37, **38**
Rodman gun, 194
Rowner, Fort, **51**, 143
Royal Commission (1859), 19–26
Royal Commission (1869), 66–8
Royal Marines, 136

St Catherine's Island Fort, 210
St Helen's Fort, 64, 134, **134**
St Nicholas' (Drake's) Island, 186
Sandown Barrack Battery, 166
Sandown Fort, 166
Scarborough, early redoubt at, 14
Scar's Elbow Battery, 104
School of Gunnery, Golden Hill, 152, 155, 160
Sconce Point Battery. 160
Scoveston, Fort, 210
Scraesdon, Fort, 195
Shaw, Lt Col G., RA, designs muzzle-pivoting carriage, 58, **59**
Sheerness Garrison Order Book, extract from, 93
Shell lifts, aid in dating a work, 183
Shornmead Fort, **34**, 106
Shotley Battery, 232
Shotley Point, Martello Towers at, 232
Shrapnel shell, 43
Singapore, armament of, 90
Slough Fort, 110, **188**
Small port carriages, 58, **59**
South Breakwater Battery, 226
South Foreland Battery, 227
South Hook Fort, 212, **213**
Southsea Castle Battery, 137, **138**
Southwick, Fort, 145
Special Committee on Iron Plates, 29
Spitbank Fort, 64, 135
Spithead Forts, 127–35

Stack Rock Fort, 89, 214
Staddon, Fort, 203
Staddon Heights Battery, 191
Staddon line, Plymouth defences, 202
Staddon Point Battery, 190
Stamford, Fort, 202
Stanhope Programme of defence improvements, 73, 86
Stevens, John, designs armoured ship, 27

Thames and Medway Defences, 93–118
Thorn Island Fort, 219
Thunderer, HMS, accident on board, 70
Tilbury Blockhouse, 93
Tilbury Fort, 98
Todleben, comments on visiting Portsmouth, 24
Tregantle Down Battery, 85, 169, 178
Tregantle, Fort, 196
Trials of 13in mortar, 164
Turnchapel, Plymouth, 202
Turntable mounting of guns, 134
Twelve Acre Break Battery, 204
Tyne defences during World War I, 89

Upnor Castle: built, 16; report by Blomefield, 17

Upton Battery, 230

Verne Fort, 229, 230
Vesuvius, USS, dynamite gun, 212
Victoria, Fort, 160

Wallington, Fort, 144
Wanstone Battery, 227
Warden Battery, 118
Warden Point Battery, 84, 160
Warrior, HMS, British ironclad, 19, 28
'Warrior' targets, 28, 164
Watch House (or Watch Tower) Battery, 190
Watkin, Capt H. S. S., RA, inventor of rangefinders, etc, 82, 83
West Blockhouse Battery, 211
Western Kings Battery, 186
Western position, Plymouth defences, 195
Whitesand Bay Battery, 180
Widley, Fort, 145
Woodlands Fort, 199

Yarmouth, Isle of Wight, battery at, 147
Yaverland Fort, 167
Yoke mounting of guns in Spithead Forts, 132

Zalinski dynamite gun, 212